Long Loan

This book is due for return on or before the last date shown

St Martins Services Ltd

THE PALGRAVE COMPANION TO
NORTH AMERICAN UTOPIAS

ALSO BY JOHN W. FRIESEN

People, Culture & Learning (Detselig, 1977);

Introduction to Teaching: A Socio-Cultural Approach (co-author), (Kendall/Hunt, 1990);

When Cultures Clash: Case Studies in Multiculturalism (Detselig, 1993);

You Can't Get There From Here: The Mystique of North American Plains Indians Culture & Philosophy (Kendall/Hunt, 1995);

The Community Doukhobors: A People in Transition (co-author) (Borealis, 1996);

The Real/Riel Story: An Interpretive History of the Métis People of Canada, second edition (Borealis, 1996);

Perceptions of the Amish Way (co-author) (Kendall/Hunt, 1996);

Rediscovering the First Nations of Canada (Detselig, 1997);

First Nations of the Plains: Creative, Adaptable and Enduring (Detselig, 1999);

Aboriginal Spirituality and Biblical Theology: Closer Than You Think (Detselig, 2000); and

In Defense of Public Schools in North America (co-author) (Detselig, 2001).

Co-authored by Virginia Lyons Friesen:

Grade Expectations: A Multicultural Handbook for Teachers (Alberta Teachers' Association 1995);

In Defense of Public Schools in North America (Detselig, 2001); and

Aboriginal Education in Canada: A Plea for Integration (Detselig, 2002).

THE PALGRAVE COMPANION TO
NORTH AMERICAN UTOPIAS

JOHN W. FRIESEN

VIRGINIA LYONS FRIESEN

palgrave
macmillan

First published 2004 by
PALGRAVE MACMILLAN™
175 Fifth Avenue, New York, N.Y. 10010 and
Houndmills, Basingstoke, Hampshire, England RG21 6XS.
Companies and representatives throughout the world.

PALGRAVE MACMILLAN is the global academic imprint of the
Palgrave Macmillan division of St. Martin's Press, LLC and of
Palgrave Macmillan Ltd. Macmillan® is a registered trademark in
the United States, United Kingdom and other countries. Palgrave is
a registered trademark in the European Union and other countries.

ISBN 1–4039–6399–1 hardback

Library of Congress Cataloging-in-Publication Data
Friesen, John W.
The Palgrave companion to North American utopias / John W.
Friesen and Virginia Lyons Friesen
    p.   cm.
    Includes bibliographical references and index.
    ISBN 1–4039–6399–1 (cloth)
    1. Collective settlements—North America. 2. Communal
living—North America. 3. Utopias—North America.
I. Friesen, Virginia Agnes Lyons. II. Title.

HX652.A3F75 2004
307.77'0973—dc22
                           2003062231

A catalogue record for this book is available from the British
Library.

Design by Letra Libre, Inc.

First edition: April 2004
10 9 8 7 6 5 4 3 2 1

Printed in the United States of America

To our children:
Bruce
Karen
Gaylene
David
Beth Anne
with whom we share the love of travel.

CONTENTS

INTRODUCTION

*Hope springs eternal in the human breast; Man never
is, but always to be blessed.*
—*Alexander Pope, "Essay on Man" (1963: 508).*

A few years back when the world moved into the new millennium, there seemed little to fear or to look forward to in North America. Although various countries around the globe were involved in military skirmishes of one sort or another, no major world crisis loomed, and North Americans generally were a bit numbed by their disillusionment with the treadmill-like progress of their existence.

Then terrorist attacks changed all that, and left North Americans bewildered and shocked. How could anything like this happen to a well-armed nation in what had been considered relatively peaceful times? The devastating damage to human trust, vision, and hope for the future from that unwarranted blow will take years, perhaps generations, to repair. We will need to muster a great deal of appreciation for the statement made by the late Norman Vincent Peale; "No matter how dark things seem to be, or actually are, raise your sights to see the possibilities—always see them, for they are always there" *(Guideposts,* June, 2003:12a).

Although American expectations for a utopian lifestyle of some sort, once so nearly realized, were severely hampered by terrorism, futuristic-minded prophets are emerging from various quarters to announce that new dreams are arising from the ashes. Evidence of the determination of many Americans to regroup and rebuild in the aftermath of unwarranted attacks on their country has already indicated that "hope springs eternal in the human breast."

If we examine North American society from a cultural perspective, other than reacting to terrorist acts, we almost have nowhere to go in the twenty-first century. Why is this so? Because we have done it all. We have permanently achieved overproduction, waste, and grotesque consumption; religious and cultural banality (if not disinterest); art without effort; low if not contradictory moral standards of all kinds; privilege without responsibility; and redundant, predictable, boring media presentations. For example, if it were not for several decades of production to mine for copy reruns, television would have virtually nothing to offer.

What then is left for the human mind to explore? Most North Americans long for a break from the monotony of treadmill industrialization, pedantic religious utterances, and cultural emptiness. Hwang (1995) may be a bit harsh when he castigates North American society for contributing to violence and lack of appreciation for work by encouraging irresponsibility and promoting false self-esteem. Youth are taught from the time of early childhood, directly or indirectly, that they need to take little or no responsibility for their behavior. They are told they are wonderful even when they spend most of their time in self-gratifying activities. Hwang blames schools for glamorizing easy success and the fast life. Current cultural values dictate that children readily challenge authority and disdain intellectual development and achievement. Not surprisingly, student apathy can be directly linked to parental apathy. Parents are so busy socializing, working at second jobs, feeding their addictions, and searching for personal fulfillment that they have no time to spend on their children's socialization.

Even if only half of these criticisms were justified, it seems logical to contend that contemporary society is ripe for a new interpretation of utopian living. Coupled with the need to regroup after the terrorist attacks, it is obvious that we desperately need a recipe for meaningful social change. This book is intended to ask how a utopian society can be formulated and even brought to fruition. It will tell the stories of thousands of optimists in various generations who dreamed up utopias and were willing to make great sacrifices to make them reality. Many of them were quite successful in their efforts, and their genius is evident in their creativity and commitment, as well as the longevity of their organizations. Some designed utopias were communal, while others were not; some had religious foundations and others did not. Most were agriculturally based, but others successfully operated on the growing edge of technological advance. What they all shared was a profound belief in the potentiality of the human spirit, and they were willing to lay aside their individual goals for the benefit of their contemporaries. They envisaged ideal forms of society in which the planners hoped to develop a form of social life that would allow them to live out their preferred set of values. In some cases utopia was perceived as a place to find release from an oppressive situation, but it was always bolstered by a strong hope for a better future.

Some questions that arise when the topic of utopian societies is discussed include: How do utopian societies (particularly communes) get started? Why would anyone participate in a utopian experiment? Why do such undertakings rarely last very long? And what are the common causes of breakdown for utopian societies? We will attempt to provide answers to those questions and examine the raison d'être for these kinds of experiments by analyzing the history and philosophy of several varied utopian societies. It should become evident that the dream of evolving an improved society must never die. Such dreams are the stuff of which new realities are born and can offer improvements to particular social segments, such as politics, economics, or religion, which would otherwise remain dull or in a deteriorating condition.

Historical research shows that utopian visions flourish in times when political and social patterns grow tedious. When the American communal experiments of the 1840s passed into oblivion, they were followed by the political ferment and Gold Rush of the 1850s, the American Civil War, and vast industrial developments in the next two decades. As the twentieth century rolled around, a new wave of sentiment and a spirit of cooperation struck the continent, placing new emphasis on the idea of communal living. The three shiploads carrying a total of 7,500 Doukhobors who relocated to western Canada from Russia in 1899 are a case in point. They left behind them many hurtful experiences of persecution and restriction. When they reached the land of opportunity where they were assigned huge pieces of land in exchange for the promise of hard work, they were elated. Within a few years they built 57 communal villages and cooperatively owned large herds of horses, oxen, and cattle.

A multiplicity of communes formed in the United States just prior to the 1900s, most of them designed by middle-class contingents who wanted to escape the drudgery of undue economic pressures. For a variety of reasons, most of them lasted only a few years. Most were not adequately prepared for the vast economic changes that occurred during their existence, while others miscalculated the intensity of pressure that often arises when individuals attempt to merge individual interpretations of utopia into a single organizational mode. Among the many relatively short-term utopian experiments were: the Progressive Community at Cedar Vale, Kansas, The Colorado Cooperative Company of Pinon, Colorado, The Ruskin Cooperative Association of Tennessee City and Cave Mills in Tennessee, The Brotherhood of the Cooperative Commonwealth at Equality, Washington, and the Christian Commonwealth at Commonwealth, Georgia.

Many cooperative experiments designed during the first half of the twentieth century emerged in response to the devastation of the two world wars. American society drifted somewhat aimlessly after World War II, probably recovering from the knowledge that humankind could now destroy itself in a very short time, thanks to atomic power. Movies of the immediate postwar era depicted happy, carefree themes, featuring the likes of Doris Day, Rock Hudson, and Marilyn Monroe. Unrealistic portrayals of family life flooded the television screen, and no one much cared if the families who played the roles in *Father Knows Best*, the *Donna Reed Show*, and *Leave It to Beaver* actually lived that way in their own personal lives. As Coontz (1992:2) suggests in her excellent study, *The Way We Never Were: American Families and the Nostalgia Trap*, "I hope to expose many of 'our memories' of traditional family life as myths. Families have always been in flux and often in crisis; they have never lived up to nostalgic notions about 'the way things used to be.' But that doesn't mean the malaise and anxiety people feel about modern families are delusions, that everything would be fine if we would only realize that the past was not all it's cracked up to be."

PROTEST MOVEMENTS

One of the more interesting reactionary crusades in North America occurred in the 1960s in the form of the hippie movement, a relatively
short-lived experiment in antiestablishment behavior. When threats of a
third world war loomed, the youth of America sprang into action to
protest. Their loudest objections were against the war in Vietnam which,
as history has shown, was not won by anybody. Hundreds of American
youth fled the country to avoid military service and were labeled draft
dodgers. A large contingent of them camped out in western Canada on
the west coast of Vancouver Island near the Village of Tofino, where they
built their own utopia of sorts—a series of temporarily constructed, ram-
shackle buildings bolstered by equally unstable arts complexes. Their
philosophy of life included such ideas as a belief in natural foods, enlightenment through drugs, and communal living. They claimed not to
value achievement, commitment, materialistic success, or competition.
Spencer (1990:70) describes their lifestyle: "Its members countered
straight culture by looking scruffy, using drugs, believing in astrology

0.1   Former hippie haven near Long Beach, British Columbia

and tarot, experimenting with unusual sexual relationships, living on yogurt and sunflower seeds, selling candles and beads on the sidewalk, and the like." Within 30 years, there were few signs that the area had ever played host to these rebels, many of them giving up the fight by melding into mainstream society.

RELIGIOUS IMPACT

A religious front was also evident in hippie protests. Not content only to bash economic and governmental institutions, some spiritual seekers with no previous church affiliation invaded the sanctuaries of various church denominations with the intent of affecting both liturgy and theology. Charismatic Pentecostal churches were prime targets of the "Jesus People Movement," and soon everybody who could claim to have had a personal experience with "the Savior, Jesus Christ," became an instant evangelist. Religious gatherings were highlighted by hours of near-chanting short Christian songs known as choruses, interrupted by frequent personal testimonial outbursts and phrases of praise. It was sometimes hard to tell if sermons were being preached or if individuals were merely responding to an inner spirit prompting them to exclaim. These meetings often ended with promises of Divine healing for the earnest seeker (Friesen, 1995a:31–36).

Observers were often quite harsh in their criticisms of charismatic religion. Columnist James Beverly made light of a Toronto revival campaign of the California-originated Vineyard movement started by John Wimber. Beverly suggested that mainline theologians might find some of the charismatic displays hard to endorse. According to Beverly, emotion ran so high in a meeting he attended that "a few individuals hit the concrete hard when they were 'slain in the spirit'" *(Faith Today,* Sept/Oct, 1994:13).

Perhaps organized Christian religion, more than any other institution, was transformed by the counterculture of the 1960s. Theology became simplified, and most larger congregations today feature two different kinds of Sunday morning worship services—traditional and seeker-oriented. The former service remains relatively untouched from its traditional mode, featuring hymns, a choir, an offering, and a sermon, while the latter is more responsive to the affective domain. Hymns are virtually nonexistent in these services, sermons are more informal and shorter, and the choir will have been replaced by a contemporary musical band featuring drums, tambourines, and other percussion instruments. The atmosphere of the seeker model is often more upbeat and joyful, and personal testimonials are frequently offered in place of sermons. Attire is informal, free from a dress code of any kind, so visitors never have to feel uncomfortable.

There were other lessons to be learned from the hippies, and for a decade or so it seemed as though the country was listening. New slogans such as a "kinder, gentler tone" appeared on the business horizon but quickly disappeared as the hippies grew up and obtained steady employment in order to better provide for their families. Orange-colored, flowered buses were replaced with smart import cars and three-bedroom houses that looked exactly like the others on the block. Clothing and hair styles were also amended; men began to shave and women abandoned their floor-length denim skirts. Now in their early to mid-fifties, many previous promoters of alternative lifestyles have adopted mainline values and behaviors.

Somewhat ironically, but not surprisingly, as the children of hippie parents grew up they often reacted against the antiestablishment zeal of their parents and strongly endorsed the leviathan of capitalism. In some ways they became even more security-minded to the point of entering the workforce and contemplating what their pension plans might look like after several decades of employment. As university students they adopted an eager but somewhat committed perspective, the former because they wanted to do well on exams, and the latter because reality dictated that academic achievement is usually correlated with economic success. During the mid-1970s, when protests had abated to something less than a feeble whisper, some academics discovered that the post-hippie generation had become so success-oriented that they were quite apt to write down the words, "Good morning class," if uttered by an entering professor. It was just as predictable that some student would raise his or her hand and ask if that utterance would be on the next examination. The utopia of antiestablishment behavior was disappointingly over.

THE UTOPIAN NEED

The fundamental premise on which this discussion is based is that utopian dreams are badly needed in modern society because our societal *Weltanschauung* (worldview) is almost entirely void of divergent thinking. Modern society is currently in need of alternative thinking with regard to the possible nature of future states. At present our inventors and creative geniuses are singly primed towards structuring a way of life that depends on more of the same—increased gadgetry, faster and more luxurious automobiles, and increased technology that will further reduce the time spent completing essential tasks. Any proposal that suggests a reduction to the rate of gadgetry production or taking more time to accomplish menial tasks is tantamount to heresy.

There is some hope, however. There are indications that people are wearying of trying to keep up with the treadmill of conformity and quick obsolescence. It can be very annoying to find oneself constantly out of step with the mad rush to update computer equipment, purchase the latest cell phone, or rid oneself of a year-old vehicle. The Y2K scare that threatened a societal shutdown unless computers were updated virtually flooded the market with new models. The result was that high-tech companies had to invent ways to relegate equipment to the scrap heap of obsolescence in less time than the usual 90-day period. Fortunately for individuals who *do* put some thought into actually designing a life pattern, a measure of resistance has emerged. Recent changes in North American institutional life have motivated some North Americans to reassess their priorities and ask the question, "Are human relationships more important than economic success?"

Without utopian dreams and "what if" conceptualizations, society would be philosophically impoverished. In following their dreams, some individuals write provocative lines of poetry and prose while others envisage inventions, and sometimes either approach can have great effects on society as a whole. The visualization of utopian societies can also have significant implications for corporate human practice. Greater numbers of people are usually involved in these experiments, and their chosen forms of lifestyle are capable of attracting a great deal of attention, particularly when they deviate significantly from the norm.

Nearly half a century ago, Andrew Hacker (1956) postulated that utopian idealism could serve as a spur to alternative thinking. Utopian vision might be a star to guide society in a new direction and offer alternative ways of perceiving life itself. Utopians do not usually perceive solutions to societal dilemmas in piecemeal ways. The only rationale for pursuing a patchwork approach would be if sufficient scraps could be blended together to resolve an unwanted situation. Hacker illustrated this point by suggesting that if a town water supply was contaminated, it would not be satisfactory to resolve the matter merely by applying chemicals to the water and then going on with life. Broader questions pertaining to the nature of an ideal society would have to be raised. Could citizens rest assured that the problem had permanently been resolved or should they look towards possible relocation? Would a pure water supply contribute to a greater degree of satisfaction with life as a whole? Would the provision of a pure water supply be made available to all citizens?

Hacker insisted that a society emphasizing such values as freedom, equality, and democracy would more likely be realized if it was filled with people who intrinsically demonstrated those attributes rather than having them enforced by law. And why not? The fundamental question, however, is not whether such people exist, but where can they be found and how can they be brought together? The late Robert Kennedy said that when complex problematic situations arise, some would be inclined to ask, "Why? How could this happen?" Speaking at the memorial service of his dead brother, the late President John Fitzgerald Kennedy, Robert Kennedy, paraphrasing George Bernard Shaw, spoke these immortal words: "Some people see things as they are, and say why. I dream of things that never were and say, Why not. Today I propose to speak of things that could be, and say, Why not?" (Spinrad and Spinrad, 1979:254). Conjuring up a vision of an ideal society allows that kind of "leap in the dark" thinking. It is not restricted by what is, but rather motivated by what could be. Futurists believe that any dismal reality can be immeasurably brightened by speculative thinking. If this premise is valid, it strengthens the need for more utopian ideas.

As one studies utopian movements one is increasingly impressed with the naivety and honesty of the people who involve themselves in these ventures. Their ideals are very explicit, not camouflaged by tricky slogans, dishonest sales pitches, or hidden agendas. Instead of sneaking their ideas in by the back door, they march them in through the front door, right into the living rooms and into the hearts of anyone who will listen. Who but utopian-minded individuals would accept the validity of such postulates as the Beatitudes found in the Bible? "Blessed are the poor in spirit, for theirs is the kingdom of Heaven. Blessed are those who mourn, for they will be comforted. Blessed are the meek, for they will inherit the earth. Blessed are those who hunger and thirst for righteousness, for they will be filled. Blessed are the merciful, for they will be shown mercy" (Matthew 5:3–7).

CRITICISMS

Utopians are not without their critics, of course, and the twentieth century has not been too kind to them. Kumar (1993) observes that the fall of the Soviet Union convinced many of its strongest supporters that their utopian formula was not workable on a large scale. For those left-wing socialists who were less than convinced that the Soviet Union constituted a legitimate example of the concept, notions of utopia were still welcome. Those leaning a little more to the right of center were, naturally, quite harsh in their attacks on the Soviet notion of utopia. This was to be expected. Utopian visionaries are generally viewed with suspicion, particularly when they espouse new doctrines that deviate significantly from or stand in direct opposition to mainstream values (Rothstein, 2003:1).

As Kumar (1993) points out, to many societal conformists, utopia is by definition an affront. To their satisfaction, the historical record is rife with examples of failed utopias, and this supports their argument that the development of new experiments is unrealistic and futile. Many such ventures were unappealing enough in their lifetime to end in division, unpleasant conflict, or even bloody revolution. The few utopias that persisted for more than three generations have more often been analyzed.

It is time that this perspective was reexamined. Perhaps reading about some of the utopian experiments outlined in this book will make it possible to gain a new appreciation for the vision and energy of individuals who sincerely try to improve society. It may also whet one's appetite for conceiving alternative lifestyles. There is ample variation in the approaches outlined in this book; some developed experiments on a strong religious and/or communal base, while others were secularly economic in outlook. We have divided the chapters of the book accordingly.

The methodology for this project was to visit, research, and photograph as many representative utopian sites as possible. There are a few exceptions, in which case we relied on published materials and the Internet. In some instances, like that of the Harmonists, the trail literally led us across the country to Pennsylvania, Indiana, Missouri, and Oregon. We spoke to as many individuals as we could who had historical connections to the organizations we researched. For example, at Bethel, Missouri, we met 80-year-old Virgil Culler, the oldest living member of the former Bethel Colony.

As we traveled and studied, it became clear to us that Canada and the United States have a rich history of foresighted men and women who saw what they perceived to be weaknesses in our social systems, and they did something about it. They attempted to build alternative institutions and lifestyles—to develop new ways of looking at society, life, and the universe. You may think of them as dreamers, but their stories make for intriguing reading.

Undoubtedly, there are many other utopian efforts that we did not make note of. However, after eight years of pursuit, we decided it was time to put pen to paper, and this book is the result. We offer our apologies to any individuals and organizations whose contributions may not be included. We hope you enjoy reading these stories; we certainly had a good time researching the topic.

Scripture quotations in this book are taken from the New International Version (NIV) of the Bible unless otherwise indicated. "KJV" denotes King James Version.

J. W. F.

V. L. F.

CHAPTER 1

THE CONCEPT OF UTOPIA

To dismiss utopia as a foolish and discredited notion without relevance to the world today would be to dismiss an ideal which has an irresistible attraction for large numbers of people and which helps to explain behavior that otherwise would seem incomprehensible.
—Peyton E. Richter (1971a:1)

Like other fields of inquiry, the social sciences have attempted to move with the times, even to the point of developing new descriptors for familiar social phenomena. The study of utopian societies is a case in point; a number of related components must be clarified at the outset of this discussion. First of all, it is important to note that not all utopian experiments are communal in nature, although the tendency to believe that they are is fairly common. Neither are utopian communities necessarily religious in philosophy, nor are they necessarily antiestablishment or delusional gatherings. It is true that many of them originated in response to the dreams or visions of a particularly charismatic individual, but others emerged as a result of rational group action or as what might be termed extended forms of social antithesis.

DEFINING UTOPIA

A sociological definition of a utopian community is a group of people who are attempting to establish a new social pattern based upon a vision of the ideal society, and who have withdrawn themselves from society at large in order to give a face to that vision in experimental form (Hine, 1983:5). A less academic definition, and one that would more obviously appeal to one's emotional side, would be "a place where the sun always shines, where Mother Nature teaches surfers who's boss, where a slice lands your ball in the ocean, and where Alaska Airlines offers you Double Air Miles" (Scott, 1997:12)

Abrahamson (1996:2f) introduces the useful concept of an enclave which he defines as a special relationship between a distinctive group of people and a place. An enclave has some characteristics of a subculture, in which a group of people share common traditions and values that are ordinarily maintained by a high rate of interaction within the group.

There is a tendency to conceive of enclaves as self-styled utopias of sorts when in effect many of them evolve due to socioeconomic pressures. A good example is San Francisco's Chinatown, which was formed due to ostracism of the Chinese after the Gold Rush of 1849 and continues today. In reality, a large proportion of Chinatown residents feel relatively dissatisfied with life in their enclave. They dislike the noise and crowded conditions and do not feel that they live in a utopia of any sort (Abrahamson, 1996:67).

Perhaps it is just human nature to dream of better days, or more efficient, easier ways of doing things. The French philosopher, Emile Descartes, once speculated that because mankind could envisage that perfection could be perceived, a form of perfection could indeed be possible. For Descartes, of course, this also meant that God must exist since mankind could conceive of such a Being. For social scientists generally, this line of reasoning means that people by their very nature will continue to envisage and pursue varying forms of the ideal. Certainly the European peasants who migrated to North America several centuries ago perceived of this continent as offering a kind of ideal location for living out their social and religious ideals.

After examining the literature on utopias, it becomes clear that an expanded definition incorporates fairly obtuse parameters. Our objective was to research at least several sites that were representative of the major utopian categories—communal and noncommunal, religious and secular, orthodox and unusual. The final chapter attempts to highlight the positive factors of the various experiments in order to show the feasibility of further utopian endeavors.

It is interesting to note that some utopian beginnings involved large numbers of people, while others started as a small gathering of committed individuals and then progressed or faded in relation to the movement's ability to attract and maintain membership. All of the visionaries discussed in this book shared consensus on one objective: to improve society directly, or at least influence what were seen to be positive developments from the outside. In light of these considerations, it is important that the study of utopian experiments not be limited to an examination of communal groups only, because that phenomenon is only one expression of the human spirit in seeking to improve life on planet earth. Although many writers employ the terms "utopia" and "commune" interchangeably (Kanter, 1972), that will not be the case in this discussion.

The concept of *intentional communities* (Shenker, 1986), has been employed by social scientists to describe utopian experiments involving both communal and noncommunal communities and other social movements aimed at preserving a unique collective purpose. Intentional communities may be differentiated from organizations, sects, and social movements by the fact that they are usually comprised of a relatively small group of individuals who have created a unique way of life for the attainment of an articulated set of goals. These groups are labeled intentional communities because they are not like a tribe or village that began spontaneously and then persisted for generations. Intentional communities are initiated through deliberate effort in order to realize a set of specific goals. Members of such a community will not have known each other before the "call was given" to fulfill a certain mission. Intentional communities are characterized by face-to-face relations, and while they frequently embrace communalism as an ethical end in itself apart from its instrumental value, they are not necessarily communal. They have collective goals and needs and expectations, and *may* prize sharing of goods as an essential ingredient. Ultimately the community will be the final authority as to what comprises appropriate behavior.

THEORETICAL INPUT

In an attempt to unpack the hidden meanings of utopianism, Davis (1984) differentiated four kinds of utopian designs: arcadianism, anarchism, millennialism, and moral reform programs. Arcadianism refers to a form of utopia with an aesthetic or moral sense, which differentiates it from anarchism because the latter exists primarily for the purpose of fulfilling individual or group goals. An arcadian kind of utopia seeks to appease these appetites but does so in a temperate way. In pursuing a form of "civil war," anarchists see themselves as restoring a social balance that existing political systems have eroded. French and French (1975:152) suggest that anarchism comes in many versions, including individualism, mutualism, collectivism, communism, syndicalism, or pacifism. The most common feature of anarchism is resistance to government infringement on what are deemed to be basic human rights. Critics of the Doukhobor movement would probably claim that such behavior was indulged in when the Doukhobors undertook their first public demonstration in southern Russia on June 29, 1895, in the "Burning of Arms." Originating in the 1650s in Russia, the Doukhobors were one of many alternative movements that took issue with the spiritual direction of the Russian Orthodox Church. Patriarch Nikon introduced Greek-theme reforms, which led to protests by many believers; the Doukhobors were one of these factions. Their form of protest was based on the concept that God exists in spirit and truth and each individual is his or her own church. They therefore rejected the priesthood, adopted communalism, and became vegetarians (Tarasoff, 2002:1–2).

At times, contempt for proposed societal variations is manifest in harsh actions. Public executions of sixteenth-century Anabaptist groups such as Amish, Hutterites, and Mennonites were intended to discourage both adherents and the public by showing that state authorities would not tolerate religious deviance. Basically, any effort to build a new social order is generally termed anarchy or some other negative label by those who wield power.

Millennialism is a third kind of utopia, which assumes that nature and humankind will be transformed by a force arising and acting independently of the wills of men and women. Rasporich (1987:220) outlines five salient features of movements that would qualify as millenarian, namely: (i) collective; (ii) terrestrial; (iii) imminent; (iii) promising a total change in the new dispensation; and, (iv) presaging a supernatural moment at a near-total end of history.

The origins of millennialist visions have a solidly Christian base, and arise out of a fear of triumphant evil rather than the triumph of chaos. The underlying motivation is the belief that the Antichrist will be defeated and Jesus Christ will establish peace on earth for a thousand years. During this time, all faithful Christians who have suffered and remained loyal will reign with Christ, and when the millennium is over there will be a comprehensive judgment of all humankind.

The fourth kind of utopian format includes those who push for a society based on a prescriptive moral order. There are many historic examples, some of which will be discussed in later chapters. Utopian moralists envisage the development of a perfect moral commonwealth, possibly following Immanuel Kant's suggestion of rationally appealing to the good will and experience of all people in perfecting an ideal society. Although the exact nature of the perceived society is often unarticulated, some groups have managed successfully to live for long periods of time in relatively exemplary premillennial formats. Perhaps the best example is that of the Hutterian Brethren, whose lifestyle has altered little despite their sojourn over several centuries on several different continents.

Moral utopians generally believe that economic inequality is anathema to reasoned living because of the poverty and suffering that it engenders; it is both an inefficient and unfair kind of social structure which causes unnecessary waste and creates unwarranted social class differences and aristocracies of wealth. Other negative results include the diminution of human dignity and the deprivation of chances for self-betterment and social mobility for certain social segments. Economic inequality is fundamentally linked to the division of labor, which implies that some jobs are more important than others, and some people's skills are more valuable then others. The attainment of fairness, then, rests on the abolition of private property and the improvement of capitalism. For most of these utopians, the former criterion can best be accomplished through group ownership and communal living. Reality dictates, however, that capitalism is still viewed as a superior method of running the economy, and socialism and communism as mainstream systems are generally rejected. Improved capitalism implies placing restrictions on income and ownership, even allowing a measure of state ownership in the formula. A number of nineteenth-century American experiments, such as Amana and Robert Owen's New Harmony, and one twentieth-century model (the Bruderhof) endorsed this paradigm on the basis that it best fulfilled the tenets of an improved capitalistic way of life (Goodwin, 1984).

COMMUNAL UTOPIAS

Communes comprise a unique (and probably the best known) form of utopianism. The concept of living together and sharing resources is probably as old as civilization itself, but communalism has rarely been accepted as an orthodox way to live. Although many observers regard communes as self-evident absurd phenomena, they do exhibit a wide variety of purposes and structures (Abrams, McCulloch, Abrams and Gere, 1976:1). More recent communes that began after the protest movement of the 1960s may be characterized as short-lived, radical, and often unorthodox in both style and character. An example would be the back-to-the-land movement, whose operations today are hardly recognizable from the original vision (Jacob, 1997). The back-to-the-land phenomenon began as a protest movement akin to that inspired by the "flower children" of that era. Later they developed a myriad of divergent lifestyles, featuring an odd admixture of self-denial and selective capitalism.

Some communes initiated during the seventeenth and eighteenth centuries when North America was being settled by Europeans enjoyed a remarkable degree of endurance. The Shakers, begun in 1772, have persisted for more than two centuries, the Harmonists lasted 90 years, and the Ephrata Cloister lasted 63 years. Many immigrants who relocated to North America during that time perceived the opportunity to settle on this continent in utopian terms. They viewed the continent as the land of the second chance (Palmer, 1972). Much of the success of their experiments could possibly be attributed to such factors as available land and freedom of opportunity, that is, enthused motivation inspired by the opportunity to build a new social order and the rise of industrialism paralleled by religious revivalism.

Definitions and classifications of communes are legion, as are their records of performance and staying power. Carter (1974) identified six major varieties of communes: self-actualizing, activist, therapeutic, practical, communes for mutual support, and religious communes. Abrams, McCulloch, Abrams, and Gere (1976:141) conducted an extensive study of modern activist communes in Britain and observed that this form of utopia could be regarded as a species of petty-bourgeois protest. These experiments failed to accommodate effectively the basic requirements of such a model for living, which includes seven criteria: (i) the challenge of dealing with generational differences; (ii) determining a workable family arrangement; (iii) deciding a format for governance; (iv) accommodating the need for recreation; (v) determining a form of identity; (vi) formulating a functional pattern for community; and, (vii) accommodating the politics of revolution. These criteria will be further alluded to in the final chapter, in which it will be shown that by borrowing from the various historical experiments, a model of a functional utopia is a reasonable undertaking. Several alternative lifestyle organizations like Amana, the Doukhobors, Zoar, and the Hutterian Brethren operated humane, satisfying, comfortable, and economically viable societies. Their concept of utopia in progress (with a few riders) fulfills virtually all of the criteria of a viable model for living.

Studies of communal life are frequently concerned with their raison d'être, fragility, and failure. Kraushaar (1980:5–6) speculated that the impulse to found a utopian society basically emerges from three kinds of considerations: religious-spiritual, political-economic, and psycho-social. Examples of all three types are described in this book. The first type has basically been characterized as Christian. The second type emerged as a potent force mainly in the mid-nineteenth century in response to the effects of the industrial revolution, that is, labor exploitation, the factory system, urbanization, pauperism, and so on. The third type arose as a result of the vision of individuals who saw society as forcing people to live in an unnatural, competitive, depersonalized, and alienated way that destroyed their human potential. Its promoters identified what they called a "sickness of the establishment" that could not be healed, and so the founding of an alternative lifestyle with greater promise was their only hope.

As European newcomers scampered to build a new life in eighteenth-century America, some groups developed a format that combined Kraushaar's first and second types; they were motivated by a religious-political push from home while seeking to fulfill the envisaged dream of peace, plenty, and prosperity. These visionaries came to build utopias that would be free from autocracy and despotism, and they were relieved when they discovered that the sufferings they endured at the hands of political dictators in Europe were finally behind them.

WHY UTOPIA?

There are many reasons why men and women have visions of building a better world, but regretfully, too many of them do not find fruition. Many utopian experiments originate because people are dissatisfied with their lot. The causes for such unhappiness may be economic, social, psychological, or spiritual. Thus, when an appropriate promising movement presents itself, these individuals will most certainly attach themselves to it. If the perceived opportunity attracts a sufficient number of people, others will likely soon join the party. Those who are not particularly prone to making decisions on their own may even join the movement on the basis that someone else, like a charismatic leader, will make all major decisions for them. This was certainly the case with communal experiments like the Bruderhof, Ephrata, Icarians, Harmonists, Mormons, Owenites, Oneida, and Shakers.

Utopian movements are sometimes undertaken by individuals living in dire straits. Sometimes it can be a matter of life or death. The

Doukhobors, for example, left Russia because of religious persecution, and the Amish, Mennonites, and Hutterites vacated Central Europe and headed to Russia for similar reasons. Later these groups found it necessary to flee from Russia when severe restrictions were placed on their religious lifestyle in that country.

Utopian ventures are sometimes undertaken because people get bored with their surroundings and therefore join an already extant experiment because they lack the personal ambition required to alter their situation. Joint experiments have a way of promising security to joiners. This was particularly so in the case of what might be called migrating utopias, namely those started in Europe and transplanted to North America. Examples include the Harmonists led by George Rapp, who brought 600 people to the new land in 1803; 350 Amana people who followed Christian Metz to America in 1803; and 225 Separatists who came to Ohio with Joseph Bimeler in 1817.

Religious motivations were probably the primary force behind the establishment of eighteenth- and nineteenth-century utopian experiments because this was a time when religious revivalism flourished. Fogarty (1990:117) postulates that in order for these utopian dreams to be operationalized it was necessary that the originators propose a unique agenda that would attract followers. For example, utopian promoters could make claims that the new way of life they were envisaging would fulfill the aspired personal needs of joiners. Some of them, like Shakers and Oneidans, claimed that their new world order would offer more freedom and security than was available in mainstream society. A number of nineteenth-century movements began in response to what was perceived to be deteriorating religious institutional life in North America. As new spiritual forms were made available, joiners quickly hopped onto virtually any bandwagon that promised spiritual renewal. The underside of this action was the perception that the evils generated by a morally deteriorating society had to be avoided at all costs. This realization made isolationist proposals very attractive to those who wished to cancel their memberships in established institutions and quickly form new ones. The Shaker movement under Ann Lee's leadership is a case in point. In 1781, Lee attracted a large number of followers in a brief preaching tour that lasted only two years. The Shakers were not able to sustain this momentum, however, and gradually their numbers began to decrease.

A STRONG DREAM

Between 1762 and 1900, more than 100 utopian societies were built in North America or transferred here, but few survived. When the immigrants first arrived, they found it more expedient to rely on cooperative than individual efforts in striving to develop the frontier. Thus they built communes. When this need dissipated, many such experiments failed because of internal deterioration and developing factions. Others simply outgrew their utopian ideals in a land quickly beset by individualistic and capitalistic realities. Still, as some utopian experiments faded into oblivion, others quickly replaced them.

Bestor (1959:7) suggests that the form of communitarianism that became peculiarly attractive in the nineteenth century was motivated by the realization that alternative methods of social reform had reached a dead end. Individualism seemed incapable of answering the need for collective action and so new communal experiments were initiated. Revolutions had shown themselves to be inadequate instruments for effective social change, as was evident in France, and the problem with industrialization was that it had outdistanced its potential to solve the very problems it was causing. Some nineteenth-century projects, like George Rapp's Harmonists, Charles Fourier's phalanxes, and Robert Owen's New Harmony experiment were deliberately planned as models of effective living. In other instances where utopian experiments failed, the cause may have been that they were originally begun as planned vehicles to tame the frontier. When that challenge had abated and prospects of individual riches rose (Zoar, for example), communalism as a way of life seemed much less attractive.

Walters (1989:59) conjectures that utopian designs are primarily about the desire to improve society based on principles reflecting a notion of transcendence. Transcendent ideas not only call into question the established conceptual, normative, and social structures of the historical context within which they arise, but they may also serve to erode the strength of those structures' authorities. Utopian ideologies, through antiestablishment behavior, may transform existing social realities into a reality that is more in accord with their own conceptions. Conversely, they may also find themselves under attack in societies that feel threatened by contrary social forms. This reality will be explored as our discussion continues.

The following chapter explores the universal desire to attain a desirable lifestyle via a series of brief historical case studies in Europe, the Middle East, Canada, and the United States. Chapters 3, 4, and 5 detail a series of utopian experiments having noncommunal, communal, religious, or economic themes. Because of its long and varied history, the Harmonist model is dealt with separately in chapter 6. Chapter 7 outlines the Ephrata and Oneida utopias, which are often viewed as unorthodox because of their unique beliefs and patterns of living. Chapter 8 underscores the fact that utopian ideals are alive and well and offers a summary of several contemporary experiments. Like the Harmonists, the Hutterian Brethren merit a separate chapter (9) because of their long and successful operation. The final chapter constitutes an attempt to show the feasibility of developing an alternative lifestyle by borrowing elements from those who have gone before.

CHAPTER 2

THE NEED FOR UTOPIA

Ah but a man's reach should exceed his grasp, or what's
a heaven for?
—Robert Browning, "Andrea del Sarto" (1942: 185).

We have outgrown the medieval view of the world and al-
most destroyed the aboriginal view. We must find a new
view, one that allows us to control the damage we are
causing to ourselves and to the universe.
—Andrew Scott (1997:17).

Plato is often credited with originating the notion of utopia with his *Republic*. Plato's conceptualizations were probably reflective of his time and comprised a dream to which his fellow citizens aspired. From the ethereal regions of his exalted metaphysics his scheme drew the imagination of his readers, emphasizing the principles of mercy, goodness, and justice as foundational concepts (Godwin, 1972:9). Sir Thomas More's political, fictional essay entitled *Utopia,* published in 1516, has been seen as an embellishment of Plato. More envisaged an ideal commonwealth having a perfect political and social system, paralleling to some extent the ideas of Plato. More's utopia was the bridge by which he sought to span the gap between the old order of the Middle Ages and the new interests and institutions of the Renaissance. No doubt such an idyllic dwelling place has been the dream of individuals in every culture and every generation. Despite centuries of searching, ultimate fulfillment for the entire human race will likely never occur, but the quest must go on. Literally dozens of schemes have been devised in every age by which to bring about such a state, and these imaginative schemes fuel the fires of human urge and desire.

There is little doubt that Edward Bellamy's book, *Looking Backward,* published in 1887, exerted more influence upon the popular imagination than any other publication. H. G. Wells's *A Modern Utopia,* published in the first decade of the twentieth century, supplemented Bellamy's work, again fueling the passion for utopia. Bellamy was a relatively unknown writer, but his book sold some 200,000 copies with its first printing. By the end of the year it was the most purchased novel in the United States except for *Uncle Tom's Cabin* published some 35 years earlier.

Bellamy's novel served as an incentive for furthering the utopian dream, as well as providing one of the primary inspirations for the growth of American nationalist political sentiment in the last decade of the nineteenth century. One of the key objectives of Bellamy's work was to defend the country's economic structure, which he defined as state capitalism. Walters (1989:211) asserts that Bellamy's position strengthened the resolve of the American petit bourgeoisie and agriculturalists who founded the short-lived Populist Party of the 1880s and 1890s. Bellamy's vision also appealed to the growing number of individuals who believed that maximization of economic efficiency could be attained through the creation of a hierarchical form of administration and a disciplined workforce.

A later attempt to elaborate the utopian urge was penned by American social philosopher Louis Mumford (1962): *The Story of Utopia.* Mumford pointed out that utopian proposals can offer fresh prospects and ideals for critical consideration. Their advantage is that by their very existence they constitute implicit criticisms of the civilizations that nurtured them and affirmations of human potentialities that have been ignored by existing institutions. Mumford went on to note that in their zeal to promote ideals, utopians often neglect concrete realities and overestimate the malleability of society. Still, their defects are minimized to some extent by their refusal to consider institutions separately but instead to view them as dynamically interrelated parts of an entire social order.

COMMUNAL VARIATION

The most obvious query that emerges when studying utopian experiments pertains to the possible motivation of their members. Some utopian experiments are probably initiated because people weary of their day-to-day status and long for a more meaningful or exciting way to live. Other would-be reformers simply desire to improve society by designing antithetical formats, which they hope will influence others to join them.

As history shows, communes are a very popular response to the utopian urge, and they are probably formed because proponents of utopian ideals perceive that philosophical consensus can be better implemented by encompassing all facets of daily living. Kanter (1972:126) emphasizes that there is comfort in commitment derived from firm group ties and strong family feelings. Speculation as to why people fall in with communal schemes has been narrowed to a series of reasons. It has been suggested that poverty alone will drive people into communalism; but when poverty is combined with ostracism due to peculiar beliefs, people are more likely to tend towards separation from the mainstream. This perception has been borne out in the case of dozens of utopian models ranging from cultic collectivities like the Texas Branch Davidians to the more tolerant Amana People, to modern-day Doukhobors and Hutterites. Ostracism has a way of reinforcing deviant beliefs and behaviors.

Patterns for the fulfillment of utopian dreams sometimes take on peculiar characteristics, showing that human beings will sometimes go to extreme lengths to fulfill their thirst for belonging and meaning. The following examples will substantiate this proposition and illustrate that utopian dreams often have strong intercontinental connections, many of them between Europe and North America.

THE MÜNSTER KINGDOM

An intriguing yet extreme commune was formed in the early part of the sixteenth century at the peak of the Protestant Reformation. The radical wing of the movement was the Anabaptists, who preached a millenarian form of gospel that implied that the end of the world was just around the corner. A popular slogan, allegedly derived from the Sermon on the Mount delivered by Jesus Christ (Matthew, chapters 5–7) was "Live as though the world were going to end tomorrow in all your dealings with your fellowman" (Rexroth, 1974:110). Reactions to this mandate varied; some Anabaptists simply interpreted their role to be to live as simply as possible without accumulating many material goods. Others interpreted it in spiritual terms and justified a certain degree of integration with the world in order to spread the Gospel and perhaps influence their peers towards a more equitable society.

The Münsterites were a radical group who perceived their role in the most literal terms and renounced all forms of societal integration, claiming that they should live together and have all things in common. In 1533 they occupied the city of Strassburg, a small ecclesiastical state in Germany, under the leadership of Thomas Münster, Melchior Hoffman, Jan Matthijs, and Jan van Leiden. Under severe persecution by state authorities almost immediately, the chiliastic seeds of Hoffman's gospel produced an evil harvest. According to Hoffman, the new age would be realized in 1533 in Strassburg where the great tribulation had already begun. When Hoffman was imprisoned, Matthijs used a new prophecy to change the location to the city of Münster in northwest Germany (Toews, 1975:7).

Residents of the "New Jerusalem" found refuge in renouncing all outside forms of life and practiced complete communalism. They also used the Bible as the sole authority for church doctrine, took up the practice of polygamy (probably because of the imbalance of the sexes within the group), and used baptism as a form of political alliance rather than a sign of discipleship. No behavioral deviance was tolerated and the wayward were severely punished (Smith, 1957:72). Roman Catholics, Lutherans, and neutrals quickly fled the city and their remaining properties were confiscated by those inside.

Münster was quickly surrounded by opposing forces and the food supply within the city dwindled, even though all available soil was planted for food. By the spring of 1535 the residents were desperate and famine and disease threatened their early demise. Small groups of dissidents tried to escape, but when caught were put to death. What happened next was as much a sad commentary on society at large as it was on the communalists. The end of the Münster revolt came when two men, Hans Eck and Henry Gresbeck, escaped and betrayed one of the city gates to outside forces who soon conquered the city. The captured Münster leaders were then paraded about the country for six months in cages and then brought back to Münster where they were tried, condemned, and tortured to death. Thomas Münster tried to recant his violent revolutionary teachings, but his victors chose to execute him along with 53 other partisans (Marty, 2003:77). Their bodies were then placed in cages and hung from the tower of St. Lambert's Church. They remained there until the end of the nineteenth century, a dismal token of opposition to utopian ideals (Rexroth, 1974:118).

METLAKATLA

Born in England in 1832 to a very poor family, William Duncan became the manager of the first, if not the only, Aboriginal commune in North America. While still a young man, Duncan emigrated to Canada with the Church of England Missionary Society. His objective was to establish a mission among the First Nations of British Columbia. He arrived in Vancouver in June 1857 and traveled to Fort Simpson, some 500 miles north, where the Anglican Church had already selected a site. A community of 2,300 souls awaited Duncan at Fort Simpson, one of the largest First Nations settlements in the province. Conveniently for Duncan, entire bands of Tsimshian people had left their traditional villages and moved their longhouses to Fort Simpson to be closer to where the fur trade flourished (Scott, 1997).

At first Duncan was a bit overwhelmed with his assignment. Although not ordained by the church, he began holding worship services and offering religious instruction wherever he could. He struggled with learning the language, eventually mastering a basic vocabulary of 1,500 Tsimshian words. Typical of missionaries of the time, Duncan bemoaned the deplorable state of Aboriginal culture, which he described as consisting of drunkenness, slavery, prostitution, and barbarous ceremonial dancing. He departed from collegial thinking when he observed that the First Nations were intelligent and industrious people, and he resolved to build on those attributes in establishing his own mission.

Duncan began a school during his first year as a missionary and within two years had attracted a group of 50 adherents. He shared his vision of a utopian Aboriginal colony with the governor of the province, and with the latter's support, made plans to develop such a site a few miles south of Fort Simpson at a location known as Metlakatla, a Tsimshian word meaning "the place where two waters meet." An advance party began the work of building the village in May 1862, followed by a company of 300 who agreed to abide by Duncan's list of 15 regulations. Then a plague struck the colony and one-third of the members died. Still, the work proceeded, eventually to include 30 houses, and a 600-seat building that doubled as a church and school. The membership of the settlement was divided into companies, each governed by several councilors, elders, and constables. The primary governing body consisted of hereditary chiefs and Duncan himself.

The economy of Metlakatla included a sawmill, a fish-processing plant, and a store. Later soap and textile factories were added, as well as a tannery, a guesthouse, a fire hall, and a dog pound. Native handicrafts and other products were taken south by a boat Duncan purchased to the city of Victoria where he marketed the goods without benefit of middlemen. This meant that Duncan essentially controlled the fur trade in the region. At its peak of development, Metlakatla was home to several other missionaries who arrived at Duncan's invitation. In 1874 the village became home to St. Paul's Church, the largest cathedral west of Chicago and north of San Francisco. It was equipped with a vestibule, gallery, belfry and spire, groined arches, and solid timber frame. It had a seating capacity of 1,200.

The beginning of the death of Duncan's Metlakatla began when he developed a dislike for his superior, Bishop Hills of Victoria. The bishop wanted Duncan to be ordained, but the latter said he did not feel called to the ministry. Duncan also resisted providing the Eucharist (Holy Communion, or The Lord's Supper) to his converts on grounds that even the little bit of alcohol consumed in the sacrament could be damaging to a people he was trying to cure of alcoholism. Another of Bishop Hill's complaints against Duncan was that he had not tried to groom local Aboriginals to become clergymen. Then a revival of sorts flared up. A newly arrived Anglican clergyman, James Hall, began to preach with an emotional enthusiasm not previously heard in the colony. Duncan became concerned, but Bishop Hills supported Hall and would not back down to Duncan's protests. In an effort to break down Duncan's influence, the mission district of Metlakatla was divided into several regions governed by a local bishop, Bishop William Ridley, who also opposed Duncan. Duncan then took his quarrel to the federal government in Ottawa. Although not likely above board, Prime Minister John A. Macdonald influenced his party to award the settlement of Metlakatla to the Anglican mission society and put Duncan out of business (Scott, 1997:36).

The loss of control over the affairs of Metlakatla did not deter the illustrious William Duncan. In 1887, after negotiating with President Grover Cleveland of the United States, Duncan managed to procure a prospective settlement in Alaska, some 75 miles north of Fort Simpson in American territory. The American government was impressed with Duncan's progress in "civilizing the Indians" and responded positively to his pleas. Eight hundred people followed Duncan to the new location. Within a few months, the new colony began to take shape. Most of the buildings at Metlakatla were dismantled and relocated to the new settlement by boat. Again, a variety of industries was established and a huge cathedral was erected. In 1908, however, there was mutiny in the ranks, with some individuals demanding their fair share of the assets. Duncan had formed a company with all assets held in his own name; it took seven years to dismantle Duncan's empire because the United States government was reluctant to "take harsh measures with a kindly old man" (Scott, 1997:39). Ultimately, things got progressively worse and Duncan became more possessive. In 1915 control of the colony was assigned to the local Indian tribal council, an arrangement that still prevails. Duncan died in 1918 at the age of 86 and was buried in front of his church.

Today Metlakatla continues to be a typical thriving northern American Aboriginal neighborhood. Several denominations have established churches in the settlement and traditional Native spirituality has made a comeback. Spiritual leaders of nearby Aboriginal settlements have provided the locals with a wide range of traditional songs, prayers, and rituals to replace those they lost when Duncan first took over. Only a few village buildings of the old Metlakatla remain as testimony to Duncan's efforts.

THE KIBBUTZ

Launched by Zionist pioneers in Palestine prior to World War I, the kibbutz has become a unique and highly successful form of socialism. The first kibbutz was established in 1909, some 39 years before Israel became a nation, and some still operate today. Zionism, which first propelled the kibbutz, has three main ideologies. The first is traditionalism, which is grounded on the belief that the process of nation-building should be unconditionally connected to the creation of a theocratic state. The second view advocates the formation of an advanced industrial state as a refuge for Jews of the world. The third position is Zionist socialism, out of which the kibbutz emerged.

Essentially, the kibbutz is a democratic cooperative of production and consumption. It is completely voluntary and its stakeholders are equal participants in the decision-making process. Theologian Martin Buber (1949:139) once called it the most impressive experiment known in alternative ways of communal living. It was an experiment that has not yet failed (Harris, 1999). Essentially socialistic in principle, the kibbutz provides housing, education, and medical care for all of its members (Neubauer, 1965; Hillary, 1968:179). Because Israel operates on a mixed economy, in which the marketplace is matched in influence by a strong labor movement, a large public sector, and numerous liberal democratic cooperatives, the kibbutz has been able to evolve in a supportive environment. In fact, the kibbutz has managed to form a powerful network of communities that are fully integrated into Israel's national economy and political process (Melnyk, 1985:54).

The founders of the kibbutz movement were young pioneers who came to Palestine from Eastern Europe during 1904–1914 and 1919–1923. They were passionate idealists with a willingness to experiment. When they first began, these innovators lived in very primitive conditions, and the work to build a cooperative was physically exhausting. They began by setting up working groups, eventually forming a federation of these groups. They also established eight working principles: voluntarism, collective ownership, the religion of labor, labor by members, self-management, direct democracy, communal education, and communal child care. Although these principles parallel those of most intentional communities, it must be noted that the kibbutz was not established as a utopian society; rather, it was specifically a response to and an outgrowth of Zionist socialism.

Kibbutz ideology rests on a number of assumptions about human nature and society. Humans are perceived as fundamentally good and inherently social. Characteristics such as being kind and cooperative with a concern for social justice flow naturally from within, provided the right setting is established. People are basically concerned with creativity, self-mastery, and the general welfare of others. If a contradiction should arise between individual desires and the desires of others, mankind's inherent sociability takes over. As Shenker (1986:83) notes, "Each person, while having a number of universal aims, realizes that others too have these aims, and he is as concerned with their achievement of them as with his own. Cooperation and concern for others are instrumental (in that they help one promote one's own ends), and they are intrinsically satisfying. The two go together. The person who sees them as primarily instrumental will not gain intrinsic satisfaction from them; the person who gains intrinsic satisfaction will also find them instrumentally valuable."

According to Harris (1999), the modern kibbutz is failing. After more than 70 successful years, its population is aging and its financial foundation is on the verge of bankruptcy. By the mid-1990s the organization had accumulated a debt of 4.5 billion dollars with a total annual output of only 3 billion dollars. The experiment has not quite reached the typical span of three generations for communes; its relatively short period of existence pales in comparison with the much longer duration of the Hutterian Brethren or the Shakers.

EARLY NORTH AMERICAN BASE

When North America was first being settled by European immigrants, the incoming pursuers of utopian ideals brought with them the belief that it was possible for people to live differently from the way they had in Europe. The plan was to organize their new lifestyle after a unique economic, social, and religious pattern (Marty, 2003:51–52). The Puritans tried it first by establishing what they perceived to be an ideal kind of lifestyle in the Massachusetts Bay Colony, and they were soon copied by others. The imported ideas and philosophies of the various incoming groups were welcomed by other immigrants because the frontier was open to philosophical as well as geographic cultivation (Calverton, 1969:15). Utopias abounded, most of them organized around a communal theme. Alderfer (1995) estimates that about 600 communal societies were formed in English American colonies and the United States between the years 1663 and 1965. Kanter (1972) suggests that the peak years were 1840–1860, during which time almost 100 such communities were founded. Kephart and Zellner (1994) and Jacob (1997) identify the years between 1965 and 1975 as a productive span for counterculture communes to form.

About one-third of the societies founded in North America were religiously sectarian, particularly those begun in the seventeenth and eighteenth centuries. Later experiments tended to be less religious (Rothstein, 2003:17). However, between 1832 and 1885, a series of religiously based communal experiments were initiated by various Mormon groups in Independence, Missouri, Preparation, Iowa, and Orderville, Utah. The settlement at Independence was started by mainline Mormons themselves, using a revelation by Joseph Smith as a basis. Then, in 1853, a dissenting Mormon leader named Charles B. Thompson established a colony in Preparation, Iowa, which lasted five years, ending in a long litigation suit. In 1874, Joseph Smith's successor, Brigham Young, attempted to initiate Smith's communal revelation at Orderville, Utah, on a strong economic base with a group of 500 members (Albertson, 1973). Besides extensive farms with large herds of sheep and cattle, the commune had a sawmill, tannery, flour mill, shoe shop, blacksmith shop, wagon shop, and a woolen mill with 200 spindles. Perhaps prosperity and the desire for independent wealth was too much for the communalists, for they disbanded in 1885. Their group commitment remained strong, however, even though individual property ownership was prized (Kephart and Zellner, 1994:259).

When settlement lands in the east became scarce, vast migrations headed west along the Santa Fe and Oregon Trails. As long as there was land available for homesteaders to claim at the end of the Oregon Trail, Horace Greeley's challenge was most appropriate: "Go West, young man, go West and grow up with the country" (Spinrad and Spinrad, 1979:249). As the supply of land diminished with the abandonment of the Oregon Trail in 1850, Greeley's slogan was amended by an anonymous observer in this manner: "Go West, young man, and drown yourself in the Pacific Ocean." America had come of age, and the undercurrents of the nation's economic outlook became institutionalized. The utopian experiments that were initiated in America in the latter part of the nineteenth century were protest movements against the effects of industrialization and offered alternative perspectives of a more humane nature. It seemed the time for new ideas that would release individuals from the tyranny of economic determinism had come.

OBERLIN COLLEGE

The arena of higher education did not remain unaffected by utopian thinking. When the Rev. John Shepherd and his associate, Philo Stewart, founded Oberlin College in 1833, they broke new ground with their radical philosophy. The Oberlin Covenant they drew up, and which every recruit was required to sign, had strong communal overtones. The founders were assisted in their drive by the American revivalist the Reverend Charles Grandison Finney. The college covenant mandated that every student promise to refrain from smoking and strong drink, and agree to contribute four hours of labor to the college farm each day. It was a school that bound students together by a solemn covenant which pledged them "to the plainest living and highest thinking."

Oberlin was clearly a leader in many respects. Physical education was viewed as an academic discipline at Oberlin, and women were admitted as students on an equal footing with men. Although stringent regulations were in place to keep the sexes separated, they did share space in the dining room and the classroom and, after 1934, in chapel services as well. In later years the Oberlin radical approach to educating both sexes drew the attention of other universities such as Cornell, Harvard, and Michigan, which sent emissaries to see how it was done. Oberlin was the first college in America to have enough sopranos in its college choir and the first to establish coed dormitories. In 1835 it became the first college to admit African American students. Truly much of what was traditionally viewed as utopian in higher education was considered a mainstay at Oberlin.

HULL HOUSE

One of the leading proponents of creating a more humane society at the turn of the twentieth century was Jane Addams of Hull House in Chicago. Although she and her colleagues were not entirely responsible for all of the turn-of-the-century reforms such as the abolition of child labor, the regulation of working hours and conditions for women, enforcement of safe working conditions, and reforms of juvenile laws, they certainly did provoke individuals who were in power to enact them. Begun in 1889, Hull House at once became an experiment and a powerhouse of social ideas. The mansion occupied by Jane Addams and her friends was built in 1856 by the Charles J. Hull family and initially leased to Addams by Hull's cousin and heir, Helen Culver. After one year of operation, Culver saw the value of Addams' vision and drew up a four-year rent-free lease for Addams and her colleagues (Polikoff, 1999:64).

As a social reformer, there was hardly a dysfunctional aspect of American life that Jane Addams did not address either in writing or by personal involvement. The complete program at Hull House is hard to describe because endeavors were often adjusted to meet the times. To begin with, Hull House was actually intended to be a kind of clearinghouse for social reform. At first boarders were taken in, reading clubs were started, and a kindergarten was begun. Handicraft, art, language, and nutrition classes were made available to neighborhood dwellers and Hull House residents offered their personal services for any community need—washing new babies, preparing the dead for burial, nursing the sick, and babysitting children. These programs were followed up with an investigation of local sweatshops, and the conclusion was drawn that the scanty pay awarded the workers was insufficient to provide for their daily needs.

At that point, Addams decided that it was not enough to provide for the needs of the poor and underprivileged. Such efforts had to be paralleled by media attention and political maneuvering, so she soon found herself lobbying the state legislature of Illinois for the enactment of a child labor law and other reforms (Addams, 1990:175). During her final years of service Jane Addams continued to spread her message of hope and equality for all by speaking at conferences and before gatherings of national leaders, always upholding the ideal that human needs must take priority over economic advancement. Addams was probably the first and last one-person female campaign for fairness and equality in North America.

KEMANO, BRITISH COLUMBIA

The notion of an idyllic, luxurious lifestyle void of any hint of inconvenience, annoyance, or difficulty is a perpetual dream. Even today, now and then a group of people will claim that they have developed such a milieu, even though it may turn out to be only a temporary respite. The town of Kemano, in northern British Columbia, is such a modern example. The town was originally built to house Alcan workers who controlled and maintained the local hydroelectric plant, which was slated to close in July, 2000 (Laird, 2000:82). Alcan's cost-cutting process caused the death of the 50-year-old settlement, which for many was an idyllic place to live. Although occupied by only 220 residents, the community was a small isolated version of modern-day living. The company provided residents with every-thing—stores, a school, daycare, restaurants, a bowling alley, a golf course, and other recreational facilities. As one single mother put it, "Its a nice place, a safe place. . . . You know, the real world is scary if you're a single mom; here it's like milk" (Laird, 2000:86).

The utopian features of Kemano were obvious. The town offered stability. In fact, some of the residents had never lived anywhere else. Alcan took care of everything. The company was landlord (with low rent), mayor, security guard, hospital, and grocery store. Families felt safe, never locking their doors at night, and there was little crime be-cause everyone knew everyone else in town. Old-fashioned pastimes like stopping to talk in the streets were universal. As one resident stated, "Every child has 50 moms and dads, aunts and uncles. And many people come here for that" (Laird, 2000:86). A major source of connection to the outside world was the two-and-a-half-hour boat ride to the northern town of Kitimat, British Columbia, which was offered twice a week. It gave an opportunity for shopping and access to services not locally available. When the company made the closure announcement in April 2000, every resident went through the various stages of the grieving process from anger to denial to gradual realization. To add to the hurt, it was learned that half of the town's homes were to be burned to the ground to provide training to British Columbia firefighters. Only 24 peo-ple were to be left on site to manage the plant.

The Kemano example leads one to speculate if this was indeed a kind of utopia, and if so, how long would it have lasted if economic con-ditions had not dictated otherwise?

MIGRANT UTOPIAS

Many utopian experiments of the past have been motivated by either push factors or pull factors, or a combination of both. Sometimes vision-aries feel unwelcome in their own country and sometimes the lure of new prospects is strong. Some utopian movements cannot so easily be classified. For these purposes, the description of them as migrant utopias might be more appropriate. Four examples may illustrate this point.

African American Migrations

Many immigrants who migrated to North America during the eighteenth and nineteenth centuries were escaping from conditions of persecution, confinement, or revolution in their home country. More than that, most of them perceived this continent as a land of promise, a place where they could build new futures and fulfill their dreams. Unlike incoming European utopian groups African Americans began their protest *in* North America. Theirs was a resistance against physical, social, political, and religious domination. It was a case of colonialism within the confines of a North American country. Unlike the immigrants who came to Canadian and American shores to start over, African Americans had to disentangle themselves from the social structures of their own homeland. In this sense, their story may best be portrayed as a counterculture movement.

The key event of the American Civil War was the freeing of African American slaves. Although the war ended in 1865, scores of runaway slaves had migrated to the American West decades before that. In fact, their westward movement had become quite substantial by the 1830s. These numbers, however, were quite limited compared to those who chose this avenue after the war. Census figures showed only 7,689 African Americans resident in western states in 1860, but 20 years later, this figure had swelled to 72,575. Some of the new arrivals came as cowboys and helped with long cattle drives through the Midwest from Texas. Others became buffalo soldiers, members of the four all-black army regiments assigned to keep the peace in the West. Large numbers of westward immigrants poured into Kansas, Nebraska, and other western states in 1879, fleeing the intolerable conditions that African Americans faced in the American South during the period of Reconstruction.

Once settled in the West, hopes for a better life were often dashed as the newcomers faced Euro-Americans who brought prejudiced attitudes and anti-black customs and laws with them. It was a sad discovery for many freed slaves who found that they were not wanted in the western territories. The Euro-Americans already settled there had not outlawed slavery because they thought it was evil, but because they did not

2.1   Oak tree marker for Underground Railroad, Nebraska City, Nebraska

want to share the new land with African Americans of any status (Yount, 1997:5–7).

Fleeing to the western states was but one safety valve for African American slaves during turbulent times. The most famous alternative was undoubtedly the underground railroad established by dedicated abolitionists, and the most esteemed location was Canada. In 1851, the Anti-Slavery Society of Canada was set up and committed to bringing African American slaves to freedom. It was a noble cause; by the time the wave of escaped slaves had subsided in the 1860s, some 40,000 to 60,000 slaves had made their way to Canada. This was a major accomplishment, despite the fact that during the days in which the slave trade flourished, as many as 10 million Africans had been subjected to the horrible fate of slavery, and at least a million had been killed.

There is an element of romance to the underground railroad, even though that in no way demeans the serious nature of its operations. Although the mythical train had no tracks and no rolling stock, in a very real sense it was a lifesaving operation carried out by courageous people who were motivated by their distaste for slavery. In the 1800s the train carried literally thousands of fugitive slaves to freedom in various northern and non-slave states and to Canada. Initiated by Quakers, an elaborate nomenclature of railroad talk was devised with which to fool the public. Volunteers bravely drove wagons loaded with slaves in hidden compartments. Stations were barns, cellars, church belfries, and underground quarters where runaways could hide temporarily till they traveled to the next station.

This secret network of people was organized in the 1780s, although its formal name originated in 1830. The new nomenclature included references to railroad "conductors" who helped the slaves find hiding places; they were responsible for moving their "cargo" from one station to another. Stations were transfer points used by conductors. One famous conductor was Harriet Tubman, who personally led more than 300 people to freedom in Canada.

The earliest African Americans to arrive in Canada came with the English Loyalists to Nova Scotia in 1776. Movements to Upper Canada did not occur until after 1793 when Canada's Legislative Assembly abolished slavery. The first major wave of African Americans arrived in Upper Canada between 1817 and 1822, most of them settling in the area around what is now Windsor, Ontario. Eventually, three African American settlements grew up in Ontario, known as Oro, Wilberforce, and Dawn. The latter is particularly significant because of the efforts of Josiah Henson, after whose life story it is sometimes thought that Harriet Beecher Stowe's book *Uncle Tom's Cabin* was patterned. Henson and a colleague, Hiram Wilson, raised money to establish an African American commune with the financial assistance of a Quaker philanthropist, James Cannings Fuller. The project began in 1842. Although the experiment lasted close to 30 years, during its time it was a safe haven for many American slaves who saw it as the ultimate utopia (Hill, 1981). Its demise was caused by a variety of factors, notably that it was operated by an outside agency and the office of management was too frequently rotated.

The most influential factor that led to the establishment of the Dawn settlement near London, Ontario, was the way in which African Americans were shut out by white society. There were separate schools for their children, only mediocre jobs were open to them, and they were not welcomed into mainstream Canadian institutional life. The promise of having their own settlement was encouraging. Even then, it took two years to formulate plans for the experiment. In 1840 Fuller went to England to raise $1,500 for "the Canada cause," and the first organizational meeting was held in London a year later. At first, about 300 acres of land were purchased by the institute and combined with the 1,500 acres already owned by incoming African American settlers. This was the site of the Dawn Settlement. Crops included corn, wheat, oats, and tobacco, supplemented by such industries as a sawmill, a grist mill, a rope factory, and a brickyard. A productive lumber industry brought profits from as far away as Boston and England. By the end of the 1840s the enterprise was estimated in value as high as $11,000 (Pease and Pease, 1963:67).

As the Dawn commune prospered, unhealthy signs that no one really wanted to address also emerged. Despite their financial income, the colony had a debt load of over $4,000. As head of the enterprise in 1849,

Henson was approached by Amos Lawrence, a Boston businessman, who offered to extend a loan to pay the debt provided that strong businesslike measures were put into place. He stipulated three measures in a letter to Henson. First, he demanded that at least 40 persons each commit themselves to advance 100 dollars to pay off communal debts. Second, Henson was to arrange for the preparation of lumber for market to ensure steady income levels for the commune; and third, Henson was to travel to England and solicit relief funds (Pease and Pease, 1963:67).

Despite Henson's attempts to meet these requests, in 1850 the Dawn property was transferred to the board of the American Baptist Free Mission Society, and the Reverend Samuel Davis arrived from England to take charge of Dawn affairs. A little later, John Scoble, a British antislavery leader, moved to Canada and became active manager of the commune. As a friend of Henson, hopes were high that financial success would be achieved, but not all trustees supported Scoble. It soon became evident that the experiment was in trouble. One thing was certain: it was not solely the fault of Josiah Henson.

Henson was primarily a preacher and motivator, even though he was completely uneducated and virtually illiterate. He certainly had a vision for the Dawn community, but there is no evidence that he was either the governor or manager of the settlement. Before 1850 the commune was managed by a six-person executive made up of local African American residents. Later it was operated by a representative of the American Baptist Free Mission Society and then by John Scoble. Like Henson, Hiram Wilson was never officially the leader of the colony, though he remained there all through the 1840s. Wilson tried to work with Henson, but his greatest source of consternation came about because he disagreed with Henson about the way funds were being spent. Henson's opinions and activities always lurked in the background, and as Pease and Pease (1963:70) suggest, Henson's "presence without that leadership precluded anyone else from assuming it." Like many unrealistic visionaries, Wilson dreamed better than he built. His critics charged that he was an "Oberlin visionary" instead of a leader, so he left Dawn virtually in midstream. He then moved to St. Catharines, Ontario, where he lived out his life.

The remainder of the Dawn story is fraught with quarrels, charges and investigations. During the five years between 1847 and 1852, the financial records of Dawn were investigated six times by the sponsoring body. The final chapter was an unfortunate quarrel between Scoble and Henson, with Scoble taking Henson to court over a mortgage matter. Scoble won the case and remained at Dawn until 1868, when it closed. It was an unfortunate ending, primarily brought about by differences in management style. Henson and Scoble were two powerful, uncompromising personalities who could not come to a consensus on matters crucial to the survival of the settlement. Rather than yield to the other, both insisted on doing things their own way. More than anything the demise of the Dawn settlement proved that utopian dreams can best be mustered and maintained if it is clear who is in charge. The talents of the three major players, Henson, Wilson, and Scoble, were not compatible. Henson was the perpetual patriarch of the settlement, Scoble was the visionary, and Wilson the frustrated and disillusioned reformer. Wilson probably came closest to being a leader, but no vehicle can be steered by three drivers with different maps.

Today visitors who make their way to Dresden, Ontario, may tour Uncle Tom's Cabin Historic Site, which includes Josiah Henson's home and other nineteenth-century buildings. The museum has exhibits dealing with Henson's career and early African American history in Canada. Henson's grave is located next to the museum.

Western Migrations

The settlers came. They were not stopped by anything. They came, first, for good land; and when gold was discovered the gold-hunters joined the ranks of the land-hungry. First a trickle, then a torrent, the migration westward became a phenomenon in American history unique in numbers and distances. For fifty years the westward migration continued, until the good land from the Missouri to the Pacific was peopled, and the frontier was declared to be past tense (Brown, 1995:29).

Although Christopher Columbus arrived just off the eastern coast of America in 1492, it took several centuries for the immigrants who followed him to discover the West. A mixture of factors motivated the westward move, among them the fact that life on many eastern settlements too much resembled that of the parent cultures from which they had been transplanted. They wanted to build a new society, develop an alternative lifestyle, and fulfill a utopian dream. Freedom-seeking citizens dreamt of forming their own institutional structures and so headed west. The abundance of traffic on the rut-laden Oregon and Santa Fe Trails testified to the sincerity of those convictions. Encountering Native Americans, who were trying to protect their hunting grounds, was only part of the challenge; food and water shortages, unexpected illness, and wagon train mutiny added to their hardships.

By the 1830s wagon trains had begun their long trek to the Great Plains on the east side of the Rocky Mountains. Two years later, the steamship *Yellowstone* transited the Missouri River to Fort Pierre and demonstrated a second means of travel to the plains. Some of the wealthier settlers managed to book passage on a steamer headed for Fort Benton, Montana, on the Upper Missouri, thus cutting off a significant part of the hazardous trail. At first the settlers arrived in a trickle, then a torrent. For the next half century the westward migration continued, until all the fertile soils from the Missouri to the Pacific had been claimed. Before land title could be claimed, however, would-be settlers had to ford rivers, conquer mountain trails, and constantly repair their wagons.

During the Civil War trained soldiers fought on the front lines of both sides, while volunteer, untrained soldiers were enlisted to stave off Native American efforts to protect their territories in the West. For settlers, the results were grim. When compared with their First Nations counterparts, they were simply not sufficiently trained in the art of warfare. Eventually things got so bad that the United States federal government sent captured Confederate troops into Native American territory to assist the settlers. One Sioux leader, Red Cloud, resisted the military incursion and issued the infamous words to the military, "It must either be war or peace. If you want peace, return at once to Powder River" (Brown, 1995:84; Utley,

1984:99). Red Cloud's mission failed, necessitating his presence at a peace conference at Fort Laramie on November 6, 1868.

It was the western-bound settlers who created the American West as it is known today. Explorers came and went, soldiers fought and were killed or retired elsewhere, and miners searched for gold and other treasures. The only remaining and committed arrivals were the settlers. They came to stay and to eke out a living in sometimes impossible conditions. These people put down roots and stayed where they were because the privilege of tilling often-stubborn soil was much more satisfying than life back home. Reminiscences of their former homes empowered their motivation to do well. After all, who in their right mind would want to go back to the stifling, crowded, religiously restricted culture of Eastern American society?

The arrival of the railroad sped up the homesteading process. When the railway reached Yankton, South Dakota, in 1873, for example, what had been a trickle of Russian and German settlers became a flood as these immigrants poured into the area. The desperate need for housing was aggravated by the long distances that materials had to be hauled, so for the first few years these utopians used materials at hand such as rocks, dirt, and grass. A little analysis shows, however, that the immigrants did not improvise much at all. They merely transplanted their home styles to the prairies, just as they transplanted their way of life and language. The situation was eased somewhat by going to work for the railroad and thus speeding up its reach to occupied areas. With the arrival of the train came more desirable building materials, eastern goods, and new settlers (Goertz, 1995:2).

Life in early western towns was often based on long-established patterns brought over from Europe via the eastern states. Physical patterns of these settlements emulated European designs, although the raw frontier had a way of dictating severe deviations. This was no less true in the case of the non-physical aspects of frontier life, including beliefs and values, social structures, mores, and folkways. Puritanical attitudes were abandoned and forced improvisations were motivated by a world of inadequate supplies. Berton (1990:71) describes the lengths to which some of the settlers went in fulfilling their immediate needs. Benches and tables were hand hewn and often dishes were hammered out of tin cans found in garbage dumps. Drinking glasses were created by cutting beer bottles in half. In most cases only temporary structures built of cheap lumber earmarked the existence of settlements, but at least the air was filled with a sense of freedom and expectancy (Friesen, 1984: chapter 11).

The standard features of immigrant towns included offices for lawyers, surveyors, dentists, and doctors, and facilities for merchants of various kinds. Churches and dance halls provided elementary forms of music until someone took the time to locate enough talent to organize a formal band. Occasionally an opera house was constructed to accommodate entertainers, traveling drama troupes, and lecturers from the East (Brown, 1995).

Barr Colonists

The occupation of the Canadian West by settlers was made possible by promoting a romanticized version of what the prairies were really like. Immigrants were informed by government and railroad officials that on the prairies they need not struggle with densely forested land in order to homestead. The government was offering the gift of a ready-made farm to all who wanted to avail themselves of the offer. An individual could arrive one day and farm the next. As the Department of Agriculture pointed out in 1887, "Nature has done her share, and done it well and generously; man's labor and industry are alone required to turn these broad rolling prairies to good account" (Francis, 1989:112). A multiplicity of ethnocultural groups took up the government's offer—Doukhobors, Dutch, Hungarians, Icelanders, Japanese, Jews, Mennonites, Mormons, Russians, Scandinavians, Ukrainians, and others (Palmer, 1972; Burnet and Palmer, 1988: chapter 3).

Many newly established utopian settlements did not last long. One Hungarian community in southeastern Saskatchewan launched in 1885 by Count Paul Esterhazy lasted only three years. Discord and conflict threatened the colony until it was rescued by an influx of new settlers in 1888. One eager group, the Barr colonists, discovered that government promises and newspaper advertisements were not quite what they purported to be.

In 1903, when over 2,000 English dreamers made their way by ship and train from England to Saskatoon, Saskatchewan, they were in for some unpleasant surprises. The last leg of their journey was by wagon train from Saskatoon across what was then the Northwest Territories. They were to travel 200 miles to points in the Northwest. They had been informed by the Reverend Isaac Barr that potentially rich farmlands lay waiting for them on the Saskatchewan prairies, all for the claiming. The land was free to anyone prepared to live on it for three years, build a house, and do a little ploughing.

The background to the Barr colony story goes back to the end of the Boer War in 1902. Troops were returning to England to a rather humdrum life. Jobs were few and hard to find and there seemed to be little hope that the economy would change in the near future. The hope of migration loomed, and the Reverend George Exton Lloyd was equal to the challenge. He was familiar with the western Canadian plains, having fought there with Colonel Otter in the Battleford front on the rugged slopes of Cut Knife Hill in Saskatchewan during the Riel wars. He therefore addressed a letter to the *London Times* requesting volunteers. After a few days' absence from town he returned to a full mailbox. One of the replies was from the Reverend Isaac Barr, who lived in England but had farmed for 15 years in western Canada. He was anxious to return, having solicited the interest of a large group of adventurers to go with him (Wetton, 1979).

The would-be colonists assembled by Lloyd and Barr were promised that the proposed settlement in western Canada would be on soil suitable for mixed farming and near a railroad depot. They were cautioned that the adventure would require a great deal of hard work in an atmosphere of isolation and loneliness. As preparations got underway, Lloyd noticed that Barr took a rather lackadaisical attitude towards finances. He simply stuffed gathered monies from the hopeful crowd into his pocket and went on his way. Later, Lloyd found it necessary to obtain the services of a clerk to handle incoming funds. A further example of Barr's inefficient way of handling things was his failure to provide for the needs of the settlers on their arrival in Saskatoon. Although he had promised that lumber, groceries, clothing, farm implements, machinery, wagons, and cattle would be available, this turned out not to be the case. His optimistic way of dealing with matters also led him to proclaim that the schools, churches, sawmills, stores, and everything they needed would "grow up spontaneously whenever they were needed" (Wetton, 1979:10).

The colonists set sail for Canada on the S.S. *Lake Manitoba* on March 31, 1903 and landed at St. John, New Brunswick on Friday, April 10. Sea sickness en route took its toll. Bachelors were forced to give up their luxury cabins to women with children and spent nights in tents on the deck. Women were also moved to the ship's emergency hospital where they could be looked after by other female passengers.

When the colonists reached St. John, they found four trains ready to move them to Saskatoon. Some bachelors elected to go only as far as Winnipeg, where they planned to work for a year in order to gain farming experience. Those who left for Saskatoon soon discovered that bedlam awaited them. There was no one to sort the baggage and there were only a few blankets to provide warmth for sleeping in tents in the cold prairie spring weather. When it came time to purchase supplies they discovered that prices had been inflated. In addition, their friend Isaac Barr had written a letter to Saskatoon merchants in advance demanding that he be paid a percentage on all goods purchased by the colonists. He then bought up all the seed oats he could for 25 cents a bushel and tried to sell them to the colonists for $1.50 per bushel. When these maneuvers were discovered there was outrage in the camp and Lloyd had to intervene to keep the peace.

Eventually Barr was stripped of his leadership role and Lloyd was asked to step in. At first he was reluctant to do so, but eventually he gave in on the condition that the decision was unanimous and a committee of 12 elected members assist him in governance (Bowen, 1994:138). The record shows that Barr eventually disappeared, but his death was reported as having happened in Australia in 1937. In the meantime he had married Christina Helberg in Nebraska and had two sons with her.

When things finally got organized, the colonists headed northwest to what is now the Battleford area. The lack of a prearranged plan for the transport of the colonists in groups led to many unnecessary hardships. Eagerly the utopians drove their heavily laden, ox-drawn wagons through sloughs, creeks, and prairie grass in the hope of reaching a land filled with milk and honey. There were few navigators among them, and their wagons were so heavily loaded that women and children had to walk most of the time. By the time they arrived at their destination, most of the travelers had used up their food, prairie fires had destroyed feed for their livestock and wood for their campfires, and icy snows had replaced heavy rains. It was difficult to keep warm and some of the children had contracted scarlet fever. It turned out that Barr's flowery rhetoric was no match for the fierce prairie weather and harsh plains soils. Years later, many settlers probably forgave Barr for his false advertisements, but no one had kind thoughts about him when they first wintered in what soon came to be called Starvation Camp—located just 30 miles from the promised land.

Bowen (1994:110) records an incident that occurred as the Barr colonists drove their wagon train to the northwest region of the province. One traveler, Thomas Edwards, had to cross a water-laden slough while his wife watched on shore. Although Edwards tried to find a way around the obstacle, he eventually decided that the way straight through was his only hope. As his wagon slowly mired its way through the slough, his plodding oxen suddenly decided to stop midstream. No amount of coaxing on Edwards' part could induce the animals to move on. As a last resort, and for whatever reason, Edwards decided to unhitch the oxen, and the lumbering beasts immediately took off. Now liberated from their heavy load, the oxen found dry ground on the shoreline. There the going was easy and Edwards soon lost sight of the animals. It took ten days for him to locate the oxen, during which time the melting snow raised the water level in the slough in which the Edwards wagon was stuck to the top of its wheels. Despite experiences such as these, these utopians prevailed, and the existence of the city of Lloydminster, Saskatchewan, and the settlement around it attests to their courage and persistence.

One source of encouragement to the Barr colonists was the experience of their immigrant compatriots, the Doukhobors. The colonists learned that this group of migrants had arrived from Russia in 1899 and developed workable farms in central Saskatchewan. One day, en route to the Battleford area, they encountered a Doukhobor communal oasis near Blaine Lake. Whitewashed log and clay-plastered houses, with their ridged roofs shaggy with thatched grass, lined the main street of the settlement. Sparkling windows trimmed in bright colors peaked out from beneath sheltering verandahs. Their machinery was up to date and corrals were filled with healthy-looking cattle. The best news was that the Doukhobors had plenty of supplies available for sale, including butter, eggs, potatoes, oats, and poultry. The Doukhobor village was a Garden of Eden on an otherwise bleak prairie plain (Bowen, 1994:116).

As events turned out, the Barr colony did not develop as originally planned. Instead of forming a tightly knit utopian community as had been envisioned, settlement was distributed over 20 or more townships and the intimacy of near neighbors was lost. Other settlers, not always of English background, took up intervening homesteads, and thus the dream of building an integrated, culturally closed community was shattered (Peake, 1983:65–66).

When the town of Lloydminster celebrated its fiftieth anniversary in 1953 there were a number of historic milestones. The Lloydminster Exhibition Association made note of the fact that the association was established by the Barr colonists and grew to be one of the most progressive farm organizations in the West. Many agriculture-related awards had been won by Lloydminster farmers in successive years. These awards were just a few of the many ways in which the work of the descendants of the original colonists was recognized and indicated the quality of farming initiated by colonists. Evidently the hardships endured by the early utopian colonists had paid off.

Cannington Manor

A would-be utopian experiment with an unusual twist was initiated south of Moosomin, Saskatchewan, by Captain Edward Mitchell Pierce in 1882. His reputation preceded him as a genteel English gentleman who had the misfortune of losing his money through a London bank failure. He then migrated to the Canadian prairies to start anew, his dream being to develop a sound farming operation with the help of unskilled apprentices. He advertised in an English newspaper for "young men of good birth and education," promising them he would teach them the art of farming. He was not altogether fortunate in the replies he received; his ad attracted a group of remittance men who wanted to learn how to be English gentlemen under his supervision.

There was an air of romance to the project, and the title, Cannington Manor, sent many hearts aflutter. The nearest railroad was miles away and applicants would have an opportunity to really test their mettle. The arrivals represented a range of backgrounds including people from England, Scotland, and Ontario. All wanted to partake of the opportunities available in the land of milk and honey.

A communal village rapidly took shape and included a church, an assembly hall that doubled as a school, a grist mill, a blacksmith shop, and a cheese factory. Work was occasionally disrupted with leisure activities such as poetry reading, choral work, painting, and discussions about farming and politics. English tea was celebrated with women wearing elaborate dresses waiting on the gentlemen. Everyone dressed for dinner and enjoyed the occasional card party, midnight frolic, or drive to the nearby lake. Eventually the railway arrived, but bypassed the colony by ten miles, putting its economic base in jeopardy. Some of the bachelors married local women, while others returned to their land of origin— and as a result, suddenly Cannington Manor was no more (Francis, 1989:114). Still, today, thanks to the careful maintenance work of the Saskatchewan government, tourists can wander what was once the main street of an unusual, unrealistic utopian experiment on a bland section of the Great Plains.

The following chapters detail the stories of some of the more extensive utopias in North America, with a view to deciphering the workable aspects of each. The main classifications of utopian experiments discussed include noncommunal utopias, communal utopias, economic-oriented utopias, unorthodox communes, and twentieth-century communes.

CHAPTER 3

NONCOMMUNAL UTOPIAS

Dreams of a better life are not necessarily encapsulated in communal terms, but frequently do involve the desire to migrate to new locations. Over the last few centuries North America has been the target of such visions, and the hope of emigrating to this continent still lives on in the hearts of many. Despite the fact that literature pertaining to North American immigration history is voluminous, it may still be helpful to outline a few historical highlights to set the stage for the discussion. One complex but relevant case emerges from the Reformation period in the form of the Anabaptist movement.

Groups like the Amish, Hutterites, and other Anabaptist communities continue to exist, reminding us that utopian ideals can span not only generations but centuries. Often labeled, "the quiet in the land" (Kraybill and Bowman, 2001), these groups feature firm religious convictions, strong family networks, and a good measure of economic success, despite remaining relatively isolated from mainstream society. In many ways outsiders consider the predominant features of their lifestyle as idyllic.

MENNONITES

A classic case of following up the passion for utopia are Mennonites, the parent group of the Old Order Amish and a variety of other Anabaptist subsects. They originated in 1536 under the leadership of Menno Simons (1496–1561), a former Catholic priest. Their sister group, the Hutterites, originated in 1530, and the Amish, under the leadership of Jacob Ammann, grew out of the Mennonite movement in 1693. Although Mennonite origins in the Reformation period were not unique, they have carved out a distinct niche for themselves in the North American cultural milieu. Today there are over one million Mennonites living in 37 countries. There are over 319,768 Mennonites in the United States and 124,150 Mennonites in Canada. Mennonites in Africa outnumber Men-

3.1 Mennonies David and Helena Friesen (author John's grandparents) circa 1920s, near Waldheim, Saskatchewan

nonites in Canada by more than three to one, thanks to an aggressive missionary program.

Mennonite migrations have taken them to countries across Europe, Russia, and North and South America, always in pursuit of the utopian dream. Because of their chiliastic (the doctrine stating that Jesus will return to earth and reign on earth for 1,000 years) orientation, Mennonites have consistently sought to occupy territories where they can prepare for the Second Coming of Christ without undue state impositions and interference. Today, essentially having run out of countries to inhabit, they remain relatively stationary and, with a few exceptions, most Mennonite groups in North America have almost completely adopted mainstream cultural affiliations.

The structural Mennonite institutions reflect mainline tendencies; Mennonites finance high schools, colleges, and seminaries, and build senior citizens' complexes and hospitals. They also sponsor life insurance companies, operate credit unions, and aid in national disaster relief. Conversely, they also have in their mosaic smaller groups who cling tenaciously to sixteenth-century modes of dress and lifestyle, although they, too, are slowly yielding to social and technological pressures of change.

Doctrines

Essentially, the fundamentals of the Anabaptist faith include the belief that the Bible is an open book for all and constitutes the sole guide for faith and practice, particularly the New Testament. The body of Christ is perceived as a voluntary group of believers banded together for the purpose of worship. This implies a rigid separation of church and state and does not support the concept of compulsory state church membership. Infant baptism is viewed as a ritual supporting the idea of a state church and therefore has no place in a voluntary institution. Christians should respect the authority of government but should not take positions in civil service. Government, however, is an institution ordained by God to protect the righteous and punish the wicked. Christians must be obedient to their rulers, pray for them, and willingly pay taxes to support the government. Christians cannot take up the sword, for love must be the ruling force in all social relations. It is wrong to kill, either as an individual or by judicial process or military force. Christians should live secluded from the evil outside world. Church discipline is to be secured through the ban, which is used to exclude the disobedient from the rights of membership. To outsiders, practice of the ban may appear to be severe but its ultimate objective is to bring the individual to repentance. The Lord's Supper (celebration of the Eucharist) is to be regarded merely as a memorial of the death and suffering of Christ, and not as containing His Real Presence. It is wrong to take an oath because Christ taught His disciples to give and keep their word without swearing (Harder, 1949:21–22).

Despite fairly strong consensus on these very basic doctrines the Anabaptists have always held strongly to the notion that individuals are to act as their own priests. Thus, in matters of faith, individuals are expected to follow the dictates of conscience—unless, of course, those convictions differed from those mandated in the Scriptures. Although conformity to congregational interpretation of the Scriptures was stressed, as their history shows, there were many instances when individuals opted to devise their own doctrines contrary to those of their local fellowships.

Menno Simons

Like many dissatisfied but searching religious individuals of the Reformation period, Menno Simons participated in the Counter Reformation in Europe. Although his followers insist that he never intended to start a new religious organization, he probably could not resist the idea (Smith, 1957; Bender, 1964; Friesen, 1977; Janzen, 1990). In 1536 he renounced the Roman Catholic Church and along with his Anabaptist peers aspired to help develop a new form of fellowship in keeping with New Testament principles. Soon his followers became known as Menno People, or Mennonites. Eventually, a price was put on Simons' head and he was forced to go into hiding. His writings were banned and his followers were persecuted by the state church. So severe was the onslaught against them that on one occasion even Menno's own followers decided to confiscate their leader's writings for their own protection. One individual, Peter von Riesen, who owned some of Menno's writings, was twice summoned before the conference of his church and ordered to deliver the whole edition of Menno's writings or be excommunicated. As Reimer and Gaeddert (1956:5) note: "Out of consideration for his family and after an intense inner struggle, he agreed. Excepting for the books destined for Russia [where they were to be sold], and a few copies for some friends, a list of which he submitted, and copies for his own family, he delivered the rest to Elder Peter Regier. The books were stored in the attic of the Tiegenhagen Mennonite Church [in West Prussia], where they were to remain for about twenty years, exposed to great damage from moisture, mould, and mice." Local church elders wrote to the Russian churches forbidding them to purchase the Menno Simons' writings from von Riesen, at a great financial loss to himself. Later the elders reversed their decision and the materials were sent to Russia. Some of them later found their way to North America, where they were more carefully preserved.

Move to America

As early as 1707 a group of Swiss Mennonites, including a number of Amish, migrated to Pennsylvania, thus starting the flow of immigrants that was to bring thousands of Mennonites to the New World. Mennonite and Hutterite immigrations to America occurred in different time periods than the Amish since these groups essentially existed as separate communities as a result of conflict over communal living. Although the Anabaptists generally shared many common beliefs, the Hutterites were virtually unaffected by Menno Simons' personal leadership because of their firm commitment to their own leader, Jacob Hutter. Although both groups were part of the Anabaptist movement, their development realized quite unique characteristics over the years.

As the Reformation swept Europe, religious persecution drove many groups to seek refuge elsewhere. In 1786 a delegation of Mennonites traveled to Russia to inspect lands offered to them for occupation and to verify other attractive terms. The Russian government offered them choice land in the southern part of the country, financial assistance for travel, and individual loans to commence farming. In addition the Mennonites were promised complete religious freedom, military exemption, no taxes for ten years, and the privilege of practicing a form of self-government that included the right to maintain their language and run their own schools.

At first things went well in Russia and the Mennonites prospered. In the course of time their success in farming was unequalled anywhere in the world. When the Ukraine became one of the world's greatest granaries in the latter part of the nineteenth century, the Mennonite economy shifted from animal husbandry to crop farming with small grain becoming one of the most important export articles to be shipped through the Black Sea ports (Francis, 1955:29). In addition to farming, the Mennonites developed a variety of industries and added these products to Russia's expanding market.

The Mennonite "honeymoon" in Russia began its demise during the 1860s when it became clear that Russian authorities were keenly interested in bringing Mennonites and other religious and cultural groups into line with official state policy. As Russia began to militarize, exemptions from conscription originally granted to Mennonites were dropped and restrictions were placed on Mennonite self-government. Mennonite functionaries immediately began negotiations with the Russian government that lasted for a decade, but to no avail. It was time for another exodus.

In 1873 a delegation of Mennonites was sent to North America; conditions were so alluring that in the next six years some 18,000 Mennonites moved to Canada and the United States. Most of them settled in the province of Manitoba and in the states of Kansas, Nebraska, South Dakota, and Minnesota. The American and Canadian governments promised the Mennonites money for passage, an ample supply of land, exclusion from military conscription, and freedom of religious practice. Although one of the conditions of Mennonite migration to Canada was the right to operate private schools where the Bible could be taught and the German language maintained, this changed in 1890 with the passing of the Manitoba Public School Act. The legislation mandated attendance at public schools for all citizens and exclusive use of the English lan-

3.2   Early Mennonite house on West Reserve, Southern Manitoba

guage. In 1921, with guarantees from the Mexican government, over 5,000 Old Colony and Sommerfelder Mennonites migrated to Mexico; another 1,700 settled in Paraguay (Heidebrecht, 1973).

Earlier a community of Mennonites had left Manitoba because of legal entanglements concerning private schools and migrated to Saskatchewan, but soon the long arm of Saskatchewan law caught up with them and the same story unfolded—public schooling or else. By 1932 members of this group embarked on yet another trek, this time to Peace River country in northern Alberta. Here they enjoyed tranquility until 1953, when the school issue drove 30 families further north to Worsley, Alberta, and 35 families to the British Honduras. Similarly, less than half a century passed before Mennonites in Mexico were again at odds with government authorities over state restrictions and many of them left for Texas and Ontario, Canada.

As a group in search of freedom and independence and the utopian dream, the Mennonites are indeed unique. Having run out of places to hide and having tasted the good life of dominant society, it is doubtful that the majority of Mennonites today would relocate because of religious convictions. Their defense would probably be that they can better deploy their energies in effecting relevant change in the land of their current domicile.

THE AMISH: MENNONITE COUSINS

The Amish of North America have a separate history reaching back over three centuries, but their religious roots also go back to the Protestant Reformation. Estimates of the American Amish population vary widely, but a conservative tally would be that there are 150,000 Amish in North America living in 230 separate communities. The largest Amish settlement is in Holmes County, Ohio, with a population of 40,000 Amish people, making a total of 50,000 Amish in the state of Ohio. Another 40,000 live in Pennsylvania, most of them in Lancaster County, which is also home to the largest Mennonite community in both North America and the world. Winnipeg, Manitoba, has the second largest Mennonite community. Almost half of the American States have Amish living in them.

Beliefs

Instead of being a people who merely cling to the traditional way of living for its own sake, the Amish hold very definite beliefs regarding social organization and religion. Fundamentally Anabaptist, the following represent principles unique to Old Order Amish.

First, Amish life is founded on the attitude of absolute submission to the *Ordnung* (church rules established by elders). When an individual is under investigation for a possible misdeed, there is no thoroughness that matches the fervor of the investigating elders. While the Amish are friendly to outsiders and give the impression of being a "gentle people," their treatment of their own kind when misconduct occurs is often very harsh. Amish life, in many ways, is grounded in implicit obedience.

Second, the Amish hold tradition in the highest regard. When modernity foists itself on them they resist as long as possible but they will go along with change in so far as they have to, and no more. Ironically, the Anabaptist sources from which they sprang rejected all tradition in the church and emphasized a direct obedience to the Scriptures. To some observers it appears as though the Amish today have reversed the relative importance of tradition and obedience to the Scriptures. According to orthodox Christian teaching, believers are to accept the grace of God and not let law or tradition be the primary governing authority in their lives. As St. Paul wrote to first century believers, "You who are trying to be justified by law have been alienated from Christ; you have fallen away from grace" (Galatians 5:4).

Well-defined Amish regulations govern all aspects of the Amish lifestyle, including choice of vocation, which is usually farming. While most Amish engage in agricultural pursuits, there are many communities where farming opportunities are limited. In these circumstances individuals may work for wages, but only in approved outlets.

Amish farms in Lancaster County, Pennsylvania, are usually about 80 acres. Amish farmers utilize a careful rotation of crops in order to feed back into the soil the nutrients required for the next crop, and thus keep the land fruitful (Kline, 1990:xvi). This careful manipulation of the soil shows a reverence for the land and guarantees its perpetual production.

Third, nonconformity with the lifestyle of mainline society is stressed as an all-inclusive Amish principle encompassing dress, transportation, and economics. Adherence to this principle often confuses visitors to Amish country because they sense elements of nonconformity that appear to contradict the commands of the *Ordnung*. A case in point is the telephone, which the Old Order Amish are forbidden to have in their homes. There are some Old Order farms that feature telephones and do so with *Ordnung* (official church rules) approval because it is necessary to their business operations. However, the telephone must be appropriately camouflaged, and hence it is relegated to an "outhouse-like" structure at the side of the road, away from the house. This arrangement is intended to discourage continual use of the device and encourage the "for business only" habit. Amish businessmen who rely on the telephone will have obtained permission for its installation, and a recent study by Kraybill and Nolt (1995:131) reports that 91 percent of Amish businessmen employ the telephone on a regular basis.

A fourth principle of Amish life is adherence to the principles of basic, very conservative Christianity. The Amish believe in such doctrines as the Trinity, the incarnation of Jesus Christ, a life of discipleship following the example of Christ, and the imminent second return of Christ. The Second Coming of Christ is always to be expected, and when He returns Christ will judge each person according to how he or she has lived out the mandate of the Gospel.

These values are central to Amish faith, but they are often hidden among a plethora of traditions and cultural trappings. Given a little time and with some personal interactive experience, outsiders will soon discover the sincere desire of the Amish to follow the teachings of Jesus Christ. In this pursuit they, like their mainline denominational counterparts, will admit that they are imperfect, but this does not mean that their discipleship is any less valid in quality. Amish faith is based on commitment (or *Gelassenheit),* which means submission to Christian practice as laid out by the *Ordnung. Gelassenheit* calls for hesitation, slowing up, backing down, and giving up one's stubborn will for the welfare of the community (Kraybill and Bowman, 2001:181). The Amish may not impress anyone with their indifference to evangelism, but neither will anyone be able to accuse them of fostering super star Christianity or seeking to build massive religious empires.

The Amish are quite communal when their neighbors are in need. When catastrophic events occur, they are quick to help one another. When an Amish barn burns down, the Amish descend on the farm in question as a unified support group. The men quickly build a new structure under the supervision of a head carpenter selected from among them, or someone acknowledged in that trade, and the women prepare food for the workers. The tragedy of the burned down barn is usually overshadowed by the enjoyment of working together. The rebuilding of the burned structure is usually an event engulfed in a spirit of neighborliness and consists of much visiting, eating, and the playing of practical jokes. Frequently the new barn is completed in a single day.

Many of the divisions that emerged among Anabaptist groups resulted from the belief that believers are their own priests. Through the centuries that the Anabaptists have persisted, a wide variety of issues

have contributed to church divisions, but, as the Amish experience illustrates, none have been as pronounced as excommunication and shunning (Warner and Denlinger, 1969). Violations that precipitate
excommunication are usually memorandized by church leaders and
guilty parties are asked to confess their sin before the local congregation. The Biblical basis that the Old Order Amish specifically utilize for
the practice of the ban (shunning) is: "But now I am writing you that you
must not associate with anyone who calls himself a brother but is sexually immoral or greedy, an idolater or a slanderer, a drunkard or a
swindler. With such a man do not even eat" (I Corinthians 5:11).

The Amish are essentially a people who strive to be secluded. This
stance is considered essential to preserving their utopia. They prefer to
have as little to do with mainstream society as possible. The only exception is usually for business reasons. Increasingly, because of a shortage of
available farmland, the Amish have been forced to take up small industries and develop Amish shops. At first these miniature factories were
agriculturally related—like blacksmithing and harness-making. Then
Amish carpenters appeared, and Amish shops began to provide goods
and services such as carriage construction, home building, and manufacturing Amish hats. The explosive growth of Amish businesses in the
1980s saw the development of a wide variety of new Amish-run retail
stores selling shoes, lighting fixtures, hardware supplies, and furniture.
The transformation of Amish work was a monumental bargain between
a tenacious people and the forces of modern, technologized social order
(Kraybill and Nolt, 1995:41)

Despite the tendency to isolate themselves, Amish leaders in Pennsylvania estimate that about 20 percent of their young people leave the
Old Order on attaining adulthood. Still, the Amish are among the fastest
growing cultural/religious groups in America. This may be attributed to
their high birth rate; they regard children as "an heritage of the Lord"
(Psalm 127:3,KJV), and the larger the family the more blessed they are
by God. The Amish population in the United States doubled between
1940 and 1960, and virtually doubled again by 1980. Improved medi-
cines, which the Amish have begun to use, have helped reduce infant
mortality and increase longevity. Today families average seven children,

3.3 Amish buggies gathering for large semi-annual sale day in Kidron, Ohio

and the Amish have found themselves pressured by their own growth (Kraybill and Nolt, 1995:29). This has forced the establishment of daughter colonies and the development of a variety of new industries. Because of these factors the trend to leave the community is real, and outside lures attract a steady flow of youthful Amish in search of a different interpretation of the ideal life.

Jacob Ammann

The Amish, also incorrectly called Plain People by their neighbors (Walbert, 2002:26), were a rather late subdivision (1693) of the Anabaptist movement. It happened that the Swiss division of the Mennonite branch of the movement in Europe was greatly influenced by the efforts of a Mennonite congregational minister named Jacob Ammann, who is usually credited with initiating the Amish movement. Ammann was probably born in 1644 but there are no records of the date of his death. Like his predecessor, Jacob Hutter, Jacob Ammann (also spelled Amman or Ammon), decided to assert his individual priestly rights and interpret the Scriptures on his own. By doing so, he incited a church split by insisting that the church was becoming too lenient both in clothing style and discipline. According to Ammann, there was evidence that worldly habits were taking over the church. Ammann's vision appears to have combined psychosocial elements, in the sense that he perceived society as unnatural, competitive, depersonalized, and alienated.

Little is known of Ammann's life except that he was born in Switzerland in the early part of the seventeenth century, and later migrated to Alsace where he became a prominent Mennonite minister and church leader (Hostetler and Huntington, 1971:3; Weaver-Zercher, 2001:124–125). The Anabaptist practices about which he showed special concern included: the celebration of Holy Communion (which Ammann believed should be practiced twice annually instead of only once); the practice of foot washing (which was not being observed consistently by some churches); and shunning, or *Meidung* (which some congregations refused to acknowledge in the strict sense that Ammann proposed). Ammann believed that members should have absolutely nothing to do with excommunicated church members. Excommunicated individuals should eat, sleep, and live completely alone (Dyck, 1967).

From the very beginning in 1693, the Amish became distinguishable from their fellows through their insistence on conservative styles of clothing, the wearing of beards for married men, and their preference for a hook-and-eye mechanism for fastening clothing instead of buttons. Initially, life was very difficult for these peasant farmers, and they became targets of very severe persecution because their new faith forbade them to swear allegiance to the state. The Amish were also unpopular because they refused to engage in military activities, which they interpreted as anti-Christian. Many Amish in Europe were burned at the stake, and in one Swiss locale it was necessary to ignite a huge bonfire in the town square to accommodate the execution of all of the alleged local heretics. In what is now Tun Castle in Switzerland, as many as 500 Amish were imprisoned at one time, awaiting their death. When burning the "heretics" at the stake attracted additional believers willing to die for their faith, the prisoners were quietly put to death by drowning. These executions were held at night to minimize publicity. Nearly 1,000 Amish died for their faith in this way before the practice of burning at the stake was abolished in 1571 (Zielinski, 1975).

American Immigration

The peak American immigration periods for Amish settlement were 1727–1770 and 1815–1860. After the Reformation waned and reprisals set in, religious persecution became the prime mover of many migrations from Europe to North America, and the Amish were no exception. By the early 1700s the Amish were able to negotiate plans to leave Europe for the United States. The first known Amish settlement in North America was established in 1736 in Berks County, Pennsylvania, and the second in Lancaster County, Pennsylvania. Once established, like most frontier congregations, the Amish met at irregular times for worship because their religious leaders had to travel extensively to reach the highly scattered settlements (Friesen and Friesen, 1996:23). Eventually bishops were ordained in every district as each community gained a measure of economic and spiritual stability. Although there were Mennonites living near some of the Amish settlements, the two groups had very little interaction during their first half century of living in America (Nolt, 1992).

Pennsylvania was part of the territory identified for the Dutch by Henry Hudson's 1609 excursion into Delaware Bay. The first permanent settlement, Gottenborg, was established on Tinicum Island in 1643 by a company of Swedes and Finns. A wide—though not complete—religious toleration was adopted in Pennsylvania under the leadership of Quaker proprietor William Penn. Penn was committed to the principle that religion is a matter of individual conscience and is not to be imposed by law and government officials (Beard and Beard, 1960:35). Naturally, this policy appealed to European immigrants, so that some 70,000 German-speaking people from the Palatinate, Swabia, Alsace, Hesse, and Switzerland migrated there between 1683 and 1775, making them a considerable presence in the colony (Weaver-Zercher, 2001:24).

By the time of the American Revolution, finalized by the Declaration of Independence in 1776, three factions of people had been satisfactorily endorsed by Penn. First, he made peace with Native Americans by dealing with them honestly and scrupulously; second, he attracted a group of hard-working people now called the "Pennsylvania Dutch," including Amish, Mennonites, Dunkards, and Moravians from Germany; and third, he encouraged a variety of other immigrants to join, notably Scots and Irish, who were eager to live under the privileges and responsibilities outlined by Penn for the new colony.

Amish Lifestyle

Amish farmers today are among the best in Lancaster County and their homes are usually identifiable by the use of the windmill or the famous waterwheel. The use of electricity or other modern forms of energy is frowned on by the Amish, as is the use of the automobile for transportation, although this has been adopted to some extent in recent years. Today many Amish industries utilize electricity to run their shops using their own power plants, although they are forbidden to tap into public utility lines (Kraybill and Bowman, 2001:106). In some communities

Amish businessmen are permitted to purchase motor vehicles for business purposes, although they are not permitted to drive the vehicles themselves. Since interstate travel between Amish communities has become quite popular, some Amish families hire Mennonite neighbors to drive them when they want to attend weddings or funerals or visit their friends and relatives in other localities (Kraybill, 1990:68f).

The Amish utilize mainly horse-drawn equipment for farming, even though such machinery is becoming exceedingly difficult to come by. As a result, Amish farmers sometimes outbid antique dealers for household and farm equipment at local auction sales. Similarly, Amish farms are rarely sold, and then mainly to other Amish. As their children reach adulthood and marry, some families will attempt to divide their farmland into smaller sections on which their married children can live. This is done in order to keep the family together. When nearby "English" farms are sold they are usually purchased by the Amish. (The term "English" is used by the Amish to denote any groups other than themselves or Mennonites).

Those familiar with the Amish ways know that they comprise three basic factions: (i) the Old Order Amish, who cling to the traditional way of life featuring the use of the home as a church, the buggy, and the avoidance of electricity; (ii) the Beachy Amish (also called Church Amish, Amish Mennonite, or Weavertown Mennonites), who allow electricity, telephones, tractors, and automobiles although their cars are subdued in color; and, the (iii) "New Amish," who represent a variety of departures from the Old Order (and often from each other) in that they may keep plain clothing but allow cars, electricity, meeting houses, and the relaxation of other particularistic regulations. New Amish religious activities tend to resemble those of conservative, evangelical, or even charismatic denominations.

It is the Old Order Amish and conservative groups of Mennonites that attract tourist curiosity because of their atypical characteristics, namely the use of the horse-drawn buggy for transportation, their simplistic lifestyle, and their conservative attire. Only the serious inquirer will discover that there is more to Amish people than meets the eye in connection with family life, courtship and marriage, church practices, and the well-publicized barn-raising. These practices will be described in more detail later on.

The Beachy Amish present an enigma to many people because of their curious mixing of the old and the new. They utilize tractors and cars, yet cling to the use of sixteenth-century clothing. Like most Mennonites, they sing in four-part harmony, something that Old Order Amish are forbidden to do because of the distraction it would cause from concentrating on "singing unto the Lord." In some Amish schools children do sing in two-part harmony but this practice is not universal.

Beachy Amish originated in 1927 from among the Old Order Amish, under the leadership of Bishop Moses M. Beachy, who saw little wrong with the practice of Sunday school, the construction of church buildings, and the use of mechanized farm machinery, the automobile, and electricity. By the 1930s the movement had spread to other states, eventually growing to about 90 congregations who, though not formalized into a conference, do function as a separate denomination (Hostetler, 1977). In 1955 the group formed the Amish Mennonite Aid, a Beachy mission, relief, and service organization. In 1970 they established Calvary Bible School at Calico Rock, Arkansas, and began a monthly church periodical named the *Calvary Messenger* (Nolt, 1992). The Beachy Amish also operate their own information center in Lancaster County as a means of acquainting visitors with their way of life and their interpretation of the Christian faith.

"New Amish" groups began to emerge in the middle of the late 1960s in both Pennsylvania and Ohio for two main reasons. One was the appeal of modern technology for farming and transportation, and the second was a spiritual concern about "cleansing of wrong ways." Adherents to "New Amish" communities began to speak of "assurance of salvation," implying that it was time to openly share their Christian faith with nonbelievers. Old Order Amish bishops warned them that to do so was an act of pride but the innovators would not desist. Old Order Amish believe that it is impossible to have assurance of salvation; at best the Christian can only hope for this status as a gift from God.

Central to the lifestyle of the Old Order Amish is the authority of local church leaders, who enforce the *Ordnung.* All members of the church must gain approval from the local church leaders for acts of behavior that are not already the norm in their particular group or face excommunication and shunning. Amish rule-breakers are usually admonished for their misconduct, and often find themselves brought up before the church body without advance warning. Practices that are permissible are well-known by church adherents even though these regulations are never written down. It is up to individual members to be aware of all rules, stipulations, and restrictions. Members of the *Ordnung* meet twice a year, before Communion Sunday, to discuss and/or amend the existing regulations, or to consider individual cases of possible indiscretion. A cohesive unit such as Amish society fosters a high degree of effective social control; it governs one's work, religious convictions, family life, and other aspects of living. What is projected is the impression of a very smoothly functioning entity (Friesen and Friesen, 1996:89).

Rules of conduct among the Amish do not necessarily correspond in every detail from one church district to another, but this lack of consistency concerning minor issues does not seem to bother adherents. Their objective is to live a simple lifestyle (preferably agrarian) under the blessing of the church. Thus, when an Amish family relocates to another Amish settlement or community it becomes essential that they immediately apprise themselves of any local doctrinal idiosyncrasies.

More than anything, tourist-type questions represent only a vague understanding of the Amish *Weltanschauung* or worldview. The Amish objective is to live as traditional a life as possible, using the advances of technology or modern value systems only when the traditional way *must* be amended. For example, when an Amish individual is no longer able to purchase "antique" farm implements for his horse-drawn operation, he may use a horse-drawn wagon to pull an engine around the field, letting the engine operate the newer machine he has had to purchase in order to stay in business. This approach does not violate any of the rules of the *Ordnung,* and chances are that the Amish man has checked beforehand with the *Ordnung* regarding the "legitimacy" of his new arrangement. To achieve peaceful relations is a major component of this form of the utopian experience.

Amish life holds many surprises for outsiders who assume that the Amish are a "backward" people who reject all forms of arts. Quite to the contrary, there are a number of modern literary pursuits among the Amish. Some Amish write poetry, keep journals, and decorate crafts with pastoral scenes. Some Amish are artists, and their works are available to tourists in local stores. Art that exalts the individual artist is unwelcome because modern art is viewed as worldly, impractical, and self-exalting, as well as a waste of money (Kraybill, 1990:40). Various crafts that are representative of Amish culture and show a high degree of artistic finesse, such as appliqued and pieced quilts, are permitted and are often sold with the artist's signature stitched into the quilt.

The Amish in America and Canada generally keep in touch with each other through a national publication, *The Budget,* and via their *National Directory of Businesses. The Budget* contains news items submitted by local correspondents, letters from individuals, or information of concern to Amish generally. It satisfies the need to know what is happening in other Amish districts and, more importantly, it is an unofficially approved channel of interdistrict communication.

Generally speaking, the Amish are not an evangelical community in the sense that they seek to attract others to their cause. They do allow people to join their ranks, but such an undertaking is perhaps more indicative of cultural conversion than religious experience. There are at least two family names, Stoltzfus (formerly an English name, "Proudfoot"), and Huyard (a French derivation) that have been drafted into the Amish family tree, one by the adoption of a 12-year-old boy and the other through adult conversion. The latter pertains to an Englishman named Proudfoot who once came to live with the Amish and later married an Amish woman. His name was promptly translated into the German equivalent, and Lancaster County has many residents by that name as a result (Friesen, 1983).

MORMONS

Like many other faith groups, the Church of Jesus Christ of Latter Day Saints (Mormons) began as a sect in the state of New York under the leadership of Joseph Smith (1805–1844). Mormonism eventually became one of the most complex and extraordinary of all religious groups to develop in that part of the country. Kephart and Zellner (1994:234) note that the area in which Mormonism developed was called the "burned over" district in western New York because so many new religious sects originated in that area during that time period. Shakers, Millerites, the Fox Sisters, and the Oneida Community (discussed in a later chapter), all drew their first converts in western New York State between 1825 and 1850.

Beliefs

Mormon theology may be characterized as polytheistic in focus. According to Douglas (1991:571), God the Father was apparently chosen in a council of the gods on the planet Kolab to be the god of the planet earth. God is both flesh and bone, is married, and has all the attributes of a human being. God and his wives created all the spirits of the world, and all of these spirits except the spirit of the man, Jesus Christ, fell from God's grace in their prior existence and are in need of redemption. Mormons believe in the historic fall of mankind, through which people discovered their sexuality. Somehow this discovery implies that procreation is essential to salvation. The Mormon church's fascination with genealogy mandates that individuals be interested in their ancestry so Mormons can be baptized for nonbelievers in one of the church's regional temples. Through this means, those ancestors who did not have a chance to receive the gospel will be given an opportunity to do so and be saved (Douglas, 1991:571).

Mormon philosophy, as it is today, was not suddenly conceived; it grew gradually and expanded as new situations and environments demanded. Mormon adherents claim that the *Book of Mormon* is the foundation of their faith because it describes the story of the descendants of the lost ten tribes of Israel, who came to the New World before the birth of Jesus. Those early settlers were part of the lost tribes, and the risen Jesus allegedly appeared to their ancestors while they were still in Jerusalem. Like most other utopian religious groups, Mormons believe that they are the chosen people to whom God has given His special blessing. Since this revelation came through Joseph Smith, he was considered God's emissary, and mandated his followers to go out into the wilderness and make converts. While Smith never claimed to be the resurrected Christ, he swore that he had seen God's angel face-to-face. Calverton (1969:133) suggests that "The Book of Mormon was founded upon theories no more fantastic than those of the Bible; it was interspersed with the doctrines of the day, rife with paradoxes and contradictions, and shot full of irrational and incredible suppositions and conceptions."

Fortunately, the Mormon doctrinal creed includes the option that their current living prophet (president), who occupies the position initiated by Brigham Young, has the authority to modify policy to meet contemporary needs. This privilege may even contradict past policies, but it shows the church's ability to transform its theology to suit time and place. A case in point was the Woodruff Manifesto of 1890 that forbade the practice of polygamy (Kephart and Zellner, 1994:251). When Mormon president John Taylor died in 1887, he was succeeded by Wilford Woodruff. In 1890, when the Supreme Court of the United States ruled polygamy to be unconstitutional, Woodruff pronounced an end to plural marriage. His decree became known as the Woodruff Manifesto. Non-Mormons saw this as a victory, and most Mormons agreed. With the abolition of plural marriages, Utah could apply for statehood.

A second example of Mormon policy change was initiated by President Spencer Kimball in 1978 which permitted nonwhites immediate rights to priesthood in contradiction to all previous authoritative teachings and practices of the church (Dieter, 1991:571). Perhaps the longevity of the Mormon church has been assured by their adaptive approach to change. Although they will probably not find it necessary to relocate geographically in the future, their method of theological modification may stimulate continuing redefinitions of utopian ideals.

Joseph Smith

One of the highlights of Joseph Smith's leadership was the frequency with which he announced visions he received from God. Smith's Scriptural interpretations did not always agree with those of orthodox Christians in the area, and local clergymen found this disconcerting. Smith claimed that an angel from God named Moroni had visited him and showed him some gold plates with spiritual messages on them. Apparently Moroni gave Smith instructions on how to translate the message of the golden plates, which resulted in the *Book of Mormon* (also entitled *Another Testament of Jesus Christ*). Critics were convinced that Smith had fabricated the *Book of Mormon* as a hoax and he should be considered a dangerous megalomaniac and con man who took advantage of his followers (Foster, 1991:125).

Smith's all-American religion was officially founded on April 6, 1830, in the state of New York. The group's beliefs were sufficiently antithetical to orthodoxy and Mormons quickly became objects of persecution. The basis of Smith's new creed was a revelation of a "new and everlasting covenant," which was to continue throughout all eternity. Perhaps the most controversial doctrine of this covenant was the belief that polygamous marriages could be justified in Scripture. On July 15, 1843, Smith privately dictated a revelation calling for restoration of polygamous marriages and set the example by being wed to 26-year-old Louisa Beaman. His wife, Emma, did not particularly endorse the doctrine and is reported to have threatened several times to leave her husband over it (Foster, 1991:134). Emma received the shock of her life one day to discover that her best friend, Eliza Snow, who had lived in her home for seven months at Nauvoo, was also one of her husband's new wives. When Emma discovered this, she became so furious that Eliza was forced to seek new places to live a number of times. Smith's followers eventually fled New York to begin colonies in Ohio, Illinois, and Missouri, finally ending up in what became the state of Utah.

When the Mormons originally decided to build a colony at Nauvoo, Illinois, in 1839, it was Joseph Smith's plan to operate the community as a state unto itself, with political and economic ramifications. To this end Smith established an upscale defensive plan. An all-Mormon militia, called the Nauvoo Legion, was formed and united more than 2,000 men. Their presence caused considerable fear among neighboring non-Mormon inhabitants. Eventually the Nauvoo settlement grew to be the second-largest city in Illinois, and appeared to hold the balance of power by alienating both major political parties.

Smith did not allow external pressures to influence the mandate he set for his followers. One such requirement was Smith's insistence that all village menfolk participate in missionary endeavors, thereby often having to leave their wives and families for long periods of time. Foster (1991:148) notes that on occasion when men were away on missionary trips, Joseph Smith would try to seduce their wives. As a result a number of Smith's followers in Nauvoo rejected polygamous marriages and left the settlement.

Joseph Smith and his brother, Hyrum, were killed in a riot in 1844 at a jail in Carthage, Illinois, where they were awaiting trial on charges arising from the dissatisfaction of some of their followers regarding polygamous marriages. After some confusion, Smith was succeeded by Brigham Young, but a division emerged and a second group headed by Smith's son began to identify itself as the Reorganized Church of Jesus Christ of Latter Day Saints. This group denounced Young's endorsement of polygamy as well as his advocacy of celestial marriage (spiritual marriage not recognized by the state), baptism for the dead, and the plurality of gods. Smith's notion that God was appointed to be the God of the universe by a council of gods, and that He is married to several wives, was unacceptable to leaders of the Reorganized Church. Unlike the larger body of Mormons, which features many more such edifices, the Reorganized Church of Jesus Christ of Latter Day Saints has only two temples, one in Independence, Missouri, and another in Kirtland, Ohio.

Dissension

Institutions with a propensity to change must always anticipate that segments of their following will not take readily to transition. This is the case with an offshoot Mormon community known as Bountiful, British Columbia. Bountiful is one of five breakaway Mormon sects in North America that still practice polygamy. To this group, "utopia" includes the spiritual privilege/obligation of populating the earth (Wood, 2001). Located in the south central part of British Columbia, not far north of the Montana border, is a village of some 50 houses, and home to Winston Blackmore, his 28 wives, and more than 80 children. A few other polygamous families live nearby, bringing the population of the settlement to nearly 1,000. Village residents tend crops and engage in seasonal work such as picking fruit, digging potatoes, processing chickens, and doing small-scale logging. In many ways their lifestyle resembles that of their neighbors in other rural parts of the province.

Essentially, colony members adhere to the teachings of a 90-year-old prophet named Rulon T. Jeffs and his right-hand man, Winston Blackmore. These leaders insist that polygamous living not only fulfills a Biblical mandate, but is protected by the Canadian Charter of Rights and Freedoms. None of the village's plural marriages are legalized, for the law would not permit it. Instead these common-law unions are know as celestial marriages, thereby avoiding prosecution under Section 293 of the Criminal Code.

Blackmore disputes critics' claims that his harem of women is primarily for his sexual convenience by insisting that the women can only have sex for the purpose of reproduction. The sole purpose of the activity, according to Blackmore, is to propagate the human race. Despite this defense, various accounts of sexual abuse have emerged from beautiful Bountiful, and a number of women have left the colony. In 1992, three men from the village were charged and convicted of sexual abuse. Also in the news were reports of dissent in the Colorado City Colony. Since the colony's prophet, Rulon T. Jeffs, is aging, the elderly prophet proposed that his son Warren replace him, but many objected to the idea. Tempers flared, lawsuits were filed, and some men openly rebelled. In retaliation, the younger Jeffs ordered 1,000 of the sect's children removed from Colorado City's public school system. In order to claim his authority, he announced that the children would now be homeschooled. Continued complaints against the community have resulted in their shipping young girls north to Bountiful to serve as celestial wives. Young men seeking wives must wait for their leader to assign someone to them or leave the community.

In response to these and other developments, the state of Utah recently tightened its anti-polygamy laws, and so charged and convicted one of the colony's members, a man named Thomas Green. The Law Commission of Canada has also indicated that an investigation into the marriage practices of Bountiful will be undertaken. Only time will tell whether or not members of this unusual group will be able to maintain their form of utopian living.

Search for Utopia

The Mormon quest for isolation initially included both escape from persecution as well as the privilege of peacefully living out their beliefs in seclusion. They traveled west across the country in search of freedom and in response to one of Joseph Smith's frequent revelations. They were not communalists in the strict sense of the word, but began as economic individualists and developed a cooperative economic system for expediency—and that only after some struggle. In Kirtland, Ohio, they met a self-styled socialist radical preacher named Samuel Rigdon who joined with them and harmonized his philosophy with Smith's notion of the United Order of Enoch and its dream of a communist commonwealth. The Kirtland experiment lasted five years, but no New Jerusalem emerged, so the Mormons moved on to Colesville, Ohio. Again, they met with opposition, and internal disagreements between Joseph Smith and Brigham Young arose, so Smith and his followers left for Nauvoo, Texas (Calverton, 1969:137–138). Soon thereafter, their community lands in Ohio were occupied by an Icarian settlement.

For the Mormons, Nauvoo was a godsend, and the settlement grew quickly from 6,000 members to 25,000. The town became incorporated as a city-state, and town leaders established an independent judiciary, built a university, and created an army of 5,000 soldiers. Smith publicly denounced slavery and advocated that all slaves in America be released immediately. He also recommended that the "parasites of the nation" (lawyers, in his opinion) be eliminated, and a national bank be set up. When he offered himself as a presidential candidate, however, it was too much for his antagonists and conflict erupted. It was then that Smith, his brother Hyrum, and Sidney Rigdon were seized and taken back to Missouri, where they were eventually killed by a hostile mob.

After Smith's death, Brigham Young became the new prophet and led his people to Utah Territory. His succession was not unanimously accepted and a dozen factions split off and settled in other parts of the country. When the Mormons arrived in Utah they built Salt Lake City and obtained large tracts of land, following a policy of segregating themselves from "the Gentiles." Their theocratic development plan represented a combination of individualism and collectivism in that individuals were allowed to own property, but this right was always subject to the rules of the theocratic state. The fundamental principle on which the community operated was that every individual had the right to have food, clothing, and a home, and enjoy the comforts of community life— but beyond that, the individual or the family were entitled to nothing. It would be the job of the theocracy to see to it that equality was attained and the surplus used for the good of all. The plan worked, and soon the Mormons turned the desert into a land of plenty. Their success brought on jealousy from their neighbors and opposition to their lifestyle arose because of what were termed outrageous revelations from Christ, John the Baptist, and other apostles. The Mormon belief in plural marriages contradicted the laws of the United States and practically led to war between the Mormons and state authorities. The practice of polygamy was finally abandoned by the Edmonds Act of 1882, paving the way for Utah to achieve statehood in 1890.

The Mormon church has always been very much involved in missionary endeavors, with some missionaries entering Canada soon after their organization (Tagg, 1968). Permanent settlements were built in southern Alberta as early as 1886, partially to escape pressures exerted by the American government against the Mormon practice of polygamy. In 1887, a conservative faction of Mormons moved to Alberta under the leadership of Charles Ora Card with the intent of launching "a Zion in the North." The Mormons believed they were fleeing from "the land of legalized persecution" when they left the United States, and they petitioned the Canadian government to allow them to practice polygamy. Although the government refused, the group persisted and established a cooperative economic system in southern Alberta, which included a sawmill, a cheese factory, and an invented form of currency that bore C. O. Card's signature (Rasporich, 1987). There are presently more than 60,000 Mormons living in Canada.

Early Mormon history is so rampant with libelous accounts that few people recognize Joseph Smith as one of America's first utopian socialists. In many ways his economic vision was far in advance of his contemporaries', and were it not for his outrageous revelations, his ideas about evangelism, sharing, and the importance of family might well have attracted the kind of attention they deserved. Even utopian visions, it seems, if they are to be publicly acceptable, must be couched in somewhat orthodox terms.

OLD BELIEVERS

Founded on religious/spiritual principles, the experiences of the Old Believers parallel those of some Anabaptist groups discussed earlier. Unlike the Mennonites, however, the Old Believers did not immigrate to Russia, but originated there as part of the seventeenth-century church revolt. During the 1650s the Russian Orthodox Church, which dominated the country, was undergoing rapid changes in appearance and structure led by the Patriarch Nikon. He decided to reform the church by introducing a series of radical innovations reminiscent of Greek culture (by which he had been influenced). The reforms included Greek themes in architecture, furnishings and rituals. Nikon also mandated a revised prayer book, the making of the sign of the cross with three fingers instead of two, the sunwise direction for processional marches, a ban on head shaving, a correction of the name of Jesus (from *Isus* to *Iiusus),* and the repetition of *alleluia* to be thrice instead of twice during services. These changes angered many members of the Orthodox Church, and dozens of new sects including the New Believers quickly formed as large groups of adherents broke away from the church (Kach, 1984).

The Russian government took serious steps to dissuade the dissidents from leaving the state church and even eliminated many of them with fire and sword. Mass burnings were undertaken, and between 1672 and 1691 some 37 incidents of mass execution were initiated by the authorities (Florinsky, 1955). These events set the Old Believers on a migration pattern to Siberia, central Asia, northwest China, Hong Kong,

Australia, New Zealand, and South America (mainly Brazil) in search of freedom. Finally, in 1967 a small group migrated to northwest Canada with short stays in Alaska and Oregon. They moved to Lac LaBiche, a small community in northeast Alberta. There they settled on small plots of farmland and engaged in various forms of mixed farming. Currently, in the springtime, some of the men accept jobs with the provincial government planting tree seedlings in northern regions of the province.

The utopian perspective of the Old Believers includes a life of simplicity, abstinence from "worldly" habits, and strict adherence to their unique interpretation of Christian prescriptions. Their belief that religion pervades all aspects of life has brought them into conflict with both neighbors and state authorities. The Old Believers maintain that their abstract ideals of peace and harmony, of love and union, have been translated into concrete forms of ritual and behavior and are not to be questioned (Kanter, 1972:75). Every aspect of community life has implications for commitment, including property, work, boundaries, recruitment, intimate relationships, group contact, leadership, and ideology. These segments of social organization have been arranged so as to promote collective unity and provide a sense of belonging and meaning. However, occasionally individuals "marry out," and are shunned by loyal adherents. Other family members are forbidden to have anything to do with them.

As modernity continues to encroach upon previously secluded pockets of civilization, the pressure to yield to its luxuries and influences becomes increasingly hard to resist. Children of Old Believer families attend public schools where they often encounter ideas not taught by their church. This has motivated them to ask hard questions of their elders, but the reply is simply to warn the children about the unfamiliar ideas of mainstream society. Almost as though having a built-in mechanism to diminish as a movement, the Old Believers have shunned a priesthood of any kind their numbers have decreased. There are no revered spiritual leaders among them who could possibly guide and reprimand them to guard and maintain their traditional values and life patterns. There are significant signs that the younger generation is finding life outside the enclave of their traditional religion very attractive and many are leaving the fold. There is no record of outside conversion to the Old Believer faith and there are only about 300 adherents left in Canada. The utopian dream appears to be melting away.

SUDETEN GERMANS

Often the pull towards a utopian goal is compelled by political motivations, as we shall see in later chapters. Dissatisfied groups often find it necessary to search for new places to live because they are being deprived of their rights, are persecuted, and even threatened with annihilation. Wars bring such groups into being, and their numbers are legion. Political and historical analysts refer to them as refugees, and their stories have emerged in every generation since time began. A representative, albeit relatively unknown case is that of the Sudeten Germans.

The Sudeten Germans are a fascinating case study of the quest for utopia away from the clutches of a totalitarian regime. Their story formally began in 1806 when a number of Germans migrated to what later became the independent country of Czechoslovakia. In 1993 the country split into the Czech Republic and Slovakia. The Sudeten Germans were lured to what was then Bohemia by the invitation of political leaders who wanted skilled Germans to cultivate frontier lands in the Sudeten Mountains. After World War I, the Imperial splendor of the Austro-Hungarian monarchy faded away and a policy statement declared by the new government included the assurance of minority rights. Despite this proclamation, which was never enforced, conflict soon broke out between Czechoslovakia loyalists and the Sudeten Germans who felt that their concerns were being disregarded (Schilling, 1989).

By 1929 the Sudeten Germans had formed two political parties, whose elected members joined a coalition cabinet with their Czech and Slovak colleagues. This, and other moves, gave rise to German nationalism and the formation of the Sudentendeutsche Heimatfront (Sudeten German Homeland Front). By the time World War II broke out there were about three million Germans in Czechoslovakia and many of them were against the Nazis (Schilling, 1989:xii). Their patriotic spirit gave them a sense of direction when Hitler's forces invaded Czechoslovakia and the Sudeten mountains in 1939, but it also resulted in the persecution of 300,000 Sudeten Germans by Hitler's forces.

Hitler's cohorts quickly identified those who were not in sympathy with their cause. Women and men were blacklisted, and the Czechoslovakian authorities could not help. Although the Sudeten people counted on assistance from the Allied forces, none was immediately forthcoming and they felt abandoned. As the "last free Germans" and anti-Nazis, during the 1940s they were overrun by Hitler's forces and many of them were persecuted, imprisoned, or thrown into concentration camps. Some fled to central Czechoslovakia; others who were more fortunate escaped to free western countries. An Englishwoman, Doreen Warriner, worked hard to relocate Czech refugees out of the Sudetenland and organized many transports of women and children to leave Prague for England.

Canada was considered a safe haven for refugees. Lengthy negotiations with the Canadian government brought some 300 Sudeten Germans to northeastern British Columbia to settle near Dawson Creek, and to St. Walberg in northwest Saskatchewan. Though none of the newcomers had a clue of what lay ahead of them, the opportunity to leave what had become enemy territory and begin anew in a peaceful location, particularly one with so much promise, gave them boundless hope. In Canada they would find a political/economic utopia and make a fresh start. Those who had spent time in Czech concentration camps were especially grateful.

When the Sudeten Germans arrived in northern Saskatchewan, the new arrivals were settled in agricultural areas despite the fact that many of them were not farmers but tradesmen. The newcomers might have done better in urban centers. Another challenge to the would-be farmers was their assignment to poor land that had been abandoned by previous settlers. The Sudeten people were flabbergasted at the resistance of the northern Saskatchewan soils to producing crops of any worth, but they persisted. At times doubts assailed their minds; they worried about relatives they had left behind and they were apprehensive about the future. Many first generation immigrants never became Canadian citizens, and were marginalized as a result. Many Sudeten immigrants were so overcome by living conditions that they wished they could return to Czechoslovakia.

One of the primary adjustment challenges faced by the Sudeten farmers was a linguistic one. Since most of the newcomers had no knowledge of the English language they initially had virtually no communication with their neighbors. They valued their heritage and attempted to keep their native language alive. It was especially difficult for Sudeten women to learn English because they had less opportunity to interact with their English-speaking neighbors while their husbands were working away from home. Still, they were grateful for the opportunity to fulfill their dreams in the new land.

When Canada officially entered World War II, many Sudeten Germans joined the armed forces as Canadian citizens or helped with the war effort in other ways. As the war progressed many locals migrated to nearby cities, giving opportunity to local farmers in the area to acquire larger tracts of land and become more productive. When the war ended a number of Sudeten German clubs sprang up in the northern regions of British Columbia and Saskatchewan. Groups of Sudetens gathered to remember their past struggles, to give thanks, and to encourage one another

3.4   Abandoned Sudetan Cemetary near St. Walburg, Saskatchewan

to meet the challenges of a rapidly changing economy. Today, three generations of Sudeten Germans still gather at various locations across Canada to celebrate their bond with one another and with their newly adopted motherland.

Unlike many "suitcase" immigrants (refugees who migrate to a new land and leave their suitcases unpacked), many Sudetens saw Canada as a place of hope for the future. "They never ceased to marvel at the freedom they found in Canada" (Schilling, 1989:172). "From the moment I set my feet on Canadian shores, I will become a Canadian," said one of the Sudetens, resolutely stamping a foot on the long wooden planks of the ship's deck (Schilling, 1989:44). Canada was not a place of escape; it was a land of new beginnings. Canada was utopia.

CHAPTER 4

RELIGIOUS COMMUNITIES

Scholars who study intentional communities seem to agree that these experiments last longer if they are undergirded by a strong underlying philosophy or religion. The communities discussed in this chapter are all of the religious-spiritual variety, and all of them had a relatively long life. The Shaker commune is the only community discussed in this chapter with active membership today. While the association reached a peak of 5,000 members in 1830, it still endures with a membership of seven.

During the nineteenth century at least 90 communal experiments were initiated in the United States, with less than a dozen of them lasting more than 16 years (Kanter, 1972:63). The four communal societies described in this chapter lasted through several generations, but their strong spiritual or philosophical base was probably not the only reason for their success. They also had capable leaders. With the exception of Ephrata, Oneida, and the Shakers, these communities were also quite reasonable in the demands they placed on their adherents. Their beliefs and daily lives reflected quite orthodox, traditional, commonplace, and ordinary behavior patterns. These communities offered a satisfying lifestyle relatively free of conflict, stress, or an unduly harsh work ethic.

AMANA

Amana was a colony whose communalism originated in the New World instead of the old: Amana communalism is thus an entirely American phenomenon. This European group had no plans to form a commune until they reached North America. Once settled, they adopted this form of lifestyle because they realized that it was probably the best way for them to survive in uncharted territory.

Beliefs

> *Religion was life to them and life was religion.*
> *—Calverton (1969:115)*

The foundation of Amana faith was a mixture of reverence for the Scriptures mingled with ongoing revelations received and interpreted by inspired prophets such as their leader, Christian Metz (1794–1867), and his successor, Barbara Heinemann (1795–1883). The application of their theology was probably more important to them than any formalized statement of creed. Basically, they believed in plain living, religious worship, and the practice of humility. They forbade anything exquisite in their houses, and did not believe in ornamental attire. People were not allowed to beautify themselves, and unduly attractive garments were regarded as sinful. Calverton (1969:112) suggests that the Amanas were as anti-intellectual, anti-ecclesiastical, and anti-progressive as the Shakers, but more backward in their attitudes towards women. Women had virtually no say on colony matters, they dined separately from the men, and they often had to sleep by themselves. Religious meetings in the Amana villages were held at least ten times a week, including every Wednesday, Saturday, and Sunday morning, with daily devotions conducted in the evenings.

Singing without musical accompaniment played an important part in Amana life, and Amana leaders wrote most of their own hymns (Shambaugh, 1988:303f). A collection of these hymns fills two gigantic volumes. Amana church buildings were unpretentious, and often indistinguishable from other colony buildings. Inside, the whitewashed walls, bare floors, and unpainted benches were a testimony to the simplicity with which these folk chose to display their faith.

The Amana community claimed to follow the Bible in all things although they did not practice baptism, which Metz regarded as a mere religious ritual. The Lord's Supper (or Eucharist) was celebrated biennially, on a date selected by the inspired leaders. On those days, a series of five communion services was held according to age and rank, with the senior or older group first partaking of the Sacrament, followed by the younger people, and ending with a service for children. Instead of partaking of bread and wine, however, the children were served coffee cake and hot chocolate, the idea being that by participating they would feel bonded to the community. Included in the service of communion was the foot-washing ritual to commemorate the washing of the disciples' feet by Jesus Christ, a custom also practiced by other conservative groups like Amish, Brethren, and Mennonites.

In many ways the Amana society paralleled the traditional Hutterian way of life (discussed in a later chapter), even though the two groups had no knowledge of one another. Both communities were governed by councils made up of local leaders who made virtually all decisions for the colony including setting budgets and determining sales of products. Their worship practices were also quite similar. Both groups seated the sexes separately during worship, and women wore mandatory shawls or bonnets. Hymn singing was a highlight of services, and elders were appointed to preach sermons. Although the Gospel was primary content for sermons, references to the testimonies of founders and leaders of the church supplemented biblical references. Both Amanas and Hutterites urged a peaceful, brotherly way of living in simple dignity and humility, with faith in Christ and in the Word of God. The primary difference between the two groups is the Hutterites' version of pacifism which historically precludes any involvement in civil courts. When Hutterites are threatened today, however, they sometimes resort to use of the courts. The Amanas were openly nonpacifist. In 1905 they were charged by state officials with violating their status as a religious organization by becoming excessively wealthy. The society immediately hired legal assistance and handily won their case on November 20, 1906. The *Cedar Rapids Gazette* reported that the Amana position had to be honored based on the conclusion that the society had originally been formed precisely to provide socioeconomic support for its members (Crum, 1998).

Christian Metz

The Amana story began in Germany in 1714 when two religious leaders of Lutheran extraction founded the Community of True Inspiration. Dissatisfied with what they saw as the dogmatism and intellectualism of the state Lutheran Church, Eberhard Ludwig Gruber and Johann Friedrich Rock came to the realization that certain individuals could be considered Divinely inspired by God. This was the Amana version of apostolic succession (Yambura and Bodine, 1986). This idea, of course, did not reflect orthodox Lutheranism, and persecution drove the group to America in 1842 under the leadership of Christian Metz, who had become their inspirational leader 20 years earlier.

A group of 350 people followed Metz to New York. They accepted Metz' prophecy of communal living and looked forward to forming a new kind of society. Metz claimed he had received a message from God telling him that anyone who did not comply with his communal plan would be cursed. There was some resistance to the proposal from some followers, but Metz continued to receive messages from God to reiterate the impact of his vision. Finally, the resisters acquiesced and communalism was realized. However, by 1855 there were several challenges that hindered Metz from realizing his vision. Almost immediately after their arrival in America, contentions arose because the Amanas had purchased land that formerly belonged to Native American tribes, but Metz wanted nothing of controversy, so he pushed his group to relocate to Iowa. In 1854 the group purchased 25,000 undulating acres of farmland along the Iowa River, almost half of it wooded with highly valued walnut, oak, and cherry trees. During the next decade Metz' followers built their homes and developed a series of very successful manufacturing industries.

The Metz people chose the name "Amana" for their new location. The word occurs in the biblical book of Song of Solomon (4:8) and means "believe faithfully." The community built seven villages, each of which was separated from the others by a distance of an hour's drive (approximately one and a half miles) by ox cart. At the time of settlement in Iowa, the Amana membership consisted of 500 souls, eventually increasing to 1,800 just before they dissolved in 1932 (Shambaugh, 1988).

The Amana community was not without elements of struggle. Their first challenge was to establish regulations about marriage. Metz was particularly displeased about the occurrence of casual liaisons and non-marital sexual relations. In the decade that followed their arrival in Iowa an approved age of marriage was established, but couples could only marry after being approved by colony elders. Even then, however, there were occasions of pregnancy before marriage: although members were temporarily shunned for their misbehavior, they were never permanently ostracized (Cavan, 1979:260). The ruling council that approved marriages was made up of males only. If approved, a couple had to wait a year until they could be married, and they were permitted to date only three times a week. If the couple lived in the same village, one of them might be transferred to another village until their wedding day. The concept was that by waiting the couple would be more sure that they were making the right decision.

At times internal struggles arose in the community because long hours of labor were required of the membership with only a small amount of remuneration to fulfill personal needs. The bulk of all income was placed in community coffers. There was also some disagreement about the sale of "personal items" for needed cash—items which, according to their philosophy, really belonged to the community. Basically everything at Amana was communal property except for individual members' clothing, toys, and other personal effects. Penalties for disobedience ranged from reprimand to public ridicule to permanent expulsion.

As the Amana people flourished they developed a series of institutions and industries—a woolen mill, a calico print factory, a furniture factory, a general store, a wine cellar, and other functional structures. They were best-known, however, for their manufacture of major kitchen appliances, and created an industry that lasted for many years. A generation ago, partly because of declining membership, this factory was sold to private ownership. It was also believed that the commune could function very well on farm income alone.

Each Amana village traditionally had a school (private, at first), and a church; Sunday schools were introduced in 1931 as part of an effort to teach religion in schools mandated by the state of Iowa. At its peak the commune amassed 26,000 acres of farmland, which today is still managed by the trustees of the Amana Society for Business Affairs. The Amana Society was governed by a Board of Trustees who were elected by members who were male, widows, or single women. Married women were not permitted to vote because it was believed that they were adequately represented by their husbands. The trustees occasionally held "mass meetings" to involve the membership in decision making, and they regularly kept people informed of fundamental changes in policy and practice. In addition to using their own judgment, they were guided by the inspiration of Sister Barbara Heinemann who assumed the role of prophetess when Christian Metz died. She served until her death in 1883 at the age of 88 (Shambaugh, 1988:43).

Village life in Amana, according to testimony of both observers and residents, was much like that in a Hutterite colony. Life was pleasant and fulfilling. There was plenty of food to enjoy, cooked in traditional German style, and eaten in good company. There were several communal kitchens in each village, each serving as many as 30 to 60 people. Men and women dined separately and meal times were 6:00 A.M., 11:30 A.M., and 6:30 P.M. Coffee breaks were at 9:00 A.M. and 3:00 P.M. Each day ended with the women and young girls cleaning the kitchens and setting tables for the next day. Homes were clean, plain, and neat. Everyone shared in the workload, and there was plenty of time for socializing. Tobacco was allowed but there were rules outlawing fancy attire.

Religious rituals were not considered important. When death came, members of the community were buried in chronologically arranged graves to demonstrate the theme, "equal in life; equal in death." Wives and husbands were not buried together because it was believed that the marriage union was not appropriate to the afterlife. This arrangement is still practiced in modern Amana, which now functions as a corporation. Each stone bears a name and the date of death.

Modern Amana

Amana remained a successful communal system for seven generations, and eventually became an industrial democracy. Like the Zoar Colony, their transformation came about as a response to increased connections with the outside world combined with broader economic forces (Rawls, 1995:73). Stresses created by outside developments occurred when a railroad passed through Amana, bringing with it a series of external influences which the elders had not expected. Passenger trains ran once a day in both easterly and westerly directions. The colony even built four hotels to accommodate outside visitors, as a means of accumulating added income. Many guests enjoyed Amana community life so much that they arranged for stays as long as a week. Later, highways were developed, which enabled even faster and increased travel to distant locations. This brought large groups of tourists to Amana who gawked curiously at the traditionally oriented people. The temptation to sell colony goods and obtain money to buy little personal extras was too great to be resisted by pretty well everyone except the most devout. Eventually the Amana residents spoke more English than German. During World War I the state imposed laws applying to all American citizens, including military conscription (Cavan, 1979:260). Naturally this kind of law was bitterly opposed by most of the Amanas. Though they were not opposed to war as such, they simply did not want to become involved in a war with Germany.

By the 1920s, temptations of modern life threatened the dissolution of the Amana Society. Young people in particular showed little interest in sacrificing their work and talent for a common purpose. They wanted less work, less religion, and more personal income. Eventually it became necessary to hire outsiders to do farm chores and till the fields. Still, the unemployed Amanas had to be supported. The flour mill and the grist mill were destroyed by fire at a time when the colony was feeling the effects of the Great Depression. Soon the colony amassed a debt of half a million dollars, and some members vacated the premises in search of more stable income and enhanced individual freedom. As a result of this trend, in 1932 the community democratically voted to dissolve, a resolution that was labeled "the big change." A complete separation of church and state occurred, and individuals could now attend church when they chose to do so. Two new respective organizations emerged; the Amana Church Society for Religion and Welfare, and the Amana Society for Business Affairs. Members were given company shares and homes were sold to individual families. There were those who grumbled about some adherents getting better houses than others, but basically the process went smoothly. Some members established small businesses. A few former members even returned to make claims on the property, having lost their allotted share through unsuccessful investment. The Amana factory and farmland continued to be operated as a corporation until the factory was sold in 1965 (Liffring-Zug, 1975). Today, the Amana Society for Business Affairs manages only farmland.

Permanent residents in Amana today receive free medical and dental care from funds provided by the Amana Society for Business Affairs and usually find employment in one of the local places of business. Some residents run local establishments, while others commute to nearby Cedar Rapids or Iowa City to work. The Amana Society provides free maintenance of streets, sewage, telephones, and electricity, although residents have to pay state and federal taxes. Several of the seven villages offer weekly church services presided over by elders who are elected on a permanent basis. One of the churches also offers a German language school. The lack of strong spiritual leadership after Metz and Heinemann died contributed to a disintegration of the society, even though family and village ties are strong for those whose roots are imbedded in the past.

A visit to Amana today enriches the mind with nostalgia and social change. Although families who live in the villages own their own homes and buy their own goods, the setting is delightfully rural and pastoral. Set in some of the nation's richest farmland in central Iowa, the seven tiny villages are open to tourists, featuring old-fashioned, attractive restaurants, as well as bed-and-breakfasts for weary travelers. Tree-lined fields reveal thick grain crops supplemented by healthy herds of cattle. Visitors can tour a modernized furniture factory, a woolen mill, bakeries, butcher shops, carpenter shops, wagon shops, and a vast range of retail stores selling gifts and collectibles. In the 1980s the woolen mill operated 24 hours a day, seven days a week making blankets for the U.S. Army. A total of 475 Amana buildings have been designated as historic land-marks, and more than one million tourists visit Amana each year. An initial response to the lure of Amana is to slow down and enjoy the moment. Visitors quickly get the impression that they could stay as long as they like and their welcome would not wear out. It is very comfortable in Amana.

If a communal utopia can possibly be imagined as a reality, Amana constitutes a very believable model. Its failing was principally due to its inability to keep in line with changing times. In the words of a former resident, the late Dr. Henry G. Moerchel, "Thanks Heavenly Father, for this little oasis of faith and devotion serving as a sanctuary for us because of America's freedom of religion, and grant that a similar magnificent spirit of affection and sincerity be imbued and found among our young people also" (Liffring-Zug, 1975).

DOUKHOBORS

Doukhobor origins may be traced to the middle of the seventeenth century, when Patriarch Nikon introduced Greek reforms into the state-approved Russian Orthodox Church. He did not anticipate the extent of opposition he would experience. Within a short time literally dozens of alternative organizations arose from within the church, condemning Nikon's actions and denouncing him as the Antichrist. Known as the *Raskol* or Great Division, the opposing factions formed several schisms rather than band together. No one individual may be credited with starting the Doukhobor organization, but their formal origins occurred around the 1730s when an unidentified wandering spiritual teacher from Moscow appeared in the Kharkov province of Ukraine. He argued that church hierarchy and priesthood were manmade inventions, as were most societal institutions. This teacher soon gained a following and in the next two generations the group formally renounced state religion and adopted the oral tradition, communalism, individualism in spirituality, sexual equality, and pacifism as basic beliefs (Tarasoff, 1982:2).

Formal designation of the term *Doukhobor* came into use in 1785 when a Russian Archbishop named Ambrosius nicknamed this dissident group *Doukhobortsi,* or "Spirit Wrestlers," arguing that the group was wrestling against the Spirit of God. The Doukhobors embraced the name, claiming instead that they were wrestling *in* the Spirit of God. Theirs was not a dead faith, they insisted; it was continually alive because of their daily struggle in the Spirit of God. The real test of Doukhobor tenacity came on June 29, 1895, when they staged a public protest (the Burning of Arms) against the militarism of the Russian government. In South Russia the Doukhobors built a series of bonfires of arms and munitions, including guns, swords, and knives, and fueled the fires with wood and kerosene. This incensed the government, which immediately took action by incarcerating some 80 Doukhobors. The event served only to strengthen the resolve of the Spirit Wrestlers and the "Burning of Arms" became an annual ritual.

Doukhobor Theology

As any folklorist knows, traditions that are handed down from one generation to another in the oral tradition are subject to constant change. In a sense this is the beauty of the oral tradition. It is difficult to synthesize Doukhobor theology into a functional whole, partially because of their disdain for social institutions. No written records are kept pertaining to fundamental beliefs and regulations and there are no managers or clerks (clergy) to supervise their maintenance. In a real sense, believers are regarded as their own priests. Despite this feature, the fundamentals of the Doukhobor faith have remained relatively intact, particularly their adherence to the doctrine of pacifism, which extends to the point of their being vegetarians; belief in individual equality regardless of race, age, or gender; and the renunciation of social institutions. Although the Doukhobors have had to acquiesce to state regulations concerning the registration of births, marriages, and deaths, they have not given in to military conscription. This was particularly evident during World War II when many young men of Doukhobor background served in various forms of alternative service (Janzen, 1990).

Orthodox Doukhobors believe that it is wrong to kill, and they have expanded this belief to the arena of refusing to kill animals for food. The creed also posits the foundational assumption that every human being has a Divine Spark (*Iskra*) within them, implying that everyone is equal before God. Spiritually speaking, this means that each individual has something to offer, and each is considered to have direct access to God. Thus, when Doukhobors gather for worship, it is expected that anyone (young or old, male or female) can lead the assembly in a psalm or hymn. Everyone will join in after the first line has been sung. In a way this practice serves to allow each one to present a testimony in the psalm they choose to sing.

The outward manifestations of early Doukhobor religion consisted of a rejection of all external rituals, images, the sign of the cross, and fasts. These were considered useless to individual salvation, which could only be attained through applied faith. The Doukhobors claimed and still believe that energies devoted to theological discussions would be better spent in the practice of brotherhood and sharing of resources. There was even one Doukhobor leader, Illarion Pobirokhin, a wool merchant from the Russian village of Goreloe in Tambov, who considered reading the Bible a waste of time; after all, God speaks only to the listening heart, not through the written page. The doctrine of the Trinity received similar short shrift because the Father, Son, and Holy Spirit, which may be likened to light, life, and peace, should be evident in daily practice, not described in literary form. In the human soul, memory may be equated with the Father, intellect with the Son, and will represents the Holy Spirit.

Much of Doukhobor thought is transmitted in poetry accompanied by music. These selections are called psalms and hymns, although the distinction between the two is not clear to the outside observer. Prayers are said without musical accompaniment. There are no hymn books or musical scores used with the songs, although they are at least partially passed on from one generation to the next via the oral tradition. Many psalms were written by Peter the Lordly (their leader from 1886 to 1924), and preserved in the oral tradition through worship and repetition. The themes reflect the Doukhobor experience at various times and places, such as the psalm of praise penned by Verigin in 1902 upon his release from 16 years of exile in Siberia. Two representative stanzas are quoted here:

O Lord, Thou art the Light of my life
And Thou I wish to praise forever—
From earth Thou has created me
And bestowed me with a soul of understanding.

How the world is created in the heights,
It brings me to ecstasies of awe—
From earth Thou has created me
And bestowed me with a soul of understanding
(Friesen and Verigin, 1996:81).

Although not a formal doctrinal creed, the following statement was formulated by the Union of Spiritual Communities in Christ (USCC) in 1934 and is still referred to by members of the organization whenever the USCC sponsors formal gatherings.

1. We the Union of Spiritual Communities of Christ, have been, are, and will be members of Christ's church, confirmed by the Lord and Savior Jesus Christ Himself and assembled by His Apostles.
2. We believe in the law and faith of Jesus as is expounded in the ten commandments and is to be adhered to on the basis of obeying God rather than man when these polarities contradict one another.
3. We do not recognize any political party nor do we support them because they symbolize the giving of body and soul to an institution. This we offer only to God.
4. We believe in "rendering unto Caesar" all things required of us by the state that do not contradict the laws of God and the faith of Jesus Christ (Popoff, 1982).

Formal Leadership

For some 22 years, beginning in 1864, the Doukhobors experienced a "Golden Age of the Commune" under the leadership of Lukeria Gubanova Kalmakoff (1841–1886). Doukhobor leaders were not democratically elected, although community input was strong. After a leader died, it was customary to appoint a successor after a six-week period of mourning. Usually the candidates were well-known to the community, and at the appointed time the people would simply bow to the candidate of choice. Often such an individual had already been groomed by the previous leader, so there were few surprises in the process. Lukeria took the reins from her 26-year-old husband, Peter Kalmakoff, at the time of his death. It was his wish that she do so. In fact, some observers noted that Peter Kalmakoff's claim to fame was his marriage to Lukeria (Friesen and Verigin, 1996:33).

During Lukeria Kalmakoff's reign she instituted a number of reforms, all of them designed to make life easier for her followers. She was very careful to see that everyone was treated equally, and she had absolutely no patience with abusive husbands. An abusive husband was locked in a chicken coop for the night. Next morning, the embarrassment alone was sufficient to help the culprit to change his ways. Lukeria also established a central welfare headquarters to serve those in need, and took a personal interest in its operation. When the time came to appoint a successor, motivated by the fact that she and her deceased husband did not have children, Lukeria selected her young cousin by the name of Peter Vasilievich Verigin (1859–1924). This action was somewhat complicated since Verigin was already "married" to Evdokia Grigorevna Koteinikoff, and Lukeria simply told him to get rid of his wife. This was not particularly difficult from a legal standpoint since the Doukhobors did not adhere to state institutions. If a man and a woman wanted to get married and had the support of their parents they moved in together, and that was that. Peter Verigin did as he was told, but the move was later to have political repercussions. Somewhat ironically, at the time of Peter Verigin's death, his son by Evdokia, Peter Petrovich Verigin, was named leader.

Lukeria trained her young charge for five years before she died. The two often went out together and stayed in a cave where Lukeria allegedly held forth on the virtues of Doukhobor life. Gossip about their personal relationship flourished, but there is no evidence to suggest that anything unorthodox occurred between them. It did transpire that on one occasion Verigin decided to visit his former wife, and when Lukeria found out about it she became very angry (Friesen and Verigin, 1996:34). Lukeria died on December 15, 1886, and since she had not directly named an heir, her brother, Michael Hubanoff, decided to fill that vacancy. A split erupted between Michael and Peter Verigin and the two factions became known as the Large Party and the Small Party. Peter Verigin (also called Peter the Lordly), ended up ruling the larger segment of this alternative group, and it was his followers who eventually made their exodus to Canada. Members of the Small Party tried to prevent Verigin from taking office, so they spread rumors about him, thereby gaining the attention of the Russian government (Tarasoff, 1982:19–20). Verigin continued to attract followers, and fearing his popularity, the Russian government immediately exiled Verigin to Siberia, from where he guided his people via correspondence. In the years following the exodus of the Large Party to Canada from Russia, the Small Party disappeared.

Tension against the Doukhobors in Russia was mounting and the Doukhobors feared the worst. They were clearly at a crossroads, but, as fortune would have it, Clifford Sifton, Canada's Minister of the Interior, was looking for immigrants to populate the western prairies. It was just what the Doukhobors were looking for.

Canadian Experience

In 1899, 7,500 Doukhobors landed on the east coast of Canada as immigrants. They spent the winter months in Winnipeg in immigration sheds and by spring were relocated to the Kamsack-Yorkton area of east-central Saskatchewan. The conditions stipulated for settlement on government lands were simple. They had to promise that they would till the land allotted to them, and satisfy the government that they would not participate in any insurrection against the government. The Doukhobors were delighted; now they would be able to live in peace and practice their beliefs without outside interference.

By 1902 the Doukhobors had built 57 communal villages and assembled a brick factory, a flour mill, and other facilities. They owned 600 horses, 400 oxen, and 865 cows. They built a bridge over the nearby river at one crossing and operated a free ferry to all passengers at another. They also established a flourishing cooperative in Yorkton. They were so successful that their neighbors got jealous and sought government assistance in squelching Doukhobor ingenuity. Critics began to accuse Sifton of going soft on immigration. He was accused of allowing unwanted groups of immigrants to engage in unfair practices. In response, on February 15, 1902, Clifford Sifton wrote a letter to the Doukhobors demanding that they swear an Oath of Allegiance to the Canadian government. The demands of the letter contradicted the Doukhobor interpretation of events. This was not the agreement they had with the government. They had faithfully tilled the soil allotted to them and they had not risen in insurrection against the government. Why did they now have to swear allegiance to the crown?

The letter caused great consternation in the Doukhobor villages. Then, to their great delight, their beloved leader, Peter Verigin, was released from exile in Russia and arrived in Canada. Despite his best efforts he was unable to persuade Sifton and his bureaucratic colleagues to exempt the Doukhobors from signing the Oath of Allegiance on religious grounds. In response, the Doukhobor ranks split into three factions. The first group, which consisted of 236 individuals (and their families), reluctantly agreed to fulfill government requirements. They did not wish to move again, and they were sure the government would respect their belief system even if they took the Oath of Allegiance. By their concession, they obtained title to settlement lands and became known as Independent Doukhobors.

The second and larger faction retained their identity as Community Doukhobors, and with Verigin plotted an alternative to swearing allegiance by relocating to British Columbia. This, of course, meant giving up their settlement lands, but they valued their faith more than material gains. The third faction, the radical segment (who called themselves Sons of God), decided to embarrass the government by staging a protest. On October 28, 1903, a crowd of 1,060 persons left their villages to endure the elements of a frosty night, and marched on Yorkton, Saskatchewan. They took few clothes and little food with them and kindly farmers who felt sorry for them gave them provisions on the way. Eventually the Royal Canadian Mounted Police rounded them up and confiscated some of their possessions in order to pay for their transportation home. Later, many of them followed their orthodox brethren to British Columbia.

During the years from 1908 to 1912, Peter the Lordly gathered up what funds he could by selling off grain, livestock, and implements, and led his faithful followers to the interior of British Columbia. Here they purchased 4,500 acres of privately owned land that did not require an oath to the government. They also built 90 multifamily communal houses and many adjoining buildings. The new Doukhobor economy included fruit farms and sawmills, a brick-making plant, and a jam factory. It was agreed that all title to land be held in Verigin's name until the organization, now known as the Christian Community of Universal Brotherhood (CCUB), was established. Several years later, true to his word, Verigin signed the assets over to the organization. The CCUB prospered, some of the men obtaining employment in surrounding communities and using their wages to pay off mortgages. Soon additional lands were purchased for the growing community; by the 1920s the CCUB owned 21,648 acres and other holdings in three provinces with an accrued value of nearly 6 million dollars.

In 1915, on Peter the Lordly's advice, the CCUB purchased 11,260 acres of land in the southern region of the neighboring province of Alberta and some 300 Doukhobors from British Columbia were settled there. Verigin bought a number of existing farms and used the buildings to house the people. He bought the farms figuring that the agricultural produce could be shipped to British Columbia in exchange for lumber and other commodities. The distance was much less than to the Saskatchewan holdings so the shipping costs were less. The arrangement worked well—another testimony to Verigin's ingenuity.

Peter the Lordly died in 1924 when an explosion rocked the train on which he was riding, and he was succeeded by his son, Peter Petrovich, who arrived from Russia in 1927. At first there was a bit of uncertainty about Verigin's successor when Anastasia Holoboff, Verigin's companion of some two decades, vied for the throne. However, of the

4,000 people gathered for leadership selection six weeks after Verigin's funeral, all but 500 of them bowed their heads towards Russia, indicating that they wanted Verigin's son, Peter Petrovich Verigin, to lead them. Naturally, Anastasia was very disappointed. She moved to Alberta where she established a colony of her own along with 165 followers.

Peter Petrovich was not able to leave Russia immediately to lead his flock, but requested that they send him funds to help the Doukhobor cause there. This was done unquestioningly, but it later proved to illustrate Peter Petrovich's single-handed method of rule. Indeed, the CCUB prospered under Peter Petrovich's leadership, but unfortunately, his personality was more abrasive than that of his father and his rule was marred by a number of personal conflicts and brushes with the law. On the positive side, Peter Petrovich contributed a great deal to Doukhobor culture by establishing Russian language schools, annual hymn festivals, and touring choirs.

In 1937 a surprise foreclosure on the CCUB was initiated by two trust companies, the National Trust Company and the Sun Life Assurance Company, with the approval of the British Columbian and Canadian governments. This action was in response to public fears that the Doukhobor commune was a threat to Canadian society.

By 1937 the Doukhobors had become very successful. The net worth of the CCUB was nearly 6 million dollars with a debt load of about four percent ($319,276.00). The debt consisted of a series of demand notes signed with banks across British Columbia and the prairie provinces. Two trust companies, the National Trust Company and the Sun Life Assurance Company, secretly bought up these notes and without warning issued a foreclosure notice. The CCUB was given 24 hours to pay up, and no bank would lend them any money in so short a time. The Doukhobors tried to avert the foreclosure via legal protection, but the Supreme Court of British Columbia ruled against them. The court announced that the Farmers' Protection Act did not apply to corporations, so the unwarranted foreclosure went ahead.

The trustees of Doukhobor lands and holdings sold some of the land to resident Doukhobors on a share basis, then liquidated the rest. After several years foreclosure proceedings came to a rest, and there remained a balance of $222,078.42, which was placed in a trust fund for Doukhobor cultural maintenance. Shortly before his death in 1939, realizing that a physical commune was no longer feasible, Peter Petrovich Verigin instituted an organization called the "Union of Spiritual Communities in Christ" (USCC), which still operates. Its basic premise is that a spiritual commune has replaced the physical one. Peter Petrovich was succeeded by his grandson, John J. Verigin. Essentially, the association sponsors annual cultural events and occasional publications as a means of keeping the Doukhobor message alive (Friesen, 1983).

In 1980, the USCC mandated a report on the future of the faith and recommended that a series of model communal villages be constructed in British Columbia. The plan was intended to attract youth who might be interested in reviving the traditional Doukhobor lifestyle. Volunteers would first serve a year of apprenticeship in training in Doukhobor beliefs and practices and then occupy homes in the model village. Local prayer homes in Castlegar and Grand Forks were targeted as sites for intensive Sunday School programs but none of these measures have aided in attracting young people. Unable to reinvent or adapt traditional motifs to contemporary forms, Doukhobor leaders have been forced to appease their utopian appetites with annual celebrations of revered holidays in constantly decreasing numbers.

The Future

Well-known Doukhobor historian Koozma Tarasoff (2002:ix) estimates that there are at least 40,000 people of Doukhobor descent in Canada, although most of them are not active in Doukhobor organizations or activities. There is no record that any Doukhobors live in the United States. Persecution and intolerance have driven many Doukhobors underground, and assimilation has taken its toll. As has been the experience of many other ethnic and religious groups, Doukhobors have not always been welcomed in the urban centers of the nation. Generally speaking, Canada has not always been receptive to ethnic diversity. Until recently, it was difficult for members of some ethnocultural backgrounds to assume roles in the country's institutions. Does this mean the

4.1   Mr. Mike and Mrs. Doris Verigin (friends of the authors), United Doukhobors of Alberta, Cowley, Alberta

ultimate end of the Doukhobor identity? Not necessarily, because the Doukhobor faith is still celebrated annually in a number of festivals. In 1995, the USCC sponsored a series of elaborate events across the nation in remembrance of the centennial of the Burning of Arms. Then, in 1999, a symposium held at the University of Ottawa brought dozens of scholars together to read papers and evaluate contributions of Doukhobor culture and faith over the past century.

If the nature of Doukhobor celebrations and the writings that emanate from them (Donskov, Woodsworth, and Gaffield, 1995; Tarasoff and Klymasz, 1995), are any indication, the message and influence of the Spirit Wrestlers will live on for a long time to come. Their cultural trappings may change, but the essential essence of their philosophy can live on in other forms. As one Doukhobor elder put it, "The disappearance of Doukhobor culture is not cause for alarm. As long as the Doukhobor message of toil and peaceful life is kept alive, it does not matter what cultural form it takes" (Friesen and Verigin, 1996:133).

Molokans

The Doukhobors were not the only sect to emerge in the period of the Great Schism in Russia. Their neighbors, the Molokans ("milk drinkers" in Russian), flourished in Russia during the 1800s and expanded to 100,000 adherents by 1900. About 2,500 Molokans migrated to North America just before the Russian Revolution. Originally anti-Orthodox and communal, the Molokans believed that a spiritual utopia could be attained by adhering to a number of fundamental, Bible-centered doctrines. No longer communal, today their 200 congregations operate in a loose federation of sorts with lay ministers and an informal council of elders. Their spiritual gatherings resemble those of Quakers, Mennonites, and Doukhobors, although culturally most of them have assimilated (Tarasoff, 2002). Most of the 20,000 active Molokans today live in Russia and the northwest United States. In the United States, except for spiritual activities, their lifestyle is virtually indistinguishable from their American counterparts.

SHAKERS

Put your hands to work and give your hearts to God
—Shaker Motto

Few communal experiments in American history have been better organized, long-lived, or culturally influential than that of the Shakers. Although their official name is The United Society of Believers in Christ's Second Appearing, most people know them as Shakers. This name originated from their practice of frenzied dancing during their religious services. During the highest growth years of the movement in the 1830s, hundreds of people joined the Shakers, making it the largest commune in America at that time. Their beloved leader was a blacksmith's daughter, Anne Lee (1736–1784). At its peak the society had over 5,000 members living in 19 settlements (Carpenter, 1975:115).

The Shakers served as an example for other utopian visionaries such as John Humphrey Noyes, Robert Owen, and Friedrich Engels. Observers have noted the Shakers' ability to sustain longstanding interest in their modes of music, crafts, and architecture. Although there are only seven Shakers left in the United States, the Shaker organization comprises a watershed advocacy organization for women's rights. The seven remaining members are all women, and live in Canterbury, New Hampshire, and Sabbath Day Lake in Maine (Religious Movements Homepage, 2003).

The Shakers promoted a campaign for the equality of the sexes long before the feminist movement struck America (Foster, 1991:17). But total and complete equality for women did not exist among Shakers, even though both men and women could serve as elders and eldresses. Although the two offices were equal in theory, in practice they were not. Men dominated the ministerial role and Shaker patents were issued only to men. Male office deacons were often called "trustees," but females were called "office sisters." Office sisters were not permitted to hold property in trust for other members, although men did (Brewer, 1986:51).

Shaker Beliefs

The Shakers believed in the bisexuality of God and therefore viewed "Mother Ann Lee" as the second and female incarnation of God. Her teachings and writings were regarded as the inspired word, a sure testimony to the fact that God's revelation had not stopped with the New Testament apostles. In her writings, Ann made a great distinction between the Holy Spirit and His temporary tabernacle, the body, which was considered evil. The Shakers thus rejected the Trinity and held the notion of a physical resurrection to be repugnant. They concluded that the only way to rid the body of its evil tendencies was to reject natural, carnal urges such as sexual intercourse and close family attachments, and devote oneself entirely to the worship of God within a communal setting. Only through this means could they possibly hope to attain salvation.

One of the ways they alleviated strong physical urges was to engage regularly in a dance form consisting of whirling, trembling, and shaking as a means of incurring exhaustion. After several hours of this kind of emotional release participants often fell onto the floor as though in a trance. A variation of the whirling, twirling type of dance was a stylized rhythmic march in which men followed close behind women in rank and file. This form of dance was called "laboring."

Ann Lee believed that God's plan of redemption had personally been revealed to her. According to her theology, Christ was only one of God's manifestations to humankind (male at that), and through her own person God was revealing the female side. Accordingly, no one could attain salvation until they had experienced the complete parenthood of God through both male and female manifestations. Having had this double opportunity, the Shakers were taught that Christ's Second Coming had occurred through Ann. It was their responsibility to see that it would continually occur through the lives of the redeemed.

Around 1800, in response to the intense religious revival that struck America, the Shakers sent three missionaries 1,000 miles on foot to verify and participate in this phenomenon. Their evangelical efforts resulted in five new Shaker communities, which were established in Kentucky, Ohio, and Indiana. Shaker membership thus peaked in 1830 at 5,000 and virtually remained there for the next quarter century (Holloway, 1966:69). By 1845, however, membership had begun to decline, and the quality of those selected to fill positions of authority diminished markedly, quickly creating a vicious cycle of membership loss (Brewer, 1986:184). What remained of Shakerism was viewed as a relic of ancient days with mostly elderly people and children making up their numbers. By this point most Americans only viewed the Shakers with curiosity and nostalgia, with little motivation to appreciate or identify with the finer aspects of their utopian ideals.

Ann Lee

Public knowledge of the Shakers first came in 1772 when a constable in Manchester, England, was called upon to quell a disturbance cited as a breach of the Sabbath. A deviant group took it upon itself to disturb a Quaker church worship service to indicate their disapproval of established religious practice. The dissidents, one of whom was Ann Lee, were fined or imprisoned. Ann had joined this reactionary group in England in 1758 at the age of 22. When the group migrated to America, their theology seemed to fit the emerging belief system of the Great Awakening of the 1740s.

Ann was particularly attracted to the movement that became Shakerism because of the Shakers' belief in direct Divine inspiration, but at first she was not very active in the movement. To please her family, Ann married a man named Abraham Standarin and delivered four children, all of whom died in infancy. In 1766, when her last child died, Ann became a more zealous follower of Shaker teachings. She reacted to the loss of her child by blaming herself, and was laden with guilt, trying to find peace and forgiveness. She became active in a Shaker group led by Jane and James Wardley and impressed them with her sincerity. Her dedication eventually resulted in her taking Jane's place, at which time she became known as Mother Ann. In 1772 she was imprisoned as a punishment for taking part in the disturbance mentioned earlier. In prison, Ann had a vision in which she "beheld the grand vision of the very transgression of the first man and women in the Garden of Eden, the cause wherein all mankind was lost and separated from God" (Andrews, 1963:11). Thereafter she was to denounce sexual intercourse and marriage as unspiritual activities.

A unique form of religious questioning of orthodoxy attracted a handful of followers to the rather rigid Shaker teachings, including the condemnation of lust, criticism of the established church for condoning marriage, and denunciation of worldliness of every kind. Soon gossip about tempestuous meetings racked with noise and fanaticism rocked local neighborhoods that the Shakers occupied. Accusations of heresy, blasphemy, and witchcraft flourished, breeding a spirit of intolerance and suspicion and leading to outright acts of oppression. The Shakers were forced to practice their religious forms in secret. Attempts to stone Ann Lee and her followers were foiled by happenstance.

Garnering little support for her message in England, where Shaker numbers never reached more than 30, in 1774 Mother Ann led eight loyal followers to New York, where her alternative organization eventually found converts. Although her husband followed her to New York, Ann made it clear to him that she would never again share the marriage bed with him. However, the divorce laws of the time made it difficult for them to legally dissolve their union. Finally, in 1775, unable to deal with a celibate married lifestyle, Ann's husband left her.

The first major Shaker breakthrough in America occurred in 1780 during the Revolutionary War and the outbreak of religious revival. In response to various requests, Ann and a few colleagues began a preaching tour throughout New England that lasted from May 1781 to September 1783 (Carpenter, 1975:124). During this period most people joined the order following what were termed "spiritual awakenings," a feature of this period of American religious life. Two years later, Ann Lee and her cohorts undertook successful preaching events at Harvard University and neighboring points and greatly enabled their cause by winning the hearts of four wealthy farmers, who financed their missionary endeavors and provided food for their extended religious meetings. Their

4.2 Dwelling house, built 1793, Canterbury Shaker Village, Canterbury, New Hampshire

success precipitated the first schism in the Congregational Church of America. It also motivated a campaign of severe opposition to the Shaker movement; one particular charge, although somewhat stretched, was that Shaker persuasion tended to alienate the minds of the people from their allegiance to the state (Andrews, 1963:34).

Shaker Routines

From its beginnings in America, Shaker philosophy centered on having "all things common," and Mother Ann Lee devised a series of strict regulations by which the meaning of this phrase could best be carried out. Each of the Shaker villages deviated only slightly from the established schedule, but essentially daily routines were quite rigid. Group units of men and women known as "families" lived in separate sections of Shaker homes, where they were under the supervision of an elder and an eldress. The various families were not allowed to visit in each others' homes, and as units they were responsible for their assigned shops, livestock, barns, and fields. Members were allowed to visit non-Shaker relatives only if they thought there was a possibility that the outsiders might convert.

Daily Shaker routines—and, in fact, every aspect of Shaker village life—was regulated, including the time of day when people arose, when they ate meals, or went to bed. All interaction between the sexes was highly regulated and any hint of a close personal relationship was broken up. Men rose "at first trump (bell)"—at 4:30 A.M. in the summer and 5:00 A.M. during the wintertime. "Put your right foot out of the bed first. Place your right knee where your foot first touched the floor in kneeling to pray. Do not speak but if absolutely necessary whisper to your room leader" (Webber, 1959:57). Women rose at second trump, making sure that all the men were safely outside, and when everyone was out of bed and prayers had been said, beds were stripped for airing and covers were folded over chairs. Backs were turned for privacy while dressing; then each room emptied, with people marching out single file to do morning chores. A third trump signaled everyone for breakfast, and while a little conversation might be allowed before entering the dining room, meals were eaten in silence and there was to be no winking or blinking.

4.3   Building complex, Canterbury Shaker Village, Canterbury, New Hampshire

When many young people joined the organization during the peak of Shaker growth in the 1830s, it increased the need for supervision, which strained leadership resources to their limits. Gradually, the traditional balance between regulation and order was threatened by rejuvenation and disorder. In order to maintain growth momentum during their period of success, attempts were made to encourage the trend by adopting orphans from England. Andrews (1963:225) notes that many women eagerly joined the order because it gave them freedom from unhappy marriages without their having to negotiate the severe divorce laws of the period.

In the workplace, individuals were always under the supervision of members of the same sex and therefore had little opportunity to cross sexual boundaries. If, for example, a man needed something from the women's shop, he would have to ask his supervisor to speak to the women's supervisor for a way to obtain the needed item. At times, more relaxed behaviors developed, but these were cut short if anything unusual occurred. Shaker men and women were occasionally permitted to visit one another in groups, but no form of physical interaction was allowed. Such meetings were carefully regimented, with women sitting on one side of the room and men on the other. The group then indulged in small talk, which included jokes, riddles, and singing, but no reference to crime, scandal, or war was allowed. These unusual restrictions were viewed as a necessary extension of celibacy but often proved to be too much for some converts who did not remain long in such solitude. There were reported instances of women who begged neighboring men to take them away by any means from the stringency of such life.

On the positive side, Shaker life also offered a great deal of togetherness or "we-spirit" (French and French, 1975:73). Everything, including very hard tasks, was done in groups, including spring planting, weeding gardens, and harvesting. These were joyous occasions and involved singing as much as they involved work. Those jobs that could not be done in groups were rotated among individuals so that no one was stuck in undesirable situations for a long time. This approach also avoided the possibility that someone might become attached to a certain task and take individual psychological ownership of it. In the majority of early American communes, work was valued by everyone and greater productivity was assured because of it. Usually individuals worked hard in order to keep the respect of their colleagues.

The economy of the Shakers was traditionally agricultural, although they supplemented their income by manufacturing furniture, weaving, broom- and basket-making, packaging seeds, and the trade of other products. They were careful to establish villages near waterways as a means of assuring transportation to possible markets. Their agricultural success was in great part attributable to their very significant appreciation for a form of hierarchical organization. Elders were appointed to guide, instruct, exhort, and sympathize with their colleagues, but they had no authority other than to encourage compliance with established rules. Prior to 1821 there were no written rules among Shakers, but increased deviancy among new converts necessitated stronger measures of compliance. Regrettably, there were individuals who disobeyed the rules, and after a sufficient number of reprimands by elders and eldresses, they were eventually excommunicated.

Occasionally elders would assume spiritual names as a mark of their appointments, sometimes taking the name of a predecessor or a name to exemplify a special trait. When the time came to replace elders and eldresses due to death, the rank and file had no say in the matter. Most took solace in the fact that those who held upper positions would be guided by the characteristics they sought in the replacements—humility, kindness, and meekness. Although elders could work their way up in the religious hierarchy, they had no special rights or privileges other than to remind their peers that each individual was responsible for his or her own salvation (Brewer, 1986:45).

Demise

The causes of the Shaker decline was attributed by Shaker leaders not to celibacy, as many outsiders thought, but by their members yielding to the temptations and lusts rampant in the world. Another way to describe it was that technological improvements and sociocultural changes in the outside world simply became too attractive to the Shaker membership (Richter, 1971b:87). The practice of celibacy made it necessary to solicit new members strictly from outside but this approach was not fruitful. Andrews (1963:226) suggests that the same economic factors that aided in tremendous growth for the Shaker movement also contributed to its demise. First, there was the matter of the expense of maintaining the order. Initially, the Shakers who joined were poor or in debt and those debts had to be paid by the community. Second, Shakers were very generous people and they were constantly giving money to help the needy. Third, their organization required a sizable financial base for maintenance; it was a large and often distant order, and as the years went by maintenance costs rose. Fourth, the Shaker policy of land ownership was in some ways illogical. Often the community bought land that was available to them for purchase, but it was not necessarily very fertile.

When Shaker membership began to dwindle, their semi-arable land became a burden on the society; the mismanagement that followed in the wake of prosperity was yet another reason for Shaker demise. As membership decreased, financial trustee appointments were often assigned to individuals who lacked the necessary experience to properly manage affairs. The fifth and final reason for Shaker demise was that they suffered from the onslaught of the industrial age. They seemed somewhat oblivious to the fact that all around them a new America was growing up. People who initially were appreciative customers soon became ruthless competitors. Perhaps the Shakers were not too deeply moved by the impending doom of their organization, as they believed that a cycle of growth and decay was common to all human institutions. Quite simply, the Shakers were thus unable to keep up with the demands of the new market, their products were obsolete, and they lacked up-to-date technology (Andrews, 1963).

During the 1840s and 1850s it became difficult for the Shakers to retain members for very long in their ranks (Foster, 1991:70). As their membership decline reached higher proportions, Shaker leaders were shocked to discover that not even the small group of the orphans they had brought into their colonies would sign the "Covenant of Confession" (statement of beliefs) required of all members. Of 197 children raised at Mount Lebanon between the years 1861 and 1900, for example, only one formally joined the movement (Newman, 1989:314). It took several decades to dismantle the various communities, beginning in 1889 with the dissolution of Tyringhamin in Massachusetts, followed by North Union in Ohio. By 1963, only three communities remained with one family in each: one in Hancock, Massachusetts, one in Canterbury, New Hampshire, and the third in New Gloucester, Maine. In 1989 there were two tiny Shaker homes left in Maine and New Hampshire with only a handful of members. Even then a strong difference of opinion about admitting new members kept them from engaging in meaningful communication.

Ann Lee did her best to prepare successors for her post when it appeared that her days were numbered. She lived to the age of only 48 despite prophecies by her followers that she would live for at least 1,000 years. Mother Ann died in 1784, and the Shakers gave their allegiance to James Whittaker, who put an end to the missionary efforts of the Shakers. Instead, he concentrated their efforts on consolidation. He died in 1786 at the age of 33, and was succeeded by Joseph Meacham whom

Ann had once described as "the wisest man that has been born of a woman for six hundred years" (Andrews, 1963:55). On assuming leadership, Meacham quickly promoted Lucy Wright to lead the women's line, where she served for 25 years. It was the combined leadership of Meacham and Wright that shaped Shakerism as a communal institution just three years after Ann's death. Meacham's plan included the establishment of a hierarchical "family system" charged with the responsibility of looking after both temporal and spiritual matters. Ironically, by the time their membership began to wane, the Shakers were organizationally in their best position.

After Mother Ann Lee died, many of her followers had visions that provided instructions from their faithful leader. These visions were not uncommon, for Shakers frequently saw spirits of people who had passed away. Webber (1959:61–62) relates the account of a Shaker meeting in which no fewer than 40,000 spirits were in attendance, including the Virgin Mary. During times of such spiritual outpouring, virtually all work except that which was absolutely necessary ceased in the village. Sometimes the spirits sang, even in an unknown tongue, but interpreters were usually appointed to translate the essence of their messages to participants.

The Shakers are an example of a utopian dream featuring a unique mixture of egalitarianism. Although racial equality was acclaimed, the small number African Americans who joined were relegated to separate quarters and served in subservient capacities. In terms of economy, the Shakers were quite traditional. Men tilled the fields and worked in the shops, while women did household chores such as cooking, sewing, cleaning, and washing. This arrangement was intended to keep the sexes apart. In spiritual terms, during her lifetime Mother Ann Lee held the reins of theological interpretation, although after her death there was a tendency to drift towards male dominance in leadership. During Ann Lee's reign, the apparent equality was virtually legislated via strict rules. As Foster (1991:19) notes, "the degree of equality that existed between men and women in religious leadership occurred in the context of a tightly controlled, celibate structure that sharply restricted individual behavior."

The last great elder of the Shaker movement during the 1860s and 1870s was Frederick Evans, who was a former associate of suffragette Frances Wright. At first he had serious doubts about the organization, but after comparing Shakerism with other religious societies he quickly became a convert. He soon rose in the ranks and attempted to recast Shakerism in its old mold. He discovered that the people had grown "rich and lazy," their looms had decayed, and they often hired outside help to accomplish necessary chores. Some of the villages permitted members to own books, newspapers, and musical instruments. They also sponsored debating societies and literary clubs and liberalized restrictions on women's clothing. It was a time for desperate measures, so Evans ordered the populations of some of the houses to combine so that the extra space could be rented out to non-Shakers. Integration also became a necessity with Abraham Lincoln's announcement of the Emancipation Proclamation in 1863, and the very few African American members were no longer required to live in secluded quarters. Even financial controls were weakened; individuals began to sell goods and keep the money for private purposes. Later, as the twentieth century approached, Shakers began to yield to the lure of modern inventions. Some bought automobiles, took train rides for pleasure, engaged in photography, and showed little interest in religious activities. Mother Ann would have had a heart attack had she known of these trends. Finally, it was all over. Some Shaker villages were sold and the money transferred to another society. As the twentieth century ended, only a half dozen elderly Shakers remained, still hoping and praying for a revival.

Prevailing Testimony

Perhaps the most amazing characteristic of the Shaker faith is its longevity. For over two centuries, the Shakers have prevailed, demonstrating that community life can be more vital than the doleful, monastic seclusion offered by some experiments (Holloway, 1966:79). Theirs was one of the first societies endowed with that practical energy that was characteristic of the revival period. Their example underscores the reality that utopian schemes do not necessarily need to adhere to the values of mainline society in order to persist. Commitment, structure, and organization are obviously key planks in building a lasting foundation for unusual visions.

Today the Shaker legacy lives on in myriad ways. Since they once comprised the largest and best-known of American communal groups, great effort has been made to preserve elements of their culture and lifestyle. In Pleasant Hill, Kentucky, the colony has been completely refurbished to the point that one can almost feel the presence of the 500 inhabitants as they move from one activity site to another. Tourist accommodations are available, and visitors can participate in a variety of activities such as river boat excursions, workshops, educational programs, and colony tours. Founded in 1805, Pleasant Hill Village served as home to the Shakers until 1961, when it was taken over by a nonprofit educational corporation known as Shakertown at Pleasant Hill, Kentucky, Inc. Thirty-three of the original buildings have been restored and 2,700 acres of farmland are being preserved. The village is listed on the National Register of Historic Places and has been declared an Historic Landmark by the U.S. Department of the Interior.

In addition to Pleasant Hill Village, there are seven other Shaker tourist sites that can be visited. These include the Shaker Historical Museum in Shaker Heights, Ohio, and the Golden Lamb Inn in Lebanon, Ohio. The Shaker Historical Museum represents the North Union Shaker Village, which operated from 1822 to 1889. In 1947 this site was established as a museum. The Golden Lamb Inn is Ohio's oldest inn and still operates for the tourist trade. Listed as a Shaker museum, the Golden Lamb houses one of the most extensive collections of Shaker furniture and artifacts in southwestern Ohio. Two large display rooms contain many excellent examples of Shaker artistry.

ZOAR

The Zoar story began in the seventeenth century as part of the Separatist movement in Germany. Disillusioned with the treadmill-like routines and lack of spirituality in the state church, a variety of groups began meeting on their own. The leadership of the state church became very intolerant of the dissidents, who chose to follow the dictates of their own consciences and rejected the rites and rituals of the church. They refused to practice Baptism, Confirmation, and Holy Communion, and withdrew their children from state schools. As a result the Separatists were flogged, thrown into prison, and had their children taken away from them. Despite these measures, they stood firm in their faith (Nordhoff, 1966:100).

One particular group became enamored with the ministry of Barbara Gruberman, a Swiss prophetess who was given to extended spiritual trances. Concerned about religious conditions in her native Switzerland where her ideas were not welcomed, Gruberman found refuge in Wurttemberg, Germany. It was there that she came into contact with what became the Zoar Separatist movement and became their spiritual prophet. Germany, it turned out, was not particularly pleased with the activities and rapid growth of the movement. Fearing the worst for her followers, Gruberman saw little hope for their safety in Germany and urged them to go to America where they might find physical and spiritual freedom. Specifically, she prophesied that they would live communally in peace and harmony in America for a lifetime. Unfortunately, Gruberman died before the group left for America (Morhart, 1981:12). As it turned out, Gruberman's prophesy was astonishingly accurate and perhaps influential in determining the longevity of the commune. Zoar lasted from 1817 to 1898, a total of 81 years. After Gruberman's death, Joseph Bimeler (1778–1853) was chosen as leader.

The historic village of Zoar operated by the Ohio Historical Society provides travelers with a rare opportunity to visit the past. Most of the original village buildings have been restored, and a celebratory festival is held every summer, which attracts hundreds of people, fun-seekers as well as descendants of the original inhabitants. A few of the original homes have not yet been made available for sale to the Ohio Historical Society and are owned by individuals with strong family links to Zoar's past.

Beliefs and Practices

The tenets of the Zoar society very much reflected the Christian orthodoxy of the time and included a firm belief in the infallibility of the

4.4   Zoar Hotel built in 1833 and famous for its delicious food and clean quarters, Zoar, Ohio

Scriptures, the Trinity, and the fall of man. As Separatists, the group adopted pacifism as an official doctrine; excluded themselves from all ecclesiastical connections; and banned the use of all ceremonies, rituals and Sacraments. Although the Zoarites observed the Sabbath, even that acknowledgement was interrupted during seeding and harvest time. Undoubtedly, they would have come into legal difficulties with German authorities over such practices. Suspicions about the orthodoxy of the Separatists had already been aroused by German authorities when the Separatists adopted pacifism (Carpenter, 1975:207).

One of the ways by which to identify members of the Zoar Separatist movement was the adornment of a seven-point star. The star represented the Star of Bethlehem and stood for peace and goodwill toward all people. They gave the star seven points because the number was considered sacred. The Separatists wore the emblem around their necks as an indication of the sincerity of their beliefs. Because of the negative attitude of state authorities towards the Separatists, it was not unusual for an officer to cut the star off with his sword when he saw it

4.5   Interior of Zoar Church, featuring the hand-carved walnut organ with hand-painted pipes, built in 1873, Zoar, Ohio

(Morhart, 1981:12). The Zoarites perceived their journey across the ocean to America as analogous with the wise men of the Bible who followed the eastern star to find the Savior, Jesus Christ. Morhart (1981:12) suggests that when someone at Zoar performed a deed that was particularly noteworthy, an additional point was added to the star they were wearing.

The Zoarites rejected the role of priests or ministers, but adopted such administrative structures as were necessary, reluctantly conceding that they had to notify civil authorities of marriages taking place at Zoar. Several challenges faced local Zoar authorities. For example, at one point an attempt was made to establish nursing homes for the elderly, but the plan did not work. Residents complained of harsh treatment and poor care and the plan was abandoned. Following the settlement of this issue, care of the elderly was assigned to each respective family. In addition, the Zoarites declined to send their children to public schools and consequently built their own school on the village grounds. Fortunately for them, the school was classified as a public institution by the county; the society maintained the building but instructors' salaries were paid by the township.

Child rearing practices in Zoar were somewhat unusual. Until they reached the age of three, children were placed in nurseries so that their mothers would be free to help with farm work. Discipline was strict and corporal punishment was frequently meted out. Although the curriculum employed was primarily religious, the McGuffy Readers were also used. Much of the philosophy of education advanced during the nineteenth century originated in the McGuffy Readers, which were first used in the state of Ohio and then published and used widely across the country (Friesen and Friesen, 2001:22) Designed by William McGuffy (1800–1873), this popular series of school readers was intended to incorporate the ideal child-raising philosophy and desired value system for the American frontier. Bernhard Mehl (1963:24) of Ohio State University estimated that during the mid-1800s the McGuffy Readers had immense impact on the minds of young Americans. This series easily outranked the political power of the time in terms of influence.

Following the McGuffy philosophy, Zoar children were taught useful skills early in life and joined the workforce as soon as it was expedient for them to do so. In the earlier years they did not remain long in school because their help was badly needed. From the 1820s to the 1850s, the village operated the school for only three months of the year. As the community grew more prosperous, however, children were allowed to attend school on a longer basis, up to the ages of 14 or 15. Since the Zoar economy grew slowly in the initial years, children were poorly clothed, often wearing patch upon patch (Morhart, 1981:107). For Christmas the children received a few apples and some dried apple "snitz" (a form of dessert).

The Zoarites met for three meetings of worship each Sunday to listen to Bimeler's discourses and engage in periods of silent prayer. The society avoided all traditional rituals including Holy Baptism, Confirmation, and the Eucharist, and aside from Bimeler's revered position, did not have a religious hierarchy. Everyone called everyone else "thou." Music was allowed, dancing and tobacco were forbidden, and the community had no library. Reading was limited to the Bible, Bimeler's writings, and hymns.

The arts, particularly music, played an important part in the Zoar configuration, and their leaders wrote many hymns and built elaborately decorated pieces of furniture. Peter Bimeler, a grandson of Joseph Bimeler, built a pipe organ in an old flour mill and operated it by water power. All parts of the organ with the exception of the pipes were locally manufactured. Zoar had a band of 30 or more musicians who performed weekly. When the ban was lifted on German folk music in 1850, the repertoire of the band expanded greatly. At times they went out of town to play, and one year won a second-place prize at the Columbus State Fair. An orchestra called the "String Band" also provided regular concerts. Following this tradition, today a number of fine arts performers live in the restored Village of Zoar.

The Garden of Happiness, which was a highlight of the village, covered a city block. The garden represented the description of the New Jerusalem in the Book of Revelation. At the center of the garden was a large Norway spruce tree, circled by a hedge, intended to represent Jesus Christ and His promise of everlasting life. Twelve juniper trees were planted outside the hedge representing the 12 apostles. A wide variety of flowers graced the garden, along with vegetables of all kinds. Twelve walks led to the center of the garden, to represent the various walks of life, and wide paths at the edge of the garden represented the outside world. The garden had a number of benches on which to sit and contemplate life. Teenage boys were assigned to tend to the garden under the supervision of a horticulturalist. In recent years the garden has been restored to its historical appearance.

The Zoarites were very productive and ingenious at finding ways to increase their financial base at times when they desperately needed it. During the years 1825–1833, they assisted in the development of the Ohio River Canal by contracting to dig the canal throughout the extent of their territory. All income went to community coffers to pay for farm lands. The excavation was 40 feet wide at the top of the canal, sloping to 26 feet in width at the bottom. The Zoarites acquired the sum of $21,000 for their efforts and made additional money by furnishing neighboring contractors with food and other supplies (Randall, 1904:52).

The Zoarites built a woolen factory, machine shop, tannery, sawmill, bakery, dye house, hotel, and many other functional structures.

They maintained a fine herd of cattle, grew orchards, and raised a variety of successful crops. Everyone was assigned a productive role and food was shared by households. Women in each household went to the respective locale (bakery, milk house, or butcher shop) to obtain the week's rations for their families. When the Civil War began, the Zoar Separatists tried to remove themselves from it. In order to escape the draft it was possible to pay the sum of $300 and have someone else go in one's place. The community gladly did this, but as the war dragged on, 12 young men left the village and voluntarily enlisted. Each man carried a copy of the ninetieth Psalm with him as a guard against harm. All of them returned safely.

Although an almost idyllic life was attained by the Zoar society, there were always a few who found the lure of life outside more desirable. From time to time members left the community, and occasionally took the society to court to obtain property settlements. Usually the dissidents lost their cases. By 1874 the Zoarites owned 7,000 acres of land and their assets were reputed to be worth about 3 million dollars.

It is not entirely clear what degree of interaction the Zoarites had with other utopian groups, although they certainly knew about the Harmonists, who originated at the same time in Wurttemburg. In America the Zoarites purchased land from Godfrey Haga, a friend of the Harmonists who had originally offered the land for sale to that group. Obviously the Zoarites would have had an opportunity to learn something about the Harmonists from Haga. It is possible that the Zoarites knew something about Shaker colonies since a number of them existed in Ohio at the time when the Zoarites arrived. In 1825 a Shaker village was built at North Union, Ohio, now part of Cleveland. Carpenter (1975:209) suggests that at one time the Shakers, Harmonists, and Zoarites considered a plan of merger amongst all three organizations but religious differences made this too difficult.

Joseph Bimeler

In 1817, Joseph Bimeler, a weaver by trade, was experiencing difficulty with the religious situation in Germany and learned about the ministry of

Barbara Gruberman. Within a short time he was asked to lead a dissident group, which grew to 225 participants. When King William ascended to the German throne early in that year, the Separatists hoped their withdrawal from the state church would become less of a national issue, but this was not to be. Religious persecution against the Separatists continued and motivated them to leave Germany. America beckoned, and with the assistance of British Quakers the Separatists sailed for the New World via Holland. The British Quakers notified Quakers in Philadelphia, Pennsylvania, that the Bimeler people were coming so a welcome party was waiting for them when they arrived. En route, the Separatists rode in the lower parts of the ship where cattle were stored because it was all they could afford. Once on American soil the Separatists purchased some 5,500 acres of Ohio land for the price of $16,500, arranging to pay for it in installments. By previous agreement, a few families were required to remain in Philadelphia to work until they had paid for their passage to America.

It was a difficult trek to Ohio along a country trail but the eagerness of the people to establish their version of utopia bore them along. The Separatists named their new settlement "Zoar" after the little town in the Bible by that name. On April 19, 1819, the group formed an official communal association by framing a constitution. The membership consisted of 53 men and 104 women. One of their unique rules decreed that women could apply for membership through marriage, but if the women married out they would be expected to leave the community.

At first the operation of Zoar was made up of individual plots of land, but after a few years a communal form of organization was adopted. During the early years the colony was under severe financial strain, so in response to this dilemma, in 1822 Joseph Bimeler decreed that the community would be celibate until they could economically afford to have children. In 1828 they began to allow marriage, Bimeler being one of the first to marry. He argued that while God did not particularly approve of marriage He tolerated it so that the human race could be propagated. Until 1845, Zoar children over three years old were raised in separate communal dwellings—one for boys and another for girls (Nordhoff, 1966:108). In 1832 the society was incorporated under the laws of Ohio with the name "The Society of the Separatists of Zoar" (Holloway, 1966:97). At the height of their growth their membership peaked at around 500.

Joseph Bimeler was a well-educated man and became the spiritual as well as temporal leader of the society. He directed the people orally, and spoke extemporaneously at length. His exhortations and instructional lectures were not to be called sermons, but "discourses." Bimeler was believed to be endowed with Divine inspiration or, as he put it, "When I come here, I generally come empty, without knowing whereof I am going to speak" (Randall, 1904:17–18). Bimeler therefore did not prepare his discourses beforehand but relied on the Holy Spirit to direct his thoughts.

Through the years Joseph Bimeler held many positions in the Zoar society such as physician, architect, cashier, postmaster, and agent-general. He died on August 27, 1853, and decreed that his grave remain unmarked. Having held all lands in his own name until ten days before his death, it was necessary at that time to name a successor and transfer ownership of the properties to the society. After Bimeler's death, Jacob Sylvan was named successor and Christian Wedel followed him. Sylvan had managed Zoar's business affairs, but he had little speaking ability and managed better with written record. Wedel served for only a few years but the board of directors was not pleased with his service and so replaced him with Jacob Ackerman in 1871. Ackerman had arrived from Germany with the original group when he was 14 years old. He was elected a trustee at the age of 28 and served the society in that capacity until his death. He was succeeded by Simon Beuter, the gardener, who retained that role until the demise of the society.

For 35 years after Bimeler's death the membership regularly gathered to listen to readings of his discourses, but his spirit was gone and the experiment was over. The Zoar society came to an end in 1898 when the membership voted to dissolve. Property was divided by share, some of the larger buildings being assigned two or three shares. The remaining goods were disposed of by public auction. According to Morhart (1981:135), the final breakup was traumatic for many of the older people, who worried that they would not be able to fend for themselves.

Dissolution

Conjectured reasons for the dissolution of Zoar are manifold, but socie-tal integration and economic failure are at the top of the list. Zoar was a utopian dream meant for a specific period of time and need. Its function was to settle and establish a certain group in the new land and this was effectively accomplished. When technological and economic changes de-manded that Zoar make significant adjustments to its protocol and op-eration, the society's trustees objected. They believed that the methods used 50 years earlier were still adequate in 1890. Antiquated machinery in the woolen mill, for example, forced the industry to operate at a loss, and it became cheaper to buy finished goods. Under Bimeler's leader-ship, community profits had been reinvested in other enterprises in order to maintain the high standards that had been established. In that way certain industries could be expanded so that exportable surpluses could be enlarged and the financial standing of the village enhanced. After Bimeler's death this practice was discontinued. During the 1860s, when railroads suffered unsteady growth, the society lost thousands of dollars from their investments. There were also instances when individu-als in Zoar sold goods privately and these monies never reached Zoar coffers (Carpenter, 1975:212).

Other explanations of the dissolution of the Zoar society abound. The first reason often discussed is that the Zoar commune had ample in-teraction with the outside world, which brought new ideas into their midst and induced changes in thinking. Second, there were signs of inter-nal dissatisfaction. One cause was the disparity between the original Zoarites and more recent members. When people joined they were often assigned newer homes, while the charter members lived in older ones. This greatly upset the original members. There were also disputes about the operation of the Zoar hotel. Some claimed that preferential treatment was accorded to those who worked and lived there.

A third possible reason was that the society was in the habit of hir-ing at least 50 outside workers to help with their trades, and this form of influence undoubtedly left its mark. Often friendly liaisons attracted younger members to the outside world. A fourth reason is that curious onlookers who came to stay at the Zoar hotel often encouraged single members to leave the confines of what they perceived to be a restricting way of life.

Before the railroad arrived, the Zoarites often used the "hack," a wagon that hauled mail and passengers. It arrived only once a week, thereby limiting outside contact. In 1884 the railroad established a station near Zoar so it was no longer possible for them to live in isolation. Holloway (1966:99) notes that the lack of religious enthusiasm by the Zoarites at a time when America was revival-inclined may also have contributed to their demise. In fact, when the society dissolved there were disagreements as to which denominational form should occupy their church. The Lutheran and Evangelical churches were the foremost contenders, and they eventually became the host denominations. Today the congregation is affiliated with the United Church of Christ and operates with little attachment to the Zoar tradition. In sum, the Zoar society was Bimeler's project, and no one after him shared his vision, energy, or leadership abilities. Like other utopian experiments of that time, Zoar was basically a one-man show.

Zoar's reputation as an interesting community was far-reaching. Ohio-born President William McKinley was an honored guest at Zoar. Although he had been a frequent visitor to Zoar before he was elected president, one summer day in 1901 he announced that he would have lunch in the village. He arrived by train with a party of 13 associates, and amid the partying mood that followed, announced that he would be visiting the exposition at Buffalo, New York, as soon as he could get away. He was assassinated in Buffalo in September of that year (Morhart, 1981:121).

The legacy of Zoar cannot be overemphasized, and their version of utopia has important implications for the twenty-first century. Originally designed for a specific time and place, the Zoar experiment illustrates that an intentional community, characterized by harmony and congeniality, is both plausible and practical. If the Zoarites had one trait that helped to maintain their way of life, it was their high regard for their leader, Joseph Bimeler. In this, their thinking paralleled that of the Amanas, Doukhobors, and Harmonists who also revered their leaders.

Critics may scoff at the concept that individuals should be held in high regard for their spiritual insights. However, when we observe the contemporary practice of worshipping media superstars, for example, the similarity of that habit to Zoar practice is just as suspect. The difference, however, is that leaders like Bimeler left a worthwhile legacy by providing a meaningful lifestyle for their people.

The next chapter examines three successful communes without particularly strong religious underpinnings. These communities illustrate that successful group efforts are not necessarily dependent on the development of doctrinal creeds. They testify to the creativity, adaptability, and genius of the human spirit.

CHAPTER 5

ECONOMIC-ORIENTED COMMUNES

Nineteenth-century immigrants to North America came with certain expectations, not the least of which was economic opportunity. Many also came to find freedom and escape from religious persecution. There may also have been some who simply sought adventure. One thing was certain: when their feet landed on North American soil, each newcomer was faced with the challenge of making a living.

Although the religious-spiritual variety of intentional communities historically outnumbered the rest, a number of political-economic models were developed as well. Many of these experiments were invented by visionaries who were not particularly religious. Three such experiments are discussed here, all of them founded on a very optimistic concept of human nature. Fourierism and Icarianism, the first two groups in this section, fared moderately well, which is surprising in light of the fact that they did not exhibit the particularly strong charismatic leadership of some of the other communities we have highlighted. Owenism, on the other hand, experienced difficulties from the beginning, in large part due to Robert Owen's extreme economic and philosophical naïveté. A visionary, Owen emphasized none of the characteristics required to make his project workable. Basically, he relied on the innate goodness of humankind and was deceived by his own optimism. Kanter (1972) suggests that the essentials for communal success are sacrifice, investment, renunciation, communion, mortification, and transcendence. Unfortunately, Robert Owen had a wonderful vision, but lacked the managerial skills and support to achieve it. In the next section we will discuss two related experiments, one historical and one contemporary. Both were founded on similar principles, but the latter (Brook Farm) appears to have built in successful maintenance structures.

THE FOURIER PHALANX

The foundations of Fourierism have sometimes been called wildly extravagant, chaotic, and entertaining, but of vital importance to the history of community experiments in America (Holloway, 1966:103).

Philosophy

The founder of the movement, François Marie Charles Fourier (1772–1837) proposed that society be divided into *phalansteries* or *phalanxes*, each with a common building housing approximately 1,600 individuals. Neighboring lands would be used for agricultural purposes and embellished with plenty of fruits and flowers. Community residents would be subdivided into smaller units of seven individuals (known as a group), and five such groups would form a "series" with specific responsibilities. All tasks were to be considered joyful exercises for the betterment of the community. Each member would be considered a full shareholder and even children would be taught to do their part. They would be encouraged to consider their assignments (the removal of garbage and the cleaning of privies) great fun. All individuals would be paid for their work and community income would be generated through shares. In Fourier's view, the essence of happiness would be assured in the following way: "There would be no discontent or discrimination, since all roles would be interchangeable. There would be a Chancellery of the Court of Love, and Corporations of Love, and an extraordinary system of organized polygamy. Not only sex, but food and all sensual pleasures, would be organized to give maximum pleasure" (Rexroth, 1974:251).

Fourier devised an elaborate cosmology as a metaphysical foundation for his scheme, following the fundamental ideas of the Enlightenment
(Riasanovsky, 1969:30). He saw nature as composed of three eternal, un-
created, and indestructible realities including God or Spirit as the *active* or
moving principle, matter as the *passive* or moved principle, and justice or
mathematics as the principle that regulates movement. Fundamentally,
Fourier was a Deist, and placed a great deal of emphasis on physics and
physical and mathematical laws, which he considered applicable to all of
creation. He believed that society could be improved by the use of reason,
and more exactly, through the realization of a scientifically correct theo-
retical model featuring cosmopolitanism and stressing human happiness
and passion. His thinking paralleled that of Jean Jacques Rousseau, and
John Humphrey Noyes of the Oneida experiment (chapter 7). To some
extent he was as optimistic about human nature as Robert Owen, but he
lacked the ability by which to implement his very detailed utopian plan.

In attempting to gather funds to finance his first phalanx, Fourier
advertised for capitalists to invest in making his dream a reality, but no
philanthropist responded. He did attracted two loyal disciples, Victor
Considérant, who started a short-lived community in Paris, and Alberta Brisbane, a young American who lectured on Fourierism in the
United States. He won over Horace Greeley, editor of the *New Yorker*,
in 1842, and Greeley gave Brisbane a regular column in which to promote Fourierism.

As a result of these efforts, Fourierism became quite acceptable in
America, and his ideas eventually made their way to Brook Farm in Massachusetts (discussed later). In the next few years some 40 to 50 phalanxes
were begun in the United States. Most of them lasted only a few weeks; a
half dozen lasted more than a year, and only three endured for more than
two years. Most phalanxes began on farms for which too much money had
been paid, and daily life was highlighted with celebrations of fun, food, and
sex. Land was heavily mortgaged and most of the party-goers were not
blessed with a particularly strong work ethic. Arguments about money and
property soon broke out, and one by one the phalanxes failed. Commitment to hard work at Robert Owen's New Harmony was weak enough,
but in the phalanxes it was virtually nonexistent. Unlike the situation in

Oneida Community, Fourier's inability to legislate the engagement of sexual pleasures contributed to its administrative fragmentation. Participants refused to heed Fourier's regulations concerning sexual relations and this form of dissidence soon stretched to other areas as well.

François Fourier

François Marie Charles Fourier was born to a relatively poor family in Besancon, France. His father died when he was nine years old, but left his son sufficient money to start a business by the time he was 20. Not particularly successful in the business world, François Fourier soon turned his hand to writing essays for local publications and one of these essays, "Universal Harmony," attracted local attention and a new teaching was born. Fourier never gave up hope that some wealthy philanthropist would enable him to realize his dreams. He kept a list of 4,000 candidates for this honor, and even inserted an advertisement in several newspapers saying he would be home at a certain hour every day if any generous benefactor cared to contact him.

Fourier devised and elaborated his scheme before he attracted adherents. He believed that his utopian plan was not only practical and workable but would preclude all forthcoming societal problems. In his carefully outlined plan, everything would be in its place and every contingency would be anticipated. Following the thinking of French philosopher Jean Jacques Rousseau, Fourier believed in the inherent goodness of people, conceiving of vice and evil as merely the result of restraints upon freedom for complete self-gratification. Ironically, Fourier agreed with Rousseau that individuals were at their best in their natural form, yet he proposed to liberate them via a most rigid form of social structure. Fourier was convinced that once he set up his model society, its operation would prove to be so alluring it would be copied the world over (Rexroth, 1974:250).

Community Development

The most successful Fourierist phalanx was established in 1843 at Red Rock in New Jersey by a group of New York entrepreneurs. Although it was not the first phalanx, it was brazenly called the North American

Phalanx. By the end of the first year the organizers had attracted 90 people who settled in, planted crops, and developed shops and mills. Applicants were carefully screened and, once accepted, had to go through a trial period of one year. The experiment worked well, partially because only a certain type of individual was admitted to membership. Regular meetings committed time to legislative and administrative matters and there were few picnics or times of frolic. Community operation much resembled the workings of a modern day Hutterite colony. Tragically, in 1854 a fire broke out and destroyed most of the colony. There was little insurance on the buildings and so, disillusioned, the stakeholders voted to close down the operation and disband. A small group of loyalists moved to the Victor Considerant Colony in Texas to start again, but this dream was never realized. Within a short time, it too dissolved.

A sister phalanx in Wisconsin was almost as successful as the North American Phalanx. It was started in 1844 by 20 hardworking individuals who eventually developed a plant worth $28,000. Included in the colony inventory was a gristmill, a dam, a millrace, a blacksmith shop, a schoolhouse, and a henhouse. The Wisconsin Phalanx was restrictive: out of every 100 applicants who applied, only one was admitted. Yet, in December of 1849, at the height of their success, they suddenly voted to put themselves out of business. The property was divided into small lots and sold mostly to members. This mysterious ending sounded the death knell for Fourierism (Rexroth, 1974:258). As one observer put it, a phalanx under Fourier's command "usually lasted until the first mortgage fell due" (Albertson, 1973:401).

If Fourierism is to teach us anything at all it is that certain forms of utopianism are not necessarily functional. In fact, as the parallel Amana, Doukhobor, Hutterite, and Zoar experiences reveal, the Fourierist dream could only have been realized with a specified form of economic planning, a very dedicated membership, and a host of restrictions (self-imposed or otherwise) on daily freedom. Loose living doth not a hive create.

Brook Farm

A copycat version of Fourierism known as Brook Farm was initiated in 1841 by the Rev. George Ripley, a Unitarian minister near West Roxbury,

Massachusetts, just nine miles from Boston. Ripley's plan was to finance the project through the sale of shares and thus form a communal society. In order to prepare for the undertaking, Ripley spent some time visiting Shaker communities, as well as New Harmony and other secular communes. He became convinced that in order to succeed he needed to avoid establishing any kind of religious foundation and instead concentrate on economic methods that worked. In his mind, everyone in the commune should share equally in work and play alike and no activity should be considered tedious. As Ripley put it, "Domestic servitude should be replaced by the love of those duties that are usually discharged by servants" (Rexroth, 1974:243).

Brook Farm became a reality through the purchase of a 200-acre plot of land with an old farmhouse on it, to which three new homes were added. Members purchased shares in the enterprise by donating funds or through labor. The workload was at first distributed by orderly committees to men and women who had the necessary skills to make the project viable—shoemakers, cooks, joiners (woodworkers), seamstresses, and so on. A school was constructed and overseen by the educated, and artists made community structures appear very attractive. In fact, Ralph Waldo Emerson (1904:125, 127) commented: "Many persons, attracted by the beauty of the place and the culture and ambition of the community, joined them as boarders, and lived there for years. . . . the art of letter-writing, it is said, was immensely cultivated. Letters were always flying not only from house to house, but from room to room. It was a perpetual picnic, a French Revolution in small, an Age of Reason in a patty-pan."

In Ripley's scheme, each individual was to be paid a small amount from the community treasury and be considered an equal participant in the decision-making process. This did not mean that everyone worked equally hard, for it was said that one man might plant all day in the fields, while another might recline and look out of the window all day, and still another might sit down and draw pictures. However, at the end of the day, all could expect to receive equal pay. Children's education was stressed, but they were also expected to participate in agricultural pursuits.

Brook Farm began with 20 adherents and eventually grew to 115 members, including such intellectuals as Nathaniel Hawthorne and Charles A. Dana (Albertson, 1973:403). Although the original intention was that the community would mix hard work with intellectual pursuits, the latter was shortchanged by the fact that the former required too much energy. To make up for this, Brook Farm leaders sponsored so many social events that they taxed people's energies, and people had little time for hard work. Because of this practice the colony never became financially self-sustaining.

Two years after it began, Brook Farm began to adopt elements of Fourierism because Ripley became a convert to Fourier's teachings. While it operated on a small scale, Brook Farm was very successful. Friebert (1993:76) suggests that it was the adoption of Fourier's scheme, which involved larger numbers of people, that ultimately led to the demise of Brook Farm. Designed for a phalanx of 1,600 people, Fourier's system was impractical for a community that never exceeded 120 persons at any given time.

Membership in Brook Farm was made available to anyone who applied. No religious test was required of new members, and no religious alternative organization would be permitted to impose its beliefs on the community. The education of the general membership stressed works of moral philosophy, poetry, and the arts. Lessons in history and foreign languages were also offered. One of the unique characteristics of Brook Farm was that it became a haven for women who were interested in developing a sense of independence and autonomy. Unlike some communal experiments, men and women in the phalanx received the same pay and everyone had the right to vote on colony matters. There was also a great deal of job-sharing. For example, in cold weather men hung out the laundry, and during harvest women worked in the fields. Because such menial tasks were community activities and completed in a spirit of recreation, gender stereotyping generally dissipated.

With the completion of the building of the colony's grand phalanstery, which was comprised of dormitories and apartments, an auditorium, and community recreation and dining rooms, the Brook Farm experiment reached its pinnacle. A great celebration was held on the evening of March 2, 1846, and everyone joined in. Shockingly, that night the building burned to the ground and Brook Farm came to an abrupt end. An investigation produced no explanation for the fire. The few buildings that were left were sold by auction. Members who believed very much in the experiment simply did not have the will to rebuild after such a catastrophic event.

Despite the great and sudden loss, a group of Brook Farm loyalists formed an alumni association and for at least the next three generations met at an annual summer camp called Summer Brook Farm to reminisce and thereby satiate their passion for utopia. Fourier's vision and enthusiasm therefore lived on for many years beyond his death. The next section of this chapter discusses a similar experiment, it too is based on the energy and motivation of a single visionary.

THE ICARIANS

Icaria was designed to be an example of rational democratic communalism in America. At its peak in Nauvoo, Texas, in 1855, just seven years after its origin, it grew to 500 members. The philosophy of the organization was hard work, honesty, and commitment, and they quickly gained the respect of their neighbors. Analysts conjecture that if Etienne Cabet (1788–1856), its leader, had been a more temperate man, he might have succeeded in establishing an ideal model of democratic communalism in the United States. As Nordhoff (1966:334) noted, "He [Cabet] had at Nauvoo at one time not less than fifteen hundred people. With so many members, a wise leader with business skill ought to be able to accomplish very much in a single year; in ten years his commune, if he could keep it together, ought to be wealthy."

Icarian Philosophy

Etienne Cabet's character has been described as philosophical, idealistic, and hotheaded, but he was also a capable politician who fit in with the political spirit of nineteenth-century America (Webber, 1959:231). Cabet studied a number of utopian writings in three different languages (English, French, and German) and from his reading developed his own utopian plan. He quickly attracted thousands of followers on both sides of the Atlantic, but he also experienced severe criticism for his radical ideas. He was once exiled from France for five years and went to Belgium, where he was exiled again, so he traveled to England. On returning to France his theories gained widespread acceptance but roused the opposition of the government, the church, the police, and the courts (Wooster, 1924:29). In 1847 there were hundreds of avid fans of Cabet's thinking in England, France, Germany, Spain, Switzerland, and other countries.

Cabet's utopian ideas were influenced by the left wing of the French Revolution and inspired by Robert Owen, with whom he had several conversations. Owen's attempts to found a commune in Texas likely motivated Cabet to give it a try. In addition, Cabet believed that communal living brought out the best in people. In such a state individuals could sacrifice their personal interests for the common good. Many people who followed Cabet were temporarily fascinated with his teachings, but like other such communities of the time, the resultant experiments died out as people grew weary. Many of Cabet's followers tended to act out the freedom of which he spoke so eloquently and were surprised when these ideas did not work in practice.

Cabet's vision of a new world, though couched in secular terms, was similar to that of a religious visionary. His teachings attracted both curious and committed individuals and even inspired a few copycat versions. Cabet was encouraged by each new venture and even dreamed of conquering the entire continent with his ideas. Although few Americans actually committed themselves to his project, many newcomers from France eagerly joined him. His philosophy of daily living included equal work for everyone. Labor was to be given freely, without financial remuneration, and with no other compulsion but a sense of duty to the community. As he put it, "We enjoy the produce in common, according to the needs of each on the principle of fraternity and equality, with no special privileges for anyone" (Calverton, 1969:355).

The primary requirement for cooperative living, according to Cabet, was good administration. Interestingly, this was one of the requirements that failed to work to Cabet's advantage. A general assembly would elect a president and chairs for such agencies as education, health and amusement, finance, provisions, clothing, lodging, and publicity. Organizationally, Nauvoo should have prospered, but Cabet had too few farmers in his fold and relied too much on the purchase of provisions outside the community. The arrangement worked as long as donations came in from France, but when these began to dry up, Cabet was in trouble. He began to travel, searching for backers to finance his schemes, but no support was forthcoming. Nauvoo was doomed to fail financially, and the schisms that evolved only aided in its demise. As with other communes, the temporary success of the Icarian dream was basically elaborated through discussions rather than implementation. In this Etienne Cabet shared an historical role similar to that of our next visionary, Robert Owen.

Etienne Cabet

Etienne Cabet inspired immigrants to New Orleans to start this secular commune in 1848. The name *Icaria* was adopted from Greek mythology and signified soaring high in adventurous flight. It was Cabet's concept of the possibilities of reasoned human ability which he hoped would result in the development of an ideal utopia. After several moves the Icarians ended up in Fannin County, Texas, along the Red River. One immediate error was that Cabet did not initially accompany his group to America to encourage his flock, but remained in France. Later when he did visit the community in New Orleans, he was shocked at their economic devastation. First of all, these would-be farmers were artisans, and knew little about tilling the soil. They were inexperienced with agricultural tools, and the shelters they created were hardly sufficient to cope with the exigencies of the natural forces. Second, it seemed as though nature was against them; the water was bad, their plows broke down, and a number of individuals contracted yellow fever. Gradually, they even questioned Cabet's vision, settlement advice, and leadership abilities (Webber, 1959:228). To make things worse, shortly after settling in America, the group learned of the revolution occurring in their home country and they grew disappointed. Perhaps they had been too hasty in moving to America. With things so stirred up in France, they fantasized that perhaps their utopian dream could have been implemented back home.

An improved location in which to develop a successful agricultural community for the Icarians was Nauvoo, Texas, where the group of 69 members relocated in 1849. The site had been occupied by a group of Mormons three years before, but they abandoned it in 1846 largely due to opposition from their neighbors. By 1855 the Icarian community had expanded to some 500 members, with a sound agricultural base supplemented by a number of related industries. They built shops, schools, and established a newspaper. They also sponsored a band of 50 musicians. Unfortunately, in the midst of this success, Cabet left Nauvoo to return to France to settle a charge of fraud against him brought by some of his previous followers. When he finally returned to Texas he found his camp in a state of administrative disarray.

A major schism developed in Nauvoo over the division of work and food distribution, and when Cabet returned he was defeated in an election. Black clouds were forming over the colony. In leaving their native land with its political and legal restrictions, the Icarians hoped to be governed in the New World solely by their utopian creed. Although it was central to Icarian philosophy that they could only minimally be influenced by local judges and courts, they were in for a surprise when Cabet himself dragged them into court. Evidently he felt that if he could not reign he could certainly ruin, and he petitioned the state legislature to repeal the act incorporating the colony. The response of his once-loyal followers was one of utter disbelief. For the Icarians, there were no other laws but Icarian laws, and Cabet himself had invented them. With Cabet's action it was necessary for the Nauvoo sheriff to intervene in colony events in order to quell several rifts (Hine, 1983:73). After Cabet's death in St. Louis in 1856, despite attempts to keep the Nauvoo community going it was forced to dissolve in 1864, at which time there were only eight members left in the colony (Calverton, 1969:355). A subgroup under Cabet's leadership had withdrawn to form a separate commune at Cheltenham near St. Louis, Missouri, but disbanded after a few years. In turn, a faction of that group established themselves at Cloverdale, California in 1881, but after a few years it too disbanded.

The few members who were left in Nauvoo decided to join the Icarian community in Corning, Iowa. Here the colony built an elaborate headquarters, but they were not prosperous until the Civil War inflated prices and they were able to sell off land. They planted vineyards and orchards and built additional houses. Some former members returned and things looked rosy for a while. However, in 1876 trouble arose between some younger members who wished to expand their holdings and older members who urged a more conservative approach. In 1878, the younger faction took the matter to court and had the colony's charter annulled. The older faction then built a new colony on the Nodaway River, in Iowa which they called the New Icarian Community. They were again threatened with legal action because inner turmoil restricted them from keeping up their financial commitments with local banks. They satisfied their creditors by giving back half the land they had purchased and arranged for a mortgage plan that would enable them to make regular payments. For the next 20 years they prospered, but the generation that followed them could not bear to maintain the old-fashioned ways of their elders and the community disbanded in 1898. The dissolution of colony assets left the remaining 21 members in comfortable circumstances. Even with this short lifespan, the New Icarian community was one of the longest running and most successful of all secular communes in American history.

The younger, more aggressive Corning Icarians tried to maintain the original Iowa colony, but the challenge proved too much for them and another split erupted. The colony at Cloverdale in Sonoma County, California grew to 54 members with ownership of 885 acres of land and $54,000 in capital. The experiment did not last long, however, and soon the property was sold and the assets peacefully divided among the membership (Wooster, 1924:33).

If the frequent migrations, relocations, and splits of one particular utopian dream are to teach us anything, it is that ready unanimity is not necessarily a byproduct of that dream. Perhaps the Icarians overemphasized the advantages of individual freedom and thus were unable to make compromised, corporate attempts work.

OWENITES

Easily one of the best-known Europeans to cross the ocean and build a utopian communal dream was Robert Owen (1771–1858), a Welsh-born industrialist in the textile business. Owen's plan for utopia in America was to change society from "an ignorant, selfish system to an enlightened one, and remove all causes for contest between individuals" (Holloway, 1966:104).

Beliefs and Structure

Owen began his version of utopia by financing the development of a new community with all necessary structures in place. These would include a large meeting hall, a school, academy, and university. There would be lecture rooms, reading rooms, committee rooms, and recreational facilities. He would include a chapel, a library, ballrooms, kitchens, dining rooms, and dormitories both for married couples (with or without children) and singles. The first and prototype community would consist of 1,000 people with about 20,000 cultivated acres of farmland. This new "empire of peace and goodwill" would operate on the principles of virtue, goodwill, enjoyment, and happiness. People of all backgrounds were welcome to join the organization, including individuals representing all trades, nationalities, creeds, and professions. Use of alcohol would be forbidden in the interests of maintaining rational conversations and exchange of ideas.

The foundation of Owen's communal plan was a rejection of the absurd notion that private or individual property was essential to happiness. "Private property," he asserted, "is entirely the child of the existing system of the world; it emanates from ignorant selfishness, and perpetuates it" (Bestor, 1959:86). On July 4, 1826, Owen therefore drafted a "Declaration of Mental Independence" intended to stand alongside the Declaration of Independence as an equally significant historical document. His paradigm for happiness centered on five main elements: environmentalism, communitarianism, gradualism, rationalism, and millenarianism (Mariampolski, 1979). Ultimately, he was given an opportunity to address the U.S. Congress; he challenged members to abandon traditional ways of viewing the economy and to dream new dreams (Holbrook, 1957:173). According to Owen, this would be done by setting up a series of utopian colonies of economic communalism. As Owen stated, "The sole objects of these communities will be to procure for all their members the greatest amount of happiness, to secure it to them, and to transmit it to their children to the latest posterity" (Calverton, 1969:181).

Although few influential individuals were moved by Owen's challenge, he managed to attract a few intellectuals. In 1824, after a surprise visit by George Rapp, who offered to sell him the town of New Harmony, Owen promptly bought the site and prepared to put his ideas into action. After negotiating the purchase of the town, Owen arranged for its settlement. He began by bringing in his famous "Boatload of Knowledge," comprised of a number of distinguished intellectuals from various cities who were to set the tone of the town. Among those who agreed with Owen by challenging the status quo was Frances Wright, an advocate for women's rights. She hoped to learn enough at New Harmony to be able to start her own colony in Tennessee. Wright was only one of a dozen visionaries to attempt to apply Owen's ideas. At the height of Owen's popularity there were nearly two dozen imitative communes in America. Owen began his first day at New Harmony with a speech designed to motivate his followers to immediate action. Unfortunately, he had no administrative plan or structure in mind and had not calculated who would occupy which position at the colony, and who would staff the various industries. His objectives were couched in terms of working during the day and partying, dancing, and socializing in the evening. Most of his intellectual followers were more skilled with pens than hammers, shovels, and ploughs, and the project seemed doomed from the start. Owen had not attracted skilled workmen in sufficient numbers to make the plan fly. There were no millers to operate the mill, which had produced 60 barrels of flour per day when George Rapp's Harmonists operated the commune. Also needed were people to handle the sawmill, the saddle and harness shop, the smithy, two large kilns, and the tannery. It turned out that the intellectuals who Owen attracted lacked the dedication and skills required to make the experiment work. Essentially, the colony did not have in place the necessary administrative structure required to function on a day-to-day basis.

The inhabitants of Owen's New Harmony were not religiously united, and everyone could go to the church of their choice, or not at all. The church building in the community had been built by the Rappites, and Owen decreed that its pulpit should be open to any minister of any denomination at any time other than Sunday morning, when Owenite doctrines were propounded in two-hour sessions. When some adherents later discovered Owen's negative attitude towards organized religion, this realization became a cause of conflict, and those with strong religious loyalties contributed to schismatic divisions in the colony (Mariampolski, 1979).

Owen decreed that children and adults should be regarded as equals in decision-making, and no significance was attached to either sex or matrimonial status. Like the Shakers, Owen believed that women had suffered through the practice of traditional marriage and family and he intended to rectify this. Unlike the Shakers, however, he based his campaign for sexual equality on economic rather than spiritual grounds. A debilitating plank in his plan was that, like Fourier, he advocated the idea that anyone who did not feel like working did not have to do so. In addition, Owen himself proposed that "No anger ought to be felt against the ... members upon their aversion to the work of cooperation; or when they brawl, quarrel, or indulge in loud talk" (Webber, 1959:147). Naturally, this policy appealed to the significant number of ne'er-do-wells in his community who were only too happy to eat at the trough of plenty without contributing anything to it. It was also noticeable that the spirit of cooperative effort was better upheld when Owen himself was present, but his excessive travels severely limited such times. These developments contributed towards initial unfavorable reports of the colony, which negatively affected its reputation.

Robert Owen was a strong advocate of education and immediately urged the construction of a school in New Harmony. Children were to be given physical education for the first five years of their lives, and afterward taught other subjects through practical experience. After sufficient absorption of the three "R's" and diverse philosophies, children were provided with technical training in such areas as taxidermy, engraving, drawing, carpentry, wheelwrighting, shoe-making, blacksmithing, cabinetmaking, and millinery. The aim of this approach was to enable children to contribute to the colony's economy and become valuable citizens. One of the most influential teachers was Joseph Neef, who had been involved with Johann Heinrich Pestalozzi's experimental child-centered school in Switzerland. Neef tried to build such a model in America. Like Pestalozzi, Neef and Owen contrived the unrealistic plan that the school would pay for its operation through the children's work efforts.

Although the concept that a member of the community was an equal shareholder was introduced by Owen early in the development of New Harmony, for the first few years he kept the title of the commune in his own name. In January 1826, the group formulated a constitution to share ownership but quarrels erupted over its interpretation. One hundred members even left the colony simply because Owen refused to change the name of the commune.

Robert Owen

Owen believed that an individual's character was wholly determined by his or her environment, and that a better environment would create better people. A man of some means, Owen tried to demonstrate this philosophy in the factory he owned and operated. Part of his financial success was attributable to his marriage to the daughter of a millionaire, but Owen was also quite capable of earning money on his own. He was in many ways a revolutionary. The eighteenth-century society into which he was born was an old system based on feudalistic modes of production. A new capitalist order was emerging with a highly motivated new middle class ready to change the system. Enter Robert Owen, son of a wage earner, and quite familiar with the hardships endured by the working class. He was proud of his background and never tried to deny or conceal it.

As the successful owner of a vast textile business in New Lanark, Scotland, Owen introduced humanitarian reforms that were significantly different from the traditional way of doing things. His charitable activities showed him to be a true egalitarian. His socialist innovations and the benefits that he provided for his workers were considered quite radical for his time. Owen profoundly believed that if people were afforded the opportunity to live in more pleasant environments, they would undoubtedly change for the better. To some extent, his plan worked. There were even profits to be made, though Owen's business colleagues thought he could have made a lot more money if he had abandoned his charitable efforts. Naturally, Owen's 1,600 workers were grateful to be part of this reform plan, and for the most part enacted Owen's utopian ideals in their daily lives. However, evaluations of his success at New Lanark are mixed. Owen himself reported that due to his reforms his workers had transformed themselves from their "dirty, idle, dissolute and drunken" patterns of living and had become an orderly, neat, and regulated people (Rexroth, 1974:219). Webber (1959:136) suggests that despite Owen's best efforts, some of his workers refused to give up drinking, riotous living, and sexual debauchery.

Owen's optimism never wavered, and he left no stone unturned in applying his theories to the various facets of his New Lanark factory. His writings attracted great audiences, and he began to travel widely to propagate his ideas. Unfortunately, the crescendo of his popularity crested when he attacked organized religion. This mistake in judgment cost him the support of many supporters and the financial success of the colony was threatened. Because of his generous invitation for anybody to join the community, Owen also attracted a variety of unusual characters to his community, who were undoubtedly upset with the established order, and they made their complaints known with bold literary attacks. The longest lasting Owenite experiment was begun by a group of Quakers. They liked Owen's approach to communal living but added the ingredient of Christian faith to the mix, which proved to be a very successful recipe.

Owen was influenced by the romantic economic doctrines of his day and based his communal dream entirely on secular grounds, premised on the principle of absolute equality. What was unique about Owen's interpretation of absolute equality was that he meant it. In his commune, everyone—men and women, young and old—was invited to share their opinions on any and every matter if they wished to do so. Every detail of communal operation could be subject to a townhouse meeting. There was so much equality that quickly the people wearied of so much opportunity to participate in decision-making.

The popularity of Owen's teachings ultimately led him to America where he arrived in 1825 with his son, William. Here he made friends with a variety of influential people, including members of the American government. Wherever he went he invited people to become part of the grand experiment he was planning. He spoke eloquently about his concept of human nature as positive, goal-oriented, cooperative, and caring. His dream was fulfilled with the establishment of the New Harmony commune in Indiana, which operated from 1824 to 1827.

On the positive side, despite the fact that Owen's experiment involved a relatively small number of people and was quite short-lived, his influence in America was significant. At the time his reputation peaked, there were some 19 communities in the United States trying to put into practice the principles he espoused.

The Colony's Demise

In January 1827, when it became clear that New Harmony would not endure, Owen lost interest in it. Gone was his dream to establish many more such experiments, and he refused to return to the community. He tried to sell off pieces of land in a desperate attempt to finance the colony's operations but the handwriting was on the wall. One entrepreneur, William Taylor, bought 1,500 acres of land at the north end of the community and took many agricultural implements that did not belong to him, thus shortchanging the colony's operations. Taylor also built a distillery on the land, thereby violating one of Owen's strict rules, against the use of alcohol. Finally, Owen's son, Robert Dale, became manager of what was left of New Harmony, and he too tried desperately to bring the community to financial stability. He was successful on some ground, however, for he succeeded in introducing into the Indiana State Legislature the most advanced divorce laws the country had ever witnessed.

In the dying days of New Harmony, criticism of Owen was rampant, both from inside the colony as well as by outside observers. Owen was accused of keeping all the property in his own name (he *had* paid for it) and absconding with funds. Splintering among the membership eventually ended in the formation of eight subcommunes, with further divisions among them. One of Owen's original supporters, a Scot named William Maclure, began to quarrel with Owen, then went to the Rapps and bought $40,000 worth of Owen's notes for a reputed $25,000 and forced Owen to accept them as a $40,000 payment on Maclure's part of community losses. Having satisfied himself by this means of havoc, Maclure tore up his will, which was supposed to have left his fortune to New Harmony, and departed.

Utopian communities like Amana, New Harmony, and Zoar faced the inevitable challenge of regulating contact with the outside world. A significant amount of interaction was obviously essential for the sale of produce or for the purchase of supplies not locally available. Thanks to Owen's love of travel, New Harmony did cultivate many contacts with the outside world. These contacts were often economic, but Owen's unorthodox religious views hindered any kind of philosophical bond. Unlike Amana and Zoar, which developed so many outside links that the lure of the outside ultimately influenced their demise, Owen opted to promote one aspect above all others. He wanted economic connections, although his own house was not in order in that regard; when his nonreligious stance became known, the attraction to New Harmony ceased. In sum, neither Amana, New Harmony, Shakers, nor Zoar could forestall the development of large scale enterprises that began after the Civil War and rendered tiny rural manufacturing plants obsolete (Bestor, 1959: 229).

In our opinion, the bottom line is that New Harmony failed because Owen was simply too optimistic about human nature. He believed in direct democracy, but since everyone in the community was invited to express their opinion on any aspect of operation, Owen's followers grew weary of the process. There were meetings about everything, and there was not enough time for work. Owen believed that people were shaped by their environments, but he had not taken into account that the people he attracted had already been influenced by previous environments that were hostile to the one he created. Within two weeks of having introduced his "community of equality," Owen's followers asked him to take over and personally direct the affairs of the community, but he was not able to meet the challenge. Owen was basically a philosopher, not an administrator (Carmony and Elliott, 1980:172). Despite this obvious miscalculation, it is important to note that Owen's influence in America was greater than the sum of his communal efforts. Because of his humanitarian concerns, many Americans were moved towards greater social responsibility and moved by his enthusiasm for social equality (Holloway, 1966:114f). While an Indiana legislator in the 1830s, Owen attempted to secure important property rights for women. He continued his efforts as a delegate to Indiana's first constitutional convention and later as a member of the General Assembly in 1851 (Wilson, 1984:195). He was able to witness great gains in this respect in the years that followed (Carmony and Elliott, 1980:183). Owen will also be remembered as a leader of British radicalism, and a founding father of modern trade unions, as well as the cooperative movement (Rexroth, 1974:228).

After New Harmony lands were sold off to inhabitants and speculators, Owen lamented that people let him down. He had given them lands, houses, implements, schools, and generous laws by which to govern themselves, but still they brought the colony to ruination. Perhaps Owen's failure at New Harmony demonstrates all too well that utopias that fare well usually combine religious or mystical beliefs with an economic ideal.

The next chapter traces the long and intriguing history of the Harmonists from whom Robert Owen bought the Town of New Harmony in Indiana in 1824. Under the leadership of George Rapp, this unique commune built towns, changed locations, and experienced a great deal of financial success. The Harmonists' story begins in Pennsylvania, moves to Indiana, and returns to Pennsylvania. A migrating faction of the Harmonists, under the leadership of William Keil, also took the movement to Missouri and Oregon.

CHAPTER 6

THE HARMONISTS

An Economic-Religious Model

INTRODUCTION TO THE HARMONISTS

The story of the Harmonists is long and involved, and for that reason merits a separate chapter. There is a great deal to tell about Harmony, as it crosses several state lines and highlights a variety of leaders. Even when this century-long empire fell into the dust, there was confusion about its exact nature and legal makeup. Reibel (1993:9) notes that when the Harmony Society dissolved in 1905 the State of Pennsylvania tried to seize the property. Their attempt was unsuccessfully fought in the courts when it was discovered that the society had never been registered as a religious organization. This shocked many observers because the origins and history of the commune were always cast in religious language. After all, their revered founder, George Rapp (1757–1847), was himself a minister of the Separatist Gospel. In 1916, the state legislature finally acknowledged the secular nature of the organization, but despite this, the state inherited only the block of the town that includes the museum. The rest was allotted to and divided among remaining members.

The end result is that today the historic town of Economy is jointly operated by the Pennsylvania Historical and Museum Commission and the Harmony Associates (Reibel, 1993:9).

Beliefs

The theological foundations of the Harmonist Society deviated little from early eighteenth-century Separatist beliefs. The Harmonists held that Adam was created in the image of God, experienced a fall from grace, and became responsible for the sins of the generations which followed. They believed that the only hope for humankind was salvation through Christ, who taught communal living. Because of the severity of man's sins, the Second Coming of Christ was imminent. It was therefore up to believers to work hard and live a life of repentance until Christ's return. Unlike the Zoarites and Amanas, they did not have a strong aversion to the practice of the Sacraments and celebrated Holy Baptism, Confirmation, and The Lord's Supper (the Eucharist).

George Rapp

George Rapp, or "Father Rapp," as he was known to his followers, was born in Würtemburg, Germany. After completing common school he became a vinedresser, a vocation that was almost inevitable in a country famous for its fruits and winemaking. At the age of 24 he married Christina Benzinger and they had a son, John, and a daughter, Rosina.

As a young man Rapp carefully studied the Bible and gradually became concerned about the lifeless condition of the church. He accused religious leaders of his day of apostasy, arguing that they had lost sight of the principles of Christian living. He was particularly convinced that civil authority and spirituality should not be connected, because the state had no right to interfere in the workings of the church. This was not a popular stance to assume in the latter years of the eighteenth century. Individuals who took this tone with the ecclesiastical upper crust of Rapp's day often ended up in jail, and so did George Rapp. Still, he persisted. On Good Friday afternoon in 1799, in protest he drove a herd of swine down the street, thereby disturbing local church services. When he was hauled up before the courts he told the judges that the service was an empty facade, and had little to do with Biblical Christianity. Evidently he did not convince the authorities and he was forced to pay a fine.

To America

The inflexibility of the state church in Germany during the latter part of the eighteenth century gave rise to the Separatist movement. Disillusioned state church adherents were looking for answers to strengthen their faith outside the church and men like George Rapp, Joseph Bimeler (Zoar), and Christian Metz (Amana) offered alternative doctrines and firm leadership. When George Rapp began his ministry he quickly attracted several hundred adherents, and determined to leave Germany to establish an intentional community in America. After selling his property, Rapp, his son John, and a fellow Separatist named Frederick Conrad Haller set sail for America in search of land. Rapp bought 4,500 acres in western Pennsylvania, just 26 miles north of Pittsburgh, and sent for his followers. He warned them that blazing a new trail in the American frontier was no easy task, and only the most committed should come to America. He was probably surprised that 839 people expressed interest, so he quickly went ahead and made plans for their departure to America. The first 300 people arrived in Baltimore on July 4, 1804. Initially 80 of Rapp's followers accompanied him to Pennsylvania to clear land and build homes. The rest would follow later. Those who stayed behind gave their money to Rapp to assist in developing their future homes.

HARMONY, PENNSYLVANIA, 1805–1814

On February 15, 1805, the Village of Harmony, Pennsylvania, became a reality as George Rapp drew up a constitution and asked his adherents to sign on. The contract stipulated that all things would be held in common, and if any member decided to leave, he or she would renounce all claims to compensation for wages or for property brought into the organization. Rapp's disciples worked hard, and in their first year they constructed nearly 50 log homes, cleared 150 acres of land, built a sawmill, tannery, and storehouse, and planted a small vineyard.

As the village of Harmony developed, George Rapp naturally became the undisputed leader. He appointed Frederick Reichert as his right-hand man, which proved to be a wise choice. Reichert had held the group together in Germany while Rapp sought land in America. Under Reichert's supervision, the village economy was organized into seven departments with an appointed manager over each. Reichert also changed his name to Frederick Rapp and became Rapp's adopted son. George Rapp himself assumed the title "Father Rapp" as a way to represent a form of spiritual authority in the community (Wilson, 1984).

In 1807, when a religious revival struck the community, George Rapp declared that celibacy would be the order of the day. Community members expressed interest in reaffirming the fundamentals of their faith, so Rapp responded by making changes to the lifestyle of the Harmonists. He reasoned that the practice of celibacy would free up time and energy for community work because people would no longer be distracted sexually. According to Rapp, women would gain an additional nine months of time in useful labor rather than nine months of pregnancy. In addition, Rapp reasoned that if all things were held in common, why divert from that theme by having individual husbands and wives? Rapp's announcement naturally led to an exodus of membership, and those who were married and remained in the colony were ordered to regard one another as brother and sister. After the edict for celibacy went out, no more children were born to colony couples. A tragic event emanating from the new rule was the death of Rapp's son, John, who allegedly died when his father castrated him as punishment for sexual indulgence (Wilson, 1984:27).

By 1813, the inhabitants of Harmony had attained a degree of economic success that would be the envy of their neighbors. In keeping with Rapp's philosophy, they provided for all of their own needs, including food, clothing, and other necessities, and they purchased few outside goods. Still, they were not satisfied, partly because of their choice of location. The village of Harmony was too far inland, and the Harmonists desperately needed a waterway to transport their produce; the closest river was 12 miles away. There was also concern that the land was not suitable for planting vineyards. In addition, having the basic elements of their utopian dreams fulfilled, the Separatists grew restless, which suggests that earthly utopias are not always what they are first envisioned to be. Rapp's solution to the dilemma was to keep his followers occupied by relocating them to a more desirable location. Their next utopia was in Indiana.

NEW HARMONY, INDIANA, 1815–1824

On May 15, 1815, a Mennonite named Abraham Ziegler appeared in Harmony, Pennsylvania, and offered to buy its buildings and its 7,000 acres for $100,000. George Rapp immediately accepted the deal and his profit on the property came to about $8,000. Land for their new location in Posey County, Indiana, had already been purchased, making Ziegler's offer even more enticing. The next location would be called New Harmony. Rapp decided that business could be enhanced if his new settlement could relocate to a waterway to ensure better trade opportunities, and the 30,000-fertile-acre plot he purchased in the Wabash Valley certainly promised that. Rapp sent 100 members ahead to prepare things for the community, and a year later the entire membership migrated to their new home, where they were joined by 130 immigrant converts from Würtemburg, Germany. By 1817 the residents of New Harmony were more than 700 strong (Nordhoff, 1966:76).

Life on the Wabash River proved successful and in a very short time, the town of New Harmony took shape. Although perceived primarily as an economic institution throughout its existence, the first building the Harmonists erected in their new location was the church. It was beautifully adorned and certainly a town landmark. Some years later the church steeple and clock were struck by a bolt of lightning, but George Rapp insisted that lightning rods should not be placed on any of the buildings; the people had to trust in the Lord for their safety. The exception to the rule was Rapp's own house, which *was* equipped with lightning rods. Rapp was very much afraid of two things—lightning and steam engines (Wilson, 1984:47). Charismatic leaders, it seems, do not necessarily have to be consistent in their philosophies.

The New Harmony settlement eventually grew to number 180 buildings, including factories, mills, and granaries, and the economy was always self-sufficient. New Harmony became an important business center for the region, and much of the commerce was carried out through its post office, bank, store, and tavern. The Harmonists also sold their products and manufactured goods in branch stores in the area, selling more than $12,000 worth of goods each year. There were very few places in the area besides New Harmony to grind grain, sell pelts, or purchase supplies. The Harmonists grew quite wealthy by this trade and gradually built a number of comfortable homes, a school, a library, and other facilities. A special home was built for George Rapp, which was surrounded by a tall wall with windows that had shutters. Whenever he wanted to peek out on his town, Rapp could open the shutters and catch a glimpse of life on the adjoining streets.

When it seemed that the economic success of New Harmony was assured, George Rapp organized a public display of his trust in the people. One day in 1818, he arranged to have a public burning of the book that contained records showing how much money each family had contributed to the original common fund. This was done as a symbol of communal unity and satisfaction. During the next few years the economic growth of New Harmony continued to expand through increased production and the obtaining of new markets. By 1824 the commercial reputation of New Harmony stretched out to 22 states and 10 foreign countries. In fact, their business including foreign shipments was so successful that Rapp proposed lending money to the state of Indiana at 6 percent interest (Wilson, 1984:78).

After just a few years in their new location, the population of New Harmony added a large membership of transported members. Most of these individuals were apprentices and German indentured servants who came to the commune from Europe on Rapp's encouragement, but few of them had sufficient funds to pay for their passage. A few former slaves also joined the society, Rapp having agreed to pay the respective slave owners for their freedom. Eventually there were so many people wanting to come to New Harmony that Rapp had to discourage them. More rigid requirements for membership quickly reduced the list of applicants (Pitzer and Elliott, 1979:231).

The success of New Harmony was in large part dependent upon the ingenuity of George Rapp. Everyone in the colony was in one way or another responsible to him. He seemed to oversee all community operations, and every supervisor, chairman, or foreman was required to consult with him. For example, when members needed hats, coats, or other personal items, they applied to the foreman of the trade and received an order signed by George Rapp himself. When nonmembers did business with a specific trade shop, they paid the respective foreman and received a receipt from Rapp. However, no one complained about this arrangement because their daily needs were well taken care of. Everyone had a job to do, plenty of food to eat, warm beds to sleep in, and various forms of entertainment such as music to indulge in. Many people sang together as they worked, and there were festive times during which an occasional drink of wine could be enjoyed. Despite the rule about celibacy, now and then there were children born in the colony. Albeit reluctant to do so, Rapp himself performed several marriages at New Harmony.

It will come as no surprise to students of history that no matter how well thought-out, no utopian plan can avoid all pitfalls, and New Harmony was no exception. New Harmony became very prosperous after ten years of hard labor, but a plague of sorts pervaded the community. The cause was a disease called *ague,* a form of malarial fever, and people fell ill in droves. An additional source of consternation was the attitude of New Harmony's neighboring businessmen, who were jealous of the commune's economic success and monopoly in certain areas. The New Harmonists owned the only landing on the Wabash River within miles, thus controlling shipping in that region. They were also accused by neighboring businessmen of charging high prices in their stores and excessive grinding fees in the mill. Eventually, disgruntled local residents took these grievances to the Indiana General Assembly, demanding that the Harmony mill be declared public property. Although Indiana legislators had privately done business with Rapp, they were somewhat apprehensive about the community's power. Despite reservations, the state eventually seized the commune mill.

This was too much for Rapp. Something had to be done, and Rapp decided that another move would be good for the membership. He told his followers that God was calling the Harmonists back to Pennsylvania and the new millennium was far into the future. A riot in the streets of New Harmony convinced Rapp that he had to take immediate action. This particular chapter of the Harmonists' utopian dream was finished. As luck would have it, a buyer for the town was lurking in the shadows. The buyer was the visionary Robert Owen. Hurriedly, the Harmonists vacated the town, many of them traveling north by boat. The *William Penn*, the *Ploughboy*, and two other steamboats, the *Bolivar* and the *Phoenix*, transported most of the Harmonists to their new location, while a few traveled the distance by Conestoga wagon. The last group left Harmony in the summer of 1825.

ECONOMY, PENNSYLVANIA, 1824-1905

In 1824 the Harmonists sold their Indiana town of New Harmony, including 20,000 acres of land, for $150,000 to Robert Owen, a visionary in his own right. It was said that George Rapp looked for the millennium, but Robert Owen thought he brought it with him (Wilson, 1984:95). Owen was soon to find out if his dream would come true.

In the meantime, always on the lookout for strong economic opportunities, George Rapp bought a parcel of land at Ambridge, Pennsylvania, a short distance north of Pittsburgh and not far from the original home of Old Harmony. An advance party went ahead to clear land and lay out the new town of Economy. Within a very short time of settlement, the commune prospered. Compared to neighboring farmers, the Harmonists lived a luxurious lifestyle, enjoying even greater prosperity than they had ever enjoyed at New Harmony. The short distance to Pittsburgh paid off, and cheap transport on the Ohio River was a real boon. The converts who had joined them from Würtemburg were young enough to provide ample labor and vigor for the New Harmonists' many enterprises. By 1825 the Harmonists had constructed cotton and woolen factories powered and heated by steam engines, and developed steam laundries and a dairy. They built shops for blacksmiths, cabinetmakers and turners, hatters, linen weavers, potters, tinners, tanners, and wagonmasters. Later they formulated a technology for high-quality silk, for which they received awards during exhibition competitions in Boston, New York, and Philadelphia.

The town of Economy was extremely well laid out, with an excellent garden equipped with a pavilion for the town's band. Flowers were cultivated with great care and locals were invited to musical concerts held on most summer evenings and Sunday afternoons. Rapp's personal home was lavishly furnished for its time, and peering out of the large living-room window he could see the statue of a young woman named "Miss Harmony" housed in a gazebo. Allegedly the statue was intended to portray Rapp's notion of peace and harmony. Rapp's admirers justified the unusually large home for their leader on the grounds that he had to entertain many visitors and strangers of distinction (Nordhoff, 1966:78).

When everything appeared to be going well in Economy—too well, perhaps—trouble was brewing behind the scenes. The aging saint, George Rapp, fell in love with a young women named Hildegard Mutschler, who had been raised within the Harmony Society. She became Rapp's constant companion and laboratory assistant in the late 1820s—to the displeasure of his son Frederick and many other Harmonists. These individuals thought Rapp was not providing a very good example of self-control. Eventually Hildegard left Rapp for a man named Jacob Klein, whom George Rapp then banished from the society. A few other members including Hildegard withdrew with Klein. In order to defend himself against criticism, Rapp scolded his followers for their gossip about him and requested that they pray for Hildegard's return. The plot thickened when Rapp's son Frederick decided he could no longer support his father's behavior. Then, in 1831, a new adherent named Bernhard Müller joined the Harmonists and incited a radical break. Calling himself "Count Maximilian de Leon," he worked his way into the confidence of the membership and began to recommend various reforms. He advocated marriage, increased participation in a livelier lifestyle, and more involvement in what had been viewed as "worldly practices" by the Harmonists. A group of 250 individuals decided to follow Müller away from Harmony to start a new society. By mutual consent they left the colony with their clothing and furnishings and a gift from the Harmonist treasury of $105,000 (Holloway, 1966:94). It was Rapp's way of trying to be fair. The money was payable to Müller's followers in three installments four months apart.

By this settlement the dissidents agreed to relinquish all rights to Economy property.

Calling themselves "The New Philadelphia Society," this group purchased 800 acres at Philipsburg, about ten miles south of Harmony. Within a few years the rebels had squandered their funds and begged Rapp for more. No further monies were forthcoming and the group relocated to Grand Encore, near Natchitoches in Louisiana, where they were able to buy cheap land. The following year Müller died of cholera and the group again divided and some of them moved to Germantown, Louisiana. None of these developments affected Economy, whose day-to-day economic activities remained very successful. Economy became the target of several lawsuits initiated by dissidents aimed at extorting money from them, but none of them was successful (Pitzer and Elliott, 1979:255–56; Holloway, 1966:95).

The Müller insurrection suffered its first setback at Philipsburg, and in 1833 Müller left the area. Those who remained divided the assets and for all intents and purposes the Philipsburg Colony ceased to exist. In 1841 the site was incorporated as a town, but the communal spirit was not lost. Some of Müller's former adherents now joined up with a self-styled physician named Dr. William Keil and traveled with him to Bethel, Missouri, where they built a commune called Bethel Colony. Keil was a charismatic individual who founded two communes, one in Bethel, Missouri, and later the Aurora Colony at Aurora, Oregon. These societies grew to accommodate some 650 people but folded four years after Keil's death (Nordhoff, 1966). A further discussion of events at Bethel and Aurora is included later in this chapter.

Aside from the fact that the population of Economy was in constant flux, life was basically enjoyable. There was plenty to eat, reading and music were encouraged, and a strong religious base, established by George Rapp, provided the society with spiritual nourishment. Families cooked for themselves from rations meted out by the head office. Tobacco was forbidden, but the group manufactured an ample supply of wine, which became quite popular in the district. The Harmonists celebrated several religious holidays including Christmas, Good Friday, Easter, and Pentecost, and three festivals: (i) February 15, which commemorated the day of their initial organization; (ii) Harvest house, which was a celebration of autumn; and, (iii) the Lord's Supper (Eucharist), which was held in October. The well-oiled village administrative machinery arranged employment for all including weaving, saddlery, tin making, shoemaking, working in the bakery, carpentry, and so on. The village operated a school that offered instruction in both English and German.

After the Müller incident, the membership of Economy began to decline. George Rapp drew up a constitution for the society, and while 625 members signed on, 42 did not. Rapp's influence was waning because his prophetic pronouncements were not reliable. He continued to insist that the Second Coming of Christ was imminent, but his message began to fall on deaf ears. Even the themes of his sermons began to change, although he did manage to maintain his schedule. Always a robust and healthy man, Rapp preached two sermons on the Sunday before his death on August 7, 1847. The economy of the nation was in transition, however, and the Harmonists were finding it necessary to adjust to the new industrialized world. Much of the machinery used by the community fell short of the more stringent standards set by the industrial revolution, because they had not kept up with the times (Reibel, 1993:9). Despite the many changes and variations that Rapp's various communes went through, George Rapp lived to the ripe old age of 90. At times it seemed as though he thrived on controversy as evidenced by his firm leadership, his influence over people, and his impatience with disgruntled members (Nordhoff, 1966:93).

After Rapp's death, the leadership of the commune fell to Rapp's son, Frederick, along with Jacob Henrici and Romelius Baker, whose spirituality and business acumen fell far short of their predecessor. Under their leadership the society practically ceased to manufacture anything for sale. They merely provided for their own needs. Although the society had money to invest, they were no longer a productive enterprise. Still, they developed one of the first oil-drilling companies in the United States, invested in railroads, and built the town of Beaver Falls. By the 1880s, however, most members were in their seventies, and because they had borne few children there were no heirs to take on the business. The society also attracted few new members, and the stress of operating the town's diverse business ventures was too much for the aging members. John S. Duss, one of the remaining members of the society, liquidated the various capitalistic endeavors and somehow the assets disappeared. There was a move to dismantle the society in 1890, but this took a few years to accomplish. By 1905 only two members of the society remained and the society was legally dissolved (Kring, 1973:202).

The unusual, and for many years successful story of the Harmonists is due almost entirely to the management of George Rapp and his son Frederick. The two of them brought 600 colonists across the ocean without a single mishap, transferred their living quarters three times, and provided members with a firm financial footing. Through the years of their existence the colony undoubtedly gained a large number of admirers. As financially propelled intentional communities go, the Harmonists' efforts have to be regarded as one of the most successful.

BETHEL, MISSOURI, 1844–1879

As a further development in the Harmonists' various phases, it is necessary to follow a little of the Bethel-Aurora communal history. Its legacy is currently being maintained by the efforts of a few surviving members who have tried to preserve some 30 buildings on the site in Bethel, Missouri. Much to the advantage of curious tourists, in 1970 these buildings were placed on the National Register of Historic Places.

The story begins with the establishment of Bethel community in 1844 by William Keil (1811–1877) in Shelby County, Missouri. The initial site consisted of 2,560 acres of farmland, but a gristmill and other industries were soon developed. Within ten years Bethel Colony attained remarkable economic stability and prosperity through its agricultural and manufacturing enterprises. In 1847 there were 476 members and by 1850 this number had grown to 650. The original land holdings had increased to 3,536 acres in Shelby County with an additional 731 acres in Adair County. Most of the membership was drawn from the German Methodist Church. The peak membership lasted only a few years because various internal factors caused divisions in the colony, which we will explore in the next sections.

Religious Beliefs

William Keil governed Bethel Colony in Bethel, Missouri; he was its spiritual leader, prophet, counselor, president, and manager. His religious heritage stemmed from the Protestant Reformation, which spawned a variety of religions. Central to these movements was the concept of a more perfect society, which some of its adherents were determined to bring into being. While there was consensus on this basic vision, there was considerable disagreement about its theological underpinnings.

William Keil elected to formulate a private theological system representing a mixture of revivalism, millennialism, and communalism. A powerful preacher, he adapted his rhetoric to meet the needs of his parishioners. He borrowed his revivalist bent from the German Methodists and his millennialist orientation from his Separatist leanings. He reasoned that communitarianism was the only way that a people committed to the Second Coming of Christ could keep themselves from worldly practices while they waited for Christ's return. Separation from the world and having all things in common combined to form a functional recipe for a temporal human organization. There were only two ways to go: the way of the world or the way of the colony.

Despite Keil's claims to mystical experiences, he almost always cited the Bible as a basis for his pronouncements and warnings. He supplemented his public gatherings with a variety of celebrations and festivities, all of which were held at his large home. Funerals always began at his house, and people at every funeral gathering sang a special hymn that Keil had written. All community events included a great deal of singing and playing of hymns and songs, many of which were specifically written for colony use. This practice served to reinforce the colony's commitment to communal life and millennialist theology.

William Keil

William Keil was born in Bleicherode, near Nordhausen in the Kingdom of Prussia on March 6, 1811. As a young man he immersed himself in the study of religion and mysticism and earned a living as a milliner in Germany. He married Louise Ritter, who became and remained his most loyal follower. Keil became a healer of sorts, using magnetism as his base, but his medical status was never legally recognized. He professed to be the keeper of an inspired book, written in human blood, containing a list of medical recipes to cure various illnesses. He eventually joined the German Methodists and became a lay preacher at Deer Creek, Pennsylvania. During this time he allegedly burned his secret book, but soon left the Methodists, taking his entire congregation along with him to form his own sect. During the time when the insurrectionist Harmonist Müller took his followers out of Economy, Keil managed to attract a few of them as adherents. He promised them nothing but bread, water, and hard work, but still they came.

Community Life

In Shelby County, Keil formed a model Harmonist-like settlement minus the celibacy principle. His people were poor and uneducated and the colony began with very little means. Still, with a lot of hard work, the commune soon became virtually self-sufficient. Bricks for building were locally manufactured, cloth was spun from colony wool, and a tailor shop produced clothing for the colony. Shoes were made and sold in the area and buckskin gloves manufactured in the colony won first prize at the New York World's Fair in 1858. Bethel plows, manufactured in the local blacksmith shop, were popular throughout the West. The best Bethel product, however, was their "Golden Rule Whiskey," which brought steady income from neighboring communities. Other industries included a gristmill, a woolen mill with carding machinery, and a sawmill. Some of the men also took up various trades needed by neighboring farmers. Colony residents also built a general store, a post office, and a church.

The Bethel community eventually owned more than 5,000 acres of land. A constitution was prepared but never signed. No records or accounts of work were kept based on the maxim that practical Christianity was more important than written records. The format of governance was characterized by simplicity, so whenever someone had a complaint Keil personally tried to appease them. At one point several families demanded a share of the property to be registered in their own name, and when Keil yielded to their demands, they took what they could and left the colony. Some left their vacant property in the colony even though it was privately registered. Keil did his best to accommodate the dissidents, though this was not an easy task. Keil's own elaborate home was at least a mile out of town and it meant a great deal of travel for him to meet with unhappy factions.

Activities at Bethel were governed by a board of trustees, but Keil had a primary supervisory role. According to Nordhoff (1966:328), the colony was never run with very strict regulations. Individuals could take flour or meal from the storehouse at will, and animals often ran loose in Bethel streets. The interiors of Bethel homes were clean. Literacy was never stressed in the community and colony members did very little reading and never printed anything. School classes were conducted in English to meet state regulations, and as a result, use of the German language eventually ceased. This did not seem to be an issue with the people. Keil was not particularly fond of higher education but a few individuals were encouraged to attend post-secondary institutions on the condition that their education would somehow benefit the community. Music played a significant role in the community; the local band played for all local festivities and often performed in neighboring communities. Individuals tended to marry while still in their teens and there were no rules about this except that if a person married outside of the community they were expected to leave. Each family received enough pigs for food, cows for milk and butter, and enough land for a garden. They were expected to raise a surplus of chickens, eggs, and vegetables for sale to outsiders.

The Bethel Colony Church, a large and impressive edifice, was completed in 1848. It was the largest church west of the Mississippi at that time. Church services were held every two weeks. There were no baptism or confirmation services, and the Eucharist was occasionally celebrated, followed by a fellowship meal. Easter and Pentecost were observed. Men and women sat separately during the services. Keil's sermons usually centered on moral living, respect for authority, and the

common good. If Keil learned that someone had violated these principles, he would bring the matter up in one of his sermons. Most of his followers put up with this embarrassing exercise but outsiders and
dissidents severely criticized the practice.

Keil's unusual habits aside, the Bethel settlement was economically
very successful, thanks to his leadership. The peak of Bethel's success occurred just four years after their first settlement. The community even
established daughter colonies at Mamri, on the south side of the North
River across from Bethel, and at Hebron, a mile northwest where a
cemetery was laid out. Then in 1855, William Keil decided to form a new
colony on the Northwest coast. His rationale for doing so may simply
have been his innate restlessness, but some of his followers were certainly pleased with being given the opportunity to avoid the Civil War
draft. Bethel Colony itself remained neutral during the war, but during
the 1860s many Bethel colonists migrated to Oregon to ensure their
noninvolvement.

AURORA, OREGON, 1856–1883

In 1855, Keil made his move to the Northwest. His yearning to head
west may have partially been motivated by the streams of pioneers who
passed through Missouri, and the fact that some of those migrants
bought their wagons at Bethel. Keil reasoned that the great Northwest
offered more opportunities for expansion and a wider range of marketable industries, so he sent representatives ahead to purchase land. In
May of 1885, a train of 25 wagons with 400 residents left on a 2,000-mile
trip to the Northwest. It took five months to complete the journey. Unfortunately, Keil's son Willie died just before the wagon train left, and
since Keil had promised Willie that he would go to Oregon, they took
Willie's body with them. The first wagon bore Willie's casket, which was
filled with alcohol to preserve the body; the journey is sometimes referred to as the longest funeral procession in American history.

The western journey undertaken by Keil and his followers was
fraught with hardships and surprises. Their route took them through Indian territory, but their passage was without altercation of any kind.

6.1   Aurora Colony lathe used to make spindles, Aurora, Oregon

Some observers suggest that Willie's casket at the head of the wagon train prompted the Native people either to respect or fear it. Others said it was Keil's appearance that allowed the travelers to make it safely through Indian territory. Keil may have been perceived as a medicine man. As Keil put it, "We met hundreds of Indians who were glad when they saw my face. I have had all power over the Indians and could do with them as I desired. [This is a reference to the often-mentioned magnetic power of his countenance.] Many times I have been surrounded by fifty to sixty Indians. I gave them tobacco which pleased them greatly" (Snyder, 1993:59). When the entourage arrived at their destination, Willie's body was buried at Willapa, Washington. The elder Keil then decided that the first location his representatives had selected was not appropriate and he ordered a move. Several families who liked the area remained there. The majority of adherents followed Keil to the Williamette Valley of Oregon, where they established their final colony.

Once settled, Keil named his new colony Aurora after his daughter, but tragedy soon struck. Between November 22 and December 14, 1862, the Keil family lost four of their six children to smallpox, a disease that had been brought into the settlement by a member who had gone to help a neighbor. These events greatly affected Keil, but he calmly accepted them as part of God's greater plan. When an additional contingent of 252 followers arrived at Aurora in 1862, they hardly recognized Keil. The responsibility of leadership had taken its toll. Undoubtedly the deaths of his children greatly affected him. He no longer appeared to be the strong, assertive, and enthusiastic leader they had known at Bethel. But despite his personal setbacks, Keil saw to it that Aurora flourished economically. The community continued to come alive through a balanced economy of agriculture and manufacturing. A hotel and restaurant business supplemented the commune's income, and the colony band drew a lot of attention in the surrounding community. Their hotel catered to passing stagecoaches as a popular meal stop and offered guests a choice of overnight or weekend stays with lavish meals.

From 1863 to 1870 the Aurora Colony flourished under the guiding hand of William Keil. A man of many talents, Keil proved to be a prudent planner. As soon as the colony was settled, he ordered that plenty of apple trees be planted. Before the trees were productive, the colonists bought apples from their neighbors for one dollar a bushel. They then saved the apple peelings to make cider vinegar, which they sold back to their neighbors at $1.50 per gallon. By this kind of shrewd planning, Keil was able to build up the treasury and pay off the mortgage on their land while other farmers went into debt.

Undoubtedly, William Keil's preaching aided in the commune's economic successes. His principal themes were humility, simplicity, self-sacrifice, prayer, and neighborly love. At the same time, he stressed the importance of hard work as a natural outcome of personal faith. Unlike Harmonist George Rapp, Keil was more subdued about his economic master plan, yet his colony did very well (Snyder, 1993:69). In a way his homiletic manner resembled his management style. He was a father figure to his people rather than a dictator, and though some of the younger set sometimes saw him as interfering, most knew that he would do his best to provide for their needs. He finally managed to draw up a constitution for the colony in April 1866, purportedly to transfer common property to a board of trustees. The transfer was made, but it did little to alter the way things were managed at the commune. In this, Keil's approach was much like that of the Doukhobor leader, Peter (the Lordly) Verigin, who benevolently ruled his members. Keil's trustees essentially took orders from him and few ever opposed his decisions.

A special source of pride for Keil was the completion of the village church in 1867. The building's steeple was 114 feet high, with two platforms around it where the local community band could play. Keil played the gracious host to any and all visitors, proudly but humbly showing off their many accomplishments. Sunday worship services were always a highlight for him.

In 1877 Keil suddenly became ill, and although no one thought it was serious, he passed away on December 30 of that year. Suddenly the glue that held the Bethel and Aurora colonies together was gone. Keil's right-hand man, Christopher Wolff, tried to persuade Keil to arrange for a successor in the event of his demise, but Keil was not concerned. The lack of agreement on the matter between the two caused a permanent rift, but Wolff continued to remain in the colony. Shortly after Keil died, the bond between the two communities was dissolved. It took many hours of keen calculation to accomplish this, since many residents of Aurora had previously contributed to Bethel's wealth. Despite these complications, an agreement was drawn up by an elected board of directors and shared with the members of the two colonies. Then the communal property was evenly and harmoniously divided among the residents. In addition, each man was paid $7.76 for every year he had worked in the colony, and women were awarded half that sum. Bethel itself, left with only 200 adherents, legally disbanded in 1879 and was incorporated as a town in 1883. A final legal decree officially ended the relationship between Bethel and Aurora in Oregon on January 22, 1883 (Schroeder, 1990:2).

When Keil's utopian kingdom was dissolved, its members continued to live in much the same way as they always had. They occupied the same houses, did the same work, and socialized with the same people. They were bonded by many years of friendship, labor, and faith. As the years went by, many members of the next generation left the area for greener pastures. No doubt the memory of being linked with one of America's short-lived but most successful utopian experiments helped to perpetuate Aurora's unusual success. Today, visitors can share in that memory by visiting the various buildings of the Aurora Colony, carefully preserved by the Old Aurora Colony Museum.

CHAPTER 7

UNORTHODOX COMMUNES

Although it is sometimes difficult to judge who has the final word on social "sanity," from time to time intentional communities have originated whose philosophy and make up have stunned even the most nonjudgmental observers. Interestingly, the lifestyles of these "unorthodox" human organizations tend to vary as much as the individual personalities of the charismatic leaders who direct them (Stoner and Parke, 1977:100). In 1978, for example, the world was shocked to learn that hundreds of followers of Jim Jones' People's Temple had committed suicide. A similar feeling of shock erupted in 1993 when 85 Branch Davidians, 17 of them children, perished in a fire after a month-long government siege of the Ranch Apocalypse in Waco, Texas. The Children of God movement, often known as The Family, was started by David Berg, a former Missionary Alliance preacher, who began his ministry in the late 1960s in California hippie communes. For many years his organization specialized in "Flirty Fishing," which meant that members should indulge in sex with outsiders as a means of luring them to the cause. After all, Berg told his disciples, "There is nothing intrinsically wrong with sex, it's a gift from God" (Milne, 1994:26).

Many social movements that sociologists label "sects" or "cults" reflect the fact that strong commitment can be a very powerful factor in keeping organizations together. Sometimes, however, commitment can be overdone (Friesen, 1995a:236f). Many alternative organizations have quite ordinary linkages. In many ways Jones' followers were no different from other people who wanted to identify with a cause. David Koresh, leader of the Branch Davidians, was a former adherent of the Seventh Day Adventist Church. Like Shakers, Ephratites, Harmonists, and many other such communities, these groups permitted their leaders to dictate their lifestyles and they took great delight in attributing superhuman attributes to them. The polygamous David Koresh was a father figure for the Branch Davidians. David Berg was called "Dad" or "Grandpa" and his wife, Maria, was called "Momma." In the Unification Church, the Rev. Sun Myung Moon and his wife were referred to as the "Perfect Parents." In Koresh's case it is difficult to understand how his followers could be absorbed into Koresh's way of thinking. Unfortunate developments like these illustrate the devastating extremes to which fanatical schemes can be carried. In the next sections we will examine two successful communities that featured somewhat unusual beliefs and practices.

EPHRATA

There is no sociological measuring technique by which to label various subcultures unorthodox or deviant. However, in layman's terms it appears that some subgroups are sufficiently different in so many respects (beliefs *and* practices) that they are considered extraordinary in nature. The two communes in this chapter certainly were that. As Alderfer (1995:3) notes, "Ephrata was different. Its frame of reference was mystical rather than rational, spiritual rather than scientific; it deliberately avoided entrapment in the 'ways of the world' and the tensions of political and social change around it."

The ruins of a unique communal experiment known as the Ephrata Cloister may be viewed in the town of Ephrata in Lancaster County, Pennsylvania. A few haunting, medieval-style buildings attest to an unusual and mystical lifestyle that lasted 63 years. Grounded in Lutheran and Reformed traditions, with input from a variety of pietist groups, the commune was originated in 1733 by Conrad Beissel (1691–1768) and operated to very strict regulations formulated by Beissel himself.

The membership of Ephrata Cloister was drawn mostly from German-speaking settlers in the area, and by 1740 there were 70 celibate brothers and sisters in the commune. At its high point in 1750, the cloister had about 100 members, with another 200 householder (married) members who were living off-site. All 300 people belonged to the Seventh Day German Baptist Church founded by Beissel. Although the commune officially folded in 1796, a handful of sisters remained in the cloister until 1814, when it was taken over by the Seventh Day German Baptist Church. The congregation used the buildings for religious activities until it dissolved in 1934.

In 1941 the Pennsylvania Historical and Museum Commission assumed administration of the Ephrata Cloister in order to restore it and preserve it as an historic site. Restoration was completed in 1968 and today the site is regularly open to tourists.

Beliefs and Practices

The Ephrata Cloister was a radical eighteenth-century religious society whose lifestyle caused many observers to shake their heads and wonder. The inhabitants became well-known for their original art and music, distinctive medieval Germanic architecture, and prolific publishing center. On many occasions the Ephrata choir performed eloquent mystical hymns written by Beissel. Members had to follow strict dietary rules in order to keep their voices sounding pure. The Ephrata press' most ambitious work was the translation and publication of the 1,200-page *Martyrs Mirror*, published for the Mennonites in 1748. At that time, it was the largest book ever published in the United States. During the peak of operation the cloister had six or eight printing presses in operation, none of which have been located to date (Alderfer, 1995:189). The economy of the settlement was based on a fairly wide variety of occupations including farming, fruit growing, basketmaking, papermaking, printing, bookmaking, carpentry, and milling.

No official statement of faith for the Ephrata Cloister was ever published by Beissel or his followers. The colony's reasoning was that once their beliefs were written down they would have to be subject to them instead of listening to the Spirit of God. This arrangement also proved useful to Beissel; he could make occasional pronouncements that became colony doctrine. The Russian Doukhobors functioned in a similar fashion. As their Doukhobor slogan proclaimed, "the letter killeth, but the Spirit giveth life." There was much disagreement among Beissel's followers because each believer could claim personal access to the Spirit. One belief that Beissel did insist upon was pacifism, and much to his displeasure, when the French and Indian war broke out in 1755, some of his followers joined the military.

What was unusual about Ephrata's belief system was that following Beissel's instruction, they ignored the biblical writings of both St. Paul and the Apostle John on certain topics. In contrast to orthodox Christianity, Beissel conjectured that God was both female and male and Divine properties were in balance between the two. Beissel blamed Satan for upsetting the Divine balance by linking the two sexes in conjugal practices. According to Beissel, God was able to withstand the attack by Satan, but it would be an everlasting struggle for humans to do the same. In addition, he proclaimed that since Adam was created first, women should be subservient to men. Since Satan was male this meant that men would forever have to bear the shame of disruption of the Divine Being (a perfect blending of male and female), and only men could provide a suitable sacrifice for this shame. They were to do this by committing themselves to a life of self-denial and suffering.

Unlike the Amana people, Beissel believed very much in the practice of two Sacraments, Holy Baptism and Holy Communion. At Ephrata these Sacraments were practiced whenever Beissel deemed it necessary, and they were preceded by a love feast or fellowship supper. Preparation for the Holy Communion required foot-washing, hymn-singing, and the kiss of charity. Eventually the group even initiated the Mormon practice of being baptized for the dead. There were also many occasions that required re-baptism of members, particularly when new orders were being established. In addition, it was customary that when new members entered the commune they were given monastic names. Beissel himself, who steadily refused to accept any position of honor, took the name *Friedsam* (peaceful or content), while his would-be successor, Isaac Eckerlin, became known as Onesimus. Beissel's followers bestowed on him the title of "Spiritual Father of the Community" (Pyle, 1889). In 1736, Beissel led his followers on a pilgrimage to preach the Gospel as he saw it. The event drew a lot of attention, with the disciples clad in pilgrim attire, walking on bare feet in inclement weather. Marching single file with heads bowed, they drew crowds of both admirers and critics and were targets of jeers and catcalls.

Like other pietist leaders of the day, Beissel believed that the Second Coming of Christ was near and people should live as though it could occur at any moment. Midnight worship services were held regularly, since this was the expected time of Christ's return. Two comets, which appeared in February 1742 and December 1743, were thought to be signs of Christ's imminent return. As time went on and no further proof of the Second Coming became evident, the colony turned its energies to other themes.

Religious mysticism was the forte of Ephrata Cloister and carnal practices in any form were shunned. Celibates were requested to comply with a series of rigid routines and commit themselves to fasting, praying, charity, chastity, poverty, and obedience to colony regulations. Adherents were to adorn themselves in plain attire that would hide the contours of the body. Women's hair was cut short, and men wore beards on which they tugged when they greeted one another. Food was meager, consisting mostly of dry bread and porridge, and utensils were made of wood or pottery. Sleep was limited, and like some monks, members rose at midnight to sing hymns and pray, and again at five o'clock in the morning for a second service.

Trying to function in the Ephrata buildings also required severe commitment. The hallways were narrow (in order to represent the way that leads to everlasting life) and doorways always had to be of a specific size (five feet high and 20 inches across). Beds were hard, and pillows were made of wood (Rexroth, 1974:177). All furnishings and floors were spotlessly clean so that it almost seemed a shame to sit on the chairs or walk on the floors. Even nail heads were polished so brightly that they glistened (Pyle, 1889:8). Spiritual and intellectual stipulations matched rigorous physical extremes. Members were required to be familiar with

Beissel's teachings and writings and discipline for deviance was severe. Each member was expected to listen to Beissel's sermons, which were delivered every week just before the Sabbath. This was also a time for self-examination and the writing of a paper of confession, which was submitted to Beissel himself.

Conrad Beissel

Conrad Beissel was born near Heidelberg, Germany, on March 1, 1691. His mother died when he was seven years old, and his father raised him in the Reform Church tradition. As a young man Beissel served an apprenticeship as a baker. One day, while attending a pietist revival meeting, he experienced a religious awakening and stopped attending state-sponsored church services. As he grew older, he continued to work as a baker and participate in pietist meetings. His religious convictions led him to conclude that his German lifestyle was too excessive and could not be justified on spiritual grounds. At one point he scolded the bakers' guild, of which he was a member, for holding parties that were too lavish. This angered his colleagues and they reported him for failing to attend state-mandated church services. After his trial he was ordered to leave the community or join one of three accepted denominations. Beissel chose to leave, so he was excommunicated and his baker's license was cancelled.

As he resumed his spiritual search, Beissel met with a variety of pietist groups from various backgrounds, but none of their beliefs entirely satisfied him. He obtained employment as a spinner of wool until, in 1720, a friend offered to loan him money to travel to America. Beissel, his friend, and two others set sail for America with the intention of joining a group called "Woman in the Wilderness," but on their arrival they discovered that the group had virtually dissolved. This group was completely communistic in its organization and seems to have owed its smoothness of operation to the complete and voluntary submission of its members. The commune was half monastic and half evangelistic, and fostered the belief that complete self-denial was the way to salvation (Holloway, 1966:30).

Beissel next took up employment with a weaver named Peter Becker, one of the leading men of the German Baptist movement in Germantown, Pennsylvania. This group was also known as "Dunkers" because they opposed military service and the taking of oaths. Beissel continued his spiritual search among Mennonites and Quakers, but he was never quite satisfied. He became convinced that the life of a hermit permitted spiritual solace better than any other. With a few friends, he took up fasting and praying and lived in isolation. The plan did not work because Beissel failed to provide food when it was his turn, or he simply gave away the group's food supply. Subsequently, the little community broke up and Beissel was alone.

Beissel resumed his connection with the German Baptists and was soon appointed leader of a congregation at Conestoga, Pennsylvania. His teachings eventually drew the congregation away from other Dunkers, and even forced a split in his own congregation. Beissel's promotion of such doctrines as celibacy, keeping the seventh day as the Sabbath, and following Mosaic dietary laws were too much for the mainstay of the congregation. This gave rise to the formation of Beissel's Seventh Day German Baptist Church in 1732. Beissel published his beliefs in a book called *Ehebuchlein,* in which he blasted marriage with such vigor that some women who read the book left their husbands and joined Beissel's solitary group. His congregation was made up of the solitary house in which only celibate people lived, and married followers who were known as "householders." There is some indication that Beissel had personally experienced unhappy relationships with women during his days in Heidelberg, and this may have influenced his distaste for the institution of marriage.

Beissel's solitary house attracted married women who abandoned their families in order to find spiritual fulfillment. They moved into quarters occupied by a group of single men and, naturally, rumors flared up over this unusual situation. At one point Beissel and a woman were even brought into court for producing an illegitimate baby, but when the case was tried it was proven that there was no truth to the charge (Carpenter, 1975:72). By 1735 the makings of an official commune had been erected, with a bakery and common storehouse, and Beissel entreated his celibate members to join him in formalizing the commune. Beissel organized the community into three "orders"—the Married Householders, the Brotherhood of the Angels (to which he belonged), and the Spiritual Virgins. A special, but plain-looking edifice of worship for women only was constructed, and named *Kedar,* which means "wandering tribe of Ismaelites" (Ezekiel 27:21). One householder encouraged his daughter and two others to become founding members of the Order of Spiritual Virgins, who practice monastic communism. They occupied the second floor of the *Kedar.* The celibate men who organized themselves as the Brotherhood of the Angels did not practice monastic communism. In 1736 the settlement became known as the Ephrata Cloister when Benjamin Franklin printed a hymnal for the colony and placed that name on it. Franklin had no connection with Ephrata but was given the printing order because he operated one of the very few printing presses in Pennsylvania.

Ending

The dying notes of Ephrata began to sound in the fall of 1744. Although a number of parents (particularly women) had formerly left their spouses and families to take up a celibate lifestyle at Ephrata, they soon began to regret their actions. The ties between parents and children won out, and by 1745 all those who were parents had left the cloister and resumed life with their families. There were also a few members of the celibate orders who found the restrictions too difficult and left the cloister to get married.

In 1745 Beissel gave up leadership of his project to Isaac Eckerlin, who had achieved great economic success for the cloister through the colony's mills. Beissel then asked to be treated like an ordinary brother, changed his mind, and began to belittle Eckerlin's leadership in order to take back the leadership. Beissel prevailed, but oddly enough, the cloister experienced true financial gain only through the years that Eckerlin operated their mills. When Beissel took over again, the cloister resumed its previous poverty. Any accumulated wealth that could be liquidated was given away. When Beissel died in 1768 at the age of 78, Peter Miller became the leader and held the position until his death in 1796. After that the Ephrata Cloister survived without particular leadership and the courts transferred property ownership to the Ephrata Seventh Day German Baptist congregation.

In the latter part of the nineteenth century, antiquarian and historical interest in Ephrata arose, some of it tinged with an air of romanticism. A few collectors showed interest in Ephrata manuscripts, artifacts, and musical scores, but there was little public demand for them. A few literary pieces about Ephrata appeared, one by Edward Eggleston called "Sister Tabea," and another by Ulysses S. Koons (under the pseudonym of Brother Jabez) entitled "A Tale of the Kloster." In 1827 the Historical Society of Pennsylvania was approached to publish accounts of Ephrata history, but it was not until 1939 that the state government authorized state acquisition of the property (Alderfer, 1995:191).

In 1940 a novel by Thomas Mann, *Doctor Faustus,* appeared, in which Beissel's philosophy and love of music were portrayed. Mann's novel is essentially autobiographical, but he weaves in elements of Beissel's story. Mann's novel came at a time when Western civilization was in the balance—1941 to 1947. Germany had made a pact with the devil and her end was near (Alderfer, 1995:200–204).

Despite its relatively long history, the Ephrata commune was racked with inner tensions and friction, scandals, and charges of exorcism and religious fanaticism. Beissel himself was frequently subject of criticism and suspicion, one charge being that he spent too much time with women. In 1735 two men whose wives had joined Beissel's commune sneaked into Beissel's cabin, when he was asleep and beat him with a knotted rope, leaving him with painful bruises (Alderfer, 1995:53). From January 1739 to June 1741, Beissel moved into the celibate women's quarters, the *Kedar,* allegedly to show that sexual temptation could be resisted. Gradually his behavior grew more erratic. In February 1765, he fell down a flight of stairs and hurt his foot, and gossips later reported that he had been drunk. In the *Chronicon,* Peter Miller at least twice referred to the "seeming drunkenness" of Beissel in his last years (Alderfer, 1995:153). These were not happy times.

The closing years of Ephrata were marked with controversy concerning leadership and property ownership, an unfortunate tribute to a man who claimed to be a pacifist to the end of his life. The legacy of the community consists of many theological writings and Ephrata-produced musical selections, as well as lingering questions. Historical analysts are still pursuing the question, "What really went on in Ephrata Cloister?"

ONEIDA

Most people who proudly purchase Oneida silverware are unaware that the product has very remarkable historical origins. The Rev. John H. Noyes (1811–1886) was the founder of the unique colony of Oneida, whose occupants were known as "the Perfectionists," a group who propounded the belief that it was possible to appear holy before God in this life. Noyes first heard of the concept of perfectionism through work done by the Reverend Charles Finney, a lawyer turned preacher who assisted in the founding of Oberlin College in Ohio. Noyes and Finney argued at length about the meaning of the term, Finney later chastising Noyes for inventing a community of free love. Noyes demurred, arguing that free love meant being free to love and leave tomorrow, and that was not what he was promoting. Finney responded by insisting that the only way to perfection on earth was to be celibate. He was so fervent in his stand that entire classes of men and women at Oberlin Theological Seminary where he taught took vows of perpetual celibacy. At times he converted whole congregations to his stand, although no one knows how long these vows were kept.

Webber (1959:365) contends that some of Finney's converts originated the idea that perfectionism without temptation was without virtue, so they placed themselves in situations where they would be subject to be temptation in order to prove themselves. Of course, temptation was to be undertaken entirely within the confines of the Christian community since they did not want to cast their "pearls before swine" (Matthew 7:6 KJV). One way to instigate temptation was through the practice of the holy kiss (I Thessalonians 5:26), so a great deal of "holy kissing" went on in some of Finney's congregations. Some churches invented the idea of "spiritual mating" by which couples could be mated with "beloved ones" and bound by love vows and oaths of celibacy. They lived together in a perpetual state of temptation but the successful maintenance of self-control assured them of salvation in the hereafter.

In his defense it must be mentioned that Finney's concept of perfection was quite inclusive. His efforts at Oberlin Theological Seminary revealed that there were many facets to his thinking, and he believed that human perfectibility could take many forms. It could involve tinkering with family relationships among husbands and wives and children. It could inspire the drive for the abolition of slavery, and form the beginnings of the women's movement. It could also include the concept of communal property, something that Noyes found particularly appealing. The point on which Noyes disagreed, however, was the notion that triumph over sexual temptation was a particularly saintly accomplishment.

Philosophy

The belief system and regulations of the Oneida community were personally set by John Noyes. Since he was trained as a clergyman he utilized some theological foundation on which to develop his unique ideas. Basically following Christian perspectives, but taking theological license, Noyes's conjectured that the Second Coming of Christ had already occurred, so he and his followers were freed from the constraints of sin, which did not exist anymore. He justified his form of communalism as analogous to that practiced by the apostles and described in the second chapter of the Book of Acts. That event (the gathering of the disciples at Pentecost) apparently underscored the need to follow the dictate of Acts 2:44, "All the believers were together and had everything in common."

Noyes' unique twist to the mandate for communalism was that there was no difference between owning things and owning persons in the sense that traditional patterns of marriage dictated. He insisted that the same spirit which abolished exclusiveness in regard to money, would abolish it, if circumstances allowed full scope to it, with regard to women and children (Richter, 1971a:135). As a result, common "possession of women and children was practiced at Oneida via Noyes' unique plan of "multiple marriage." This was a form of group marriage by which everyone could consider themselves married to everyone else. This way, everyone would have the opportunity to enjoy a wider range of satisfaction for their sexual desires. This would reduce the temptation for adultery and allow young people to satisfy their sexual appetites much sooner than they would be allowed in conventional marriages. Of course, the actual procedure for multiple marriage was quite complicated. A committee of men and women received applications from a member who identified someone they desired, and if the committee considered the pairing suitable, they arranged for the meeting or obtained a refusal, which was relayed to the applicant. It was a rule of the colony that no one had to receive the attention of someone they did not like (Webber, 1959:395).

In Noyes' view, multiple marriage should not be confused with licentiousness, because unlike the wanton fulfillment of sexual desires, multiple sexual unions were based on responsible action and on love, rather than lust. Any children born to such a union would naturally become the responsibility of the colony as a whole. Noyes contended that modern civilization had corrupted the meaning of marriage and clouded true relations between the sexes. Since sexual relations were deemed to be second in importance only to the relation of humans to God, the matter was in need of serious attention. Salvation was possible only if the traditional view of sexual relations was modified. After that, attention could be given to industrial matters.

In order for Noyes' view of multiple marriage to be effective it had to be controlled. Noyes saw it as essential that two related practices be introduced, namely "male continence" and "mutual criticism." Male continence simply meant that males were not allowed to bring the sex act to completion (ejaculation) during intercourse. Men were expected to control themselves during the sex act until women had one or two orgasms, and then withdraw without ejaculation. Rexroth (1974:212) suggests that various erotic yoga practices demonstrate that this form of self-control is quite viable, and it created a positive union.

Noyes reasoned that the practice of continence naturally avoided the danger of unwanted pregnancies, a safeguard that was particularly important during the early years when the colony was establishing itself economically. Such self-control would also allow men and women to enjoy "amative" or erotic love independently of propagative love.

"Mutual criticism" decreed that members had the right and were expected to criticize one another at meetings scheduled for that purpose. It was expected that individuals would be grateful to have their shortcomings and failings pointed out in general meetings so they could improve themselves and grow as human beings. The practice was designed as a form of therapy and substitute for backbiting. The end result would be moral improvement and more effective community functioning.

At Oneida, young boys in their early teens were usually matched up for their first sexual experience with an older woman who had reached menopause. This way pregnancy was not a likelihood and such matches were continued until the boys learned to practice continence. Young girls were taught that their first sexual experience was very special because it was believed that unlike boys, they probably would be less inclined towards self-gratification through the act. Noyes himself often initiated very young girls to this privilege, sometimes targeting children who were so young that he was eventually accused of pedophilia and had to flee to Canada to escape being charged under the law. Strong disapproval was expressed toward young couples who sought to cling to a particular partner their own age, thus voiding the value of regarding everyone as equals in the group-marriage plan. Special love for one particular person was the worst sin an Oneidan could commit, although Noyes seemed to have shown special favor towards a certain Mrs. George. She seemed to have privileges that other women in the commune did not have. The Noyes and the Georges spent a great deal of time together as couples at Willow Place in Brooklyn, New York, which consisted of two neighboring houses that had been joined together to form a publishing house (Webber, 1959:398).

Noyes targeted diet as another mode of attaining health and happiness, and mandated that his people become vegetarians. They were allowed to eat only two meals a day, accompanied by tea or coffee. Alcohol and tobacco were forbidden. Noyes believed that disease was a result of imperfect living and healing was to occur via a combination of group therapy (mutual criticism) and faith healing. Clothing worn by the Oneida folk was plain and conventional. Women wore short hair, skirts to the knee, and a good deal less underwear than was the custom. As with clothing and food practices, daily life at Oneida was governed by a series of built-in checks, and controls designed to prevent, abort, or cure every vestige of selfishness and acquisitiveness.

John Humphrey Noyes

John Humphrey Noyes was born in Brattleboro, Vermont, on September 3, 1811. When he was six years old his family moved to Dummerton, Vermont, where Noyes received his early schooling. He entered Dartmouth College at the age of 15, and the following year came under the influence of Charles Finney, a Congregational clergyman. This was the period of the Great Awakening in America and revivalism was flourishing. On July 1, 1832, Noyes wrote in his diary, "On the 18th of September 1831, I gave my heart to God. This was with much delight and . . . I became so much absorbed in meditation on the goodness of God and on the novelty of my situation, that my mind seemed to lose its faculty of self-control" (Noyes, 1923:42). Noyes was convinced that he was called to preach the Gospel so he enrolled at Andover Seminary to fulfill that goal. Convinced that he would be offered more profound studies at Yale Theological Seminary, he transferred there for his second year.

Noyes's heretical side came out while he was still a theological student. When he countered an orthodox belief in conversation with his father one day, the elder Noyes warned, "Take care, that is heresy. If you get out of the traces, the ministers will whip you in." John replied, "Never will I be compelled by ministers or any one else to accept any doctrine that does not commend itself to my mind and conscience" (Noyes, 1923:69). Thus the stage was set for the alternative theological beginnings of the Oneida community.

In 1845 Noyes and his followers formed the Association of Perfectionists at Putney, Vermont, but moved to Oneida, New York three years later. There they purchased 40 acres of land and a run-down house; they later established communities at Wallingford, Connecticut; Newark, New Jersey; Cambridge, Vermont; and Manlius, New York, but their communal activities were concentrated at Oneida. By 1848 Noyes' followers numbered over 200, and they worked hard to raise their community from its substandard condition. They grew crops and sold them, and ran a sawmill and a blacksmith shop. They invented animal traps, first making them by hand and later manufacturing them to the point that they comprised a major Oneida enterprise. Twenty-five years after they began, Oneida was a very profitable company, employing a number of domestic servants. In 1874 their membership peaked at 300 people, with an accumulated wealth of half a million dollars in property.

Oneida Shifts

The Oneida community experienced a golden age during the 1860s when they built a huge mansion, and Noyes decided that it was time for the colony to increase its population. The Oneida mansion still stands as a monument to the ingenuity of the commune. Constructed between 1861 and 1914, it is 93,000 square feet in area and today houses a museum, lecture hall/performance center, 35 apartments, eight guest rooms, and a dining room. It is currently operated as a historic site, private residence,

7.1   Oneida Community Mansion today, Oneida, New York

and conference center. It is open to the public for guided tours, meals, and overnight lodging.

Noyes' plan to increase the Oneida population was unusual from the start. In fact, it was probably America's first experiment in selective breeding. Noyes called it "stirpiculture," or scientifically planned procreation, and if properly implemented, it would hopefully produce superior specimens of human beings. Of course, children had been born at Oneida before this, but they were considered "accidents," or perhaps the result of the activity of a young couple who chose to defy colony laws and take matters into their own hands. When Noyes made his announcement about selective breeding, 53 young women volunteered to take part in the experiment. Eventually 58 stirpiculture babies were produced. The fact that Noyes himself sired nine of these children and his son, Theodore, fathered eight is a good indication that the committee that approved the selection of males and females for the experiment regarded Noyes' biological and intellectual characteristics at least as highly as he did himself.

During the glory days of Oneida, Noyes insisted that his members spend several hours a day in religious discussion, study and contemplation. By 1864 he was encouraging clubs for mutual improvement, and suggesting that his followers experiment with "how to spend Sunday in a scientific manner" (Carden, 1998:91). He even encouraged them to give attention to spiritualism, something that had been off limits 30 years earlier. As John Noyes began to age, his leadership was questioned by those who thought they could handle the job better. One such man was James W. Towner, who had joined the commune in 1874 and who eventually hoped to replace Noyes. As the time neared, Noyes surprised him by naming his son, Theodore Noyes, a physician and a declared agnostic, as president.

The appointment of Theodore Noyes as leader did not last long because he was not fully committed to Oneida philosophy. He was also not reliable. Right from the beginning he insisted that he must be free to think and act for himself. Twice, first in 1873, and again in 1878, he left the community with the declared intention of seeking his fortune elsewhere, and twice he returned and requested to be readmitted to membership (Robertson, 1972:33). When he temporarily assumed leadership of Oneida, Theodore began by demanding hourly work reports of the members, and he refused to live in the community since he and his wife were an "exclusive" couple. His father again took over the reins of rule and advised his followers to abandon the communal way of life, including group marriage, in order to save what was left of their organization. Many were shocked at the elder Noyes' command. Theodore Noyes served as president until the community reorganized to become a joint-stock company. They also shifted their product line from traps to tableware, which proved to be very successful. Oneida heirs still manage the company and retail excellent silverware. In August 2003 the company was worth $106.3 million.

As Oneida came to an end, company shares were divided among the members, with some selling their shares to other shareholders so they could leave town. For some members the adjustment was particularly hard since they were personally handling money for the first time. Another challenge was for couples to organize themselves into families of some sort. This was particularly complicated since some children were unable to identify their parents. Children were expected to go with their mothers, who sought to find consensus with some male in the exercise of monogamy.

Noyes himself faced the prospect of criminal charges of statutory rape being filed against him by the state of New York. As young girls in the colony experienced their first menstruation, they were immediately introduced to "complex marriage," and usually had their first sexual experience with the "first husband" in the commune, namely John Humphrey Noyes. Medical examinations by Dr. Van de Walker in 1877 confirmed that of a group of 42 women whom he examined, 23 had been introduced to sex at ages ranging from 10 to 18 years. The average age for initial intercourse was just over 13 years (Carden, 1998:100).

In order to avoid criminal action against him, and with his plans known only to two trusted friends, stealthily in the night John Humphrey Noyes fled 200 miles north into Canada on June 22, 1879. His granddaughter, Constance Noyes Robertson, suggests that he may have fled in order to draw the fire of critics away from his community so that they might be left in peace (Robertson, 1972:111). Noyes died in Niagara Falls, Ontario, on April 16, 1886, surrounded by a small company of former followers. His body is buried at Oneida and bears only his name and the dates, 1811–1886.

The financial success of the Oneida silverware company did not happen overnight. Like other utopian ventures such as Amana, Harmonists, Shakers, and Zoar, Oneida faced the difficult challenge of adjusting nineteenth-century business methods to modern ones. By the last decade of the nineteenth century, American industry had expanded considerably and any rising firm had to take advantage of improved mechanical skills, newly developed production processes, and more modern promotional and distributional techniques. Enmeshed in outmoded practices, Oneida's directors had to scurry to meet the challenges of rapidly changing times. The man for the time was Pierrepont Burt Noyes, stirpicult son of John Noyes and Harriet Maria Worden. In 1893, Pierrepont and his half-brother, Holton V. Noyes, began a successful business called Noyes Brothers, Wholesalers of Silverware and Novelties. In 1894 he became a director of the Oneida company and shortly thereafter, superintendent. It was he who convinced the board of directors to stop making animal traps and concentrate on tableware.

The Oneida commune provides a good example of cultural relativism. Noyes was able to justify his beliefs and practices within the parameters of the community and ignore the value frame of the greater society. Oneida's appeal was limited because its value system was so far removed from the American mainstream, but it broke new ground in demonstrating that radical alternative lifestyles could be quite feasible. Common sense dictates that even if Oneida were functioning today its antics would probably be ignored by a significant portion of the population.

CHAPTER 8

TWENTIETH-CENTURY COMMUNES

The nineteenth century witnessed an upsurge of utopian activity, which continued well into the next century. The dream did not die. In many regions of North America, the formation of intentional communities proceeded with the same degree of speed and enthusiasm as it had before. From 1850 to 1950, for example, the state of California witnessed the formation of a larger number of utopian experiments than any other state in the union. During this period at least 17 new utopian groups emerged, 6 of which were religiously based and 11 of which were secular. Contributing factors to this phenomenon included vigorous bursts of population growth caused by the Gold Rush of the 1880s, as well as the economic boom of the 1920s. California's attractive climate also brought in large numbers of elderly and retired people who were frequently lured into retirement schemes advertised as panaceas. The railroads, real estate promoters, and chambers of commerce likely contributed to population growth with their lavish descriptions of the oceanside climate, fertile soil, and luxurious living conditions (Hine, 1983:10). While California continued to beckon utopians into the latter half of the twentieth century, other parts of the country were also playing host to groups wanting to develop what might be termed unorthodox but promising social structures.

BACK-TO-THE-LANDERS

The decade of the 1960s was probably the most interesting of the twentieth century in terms of giving birth to a myriad of social movements emphasizing civil rights, government protests, religious realignments, and alternative lifestyles. The back-to-the-landers comprise one segment of this philosophical orientation, representing both a breakthrough in agrarian pursuits as well as a protest movement.

The underlying philosophy of the back-to-the-land movement involved disillusionment with what was described as the treadmill of American middle-class living. The tedium of urban life was too much for these reformers, and though they often liked to combine the best of both worlds, urban and rural, no adequate characterization exists by which to describe them all. In fact, in his original research on the movement, Jacob (1997) identified seven different interpretations of the "going back to the land" orientation. His typology includes the following breakdown: weekenders, pensioners, country romantics, country entrepreneurs, purists, microfarmers, and apprentices.

According to this typology, "weekenders" are people who have full-time jobs in nearby urban centers but like to spend their weekends working on plots of land they have purchased. These individuals maintain a homestead in the country and spend all of their free time working on their rural properties. Sometimes they ride horses, mend fences, prune orchards, shear sheep, grow gardens, or make improvements to their buildings. They often spend more time working on their homesteads than they do at their jobs. When vacation time comes, they are apt to spend their time in the country.

Pensioners may be divided into two categories, and are usually retired people. There are "snowbirds" who work as farmers during the summer, then migrate to warmer climates in the wintertime. The other type of retired back-to-the-landers devote all of their energies to building up a self-reliant homestead, to which they can eventually retire (Jacob, 1997:70). This group is characterized by limited incomes; these are people who are finally able to realize the lifelong dream of living in the country. Having a pension to fall back on enables them to make small improvements to properties they manage without having to seek additional employment. Self-sufficiency is a basic goal and includes growing much of their own food and cooking on a wood stove.

The country romantics are small landholders who like to spend as much time in the country as possible. They place a great deal of emphasis on the joy of country living and take a casual attitude towards systematically exploiting it for a cash income. They spend little time in looking for outside work, trying to make do with what they can raise or make themselves. Some of them may have part-time jobs away from home or even run a small business. Philosophically, they tend to be carefree and serendipitous in outlook, always preferring to let nature take its course. They are closely linked to the country entrepreneurs, who are fulfilling their lifelong dream of owning and operating a small rural business. Since many small business establishments fail because of competition from larger companies, these entrepreneurs pride themselves on having their land to fall back upon. As a backup, the land can be used to produce agrarian products both for family use as well as for sale.

The purists best fit the stereotypical image of this movement. Their homesteads in many ways resemble the pioneering efforts of a century ago. These individuals are almost completely self-sufficient in terms of food, clothing, utilities, and shelter. They use natural materials for constructing buildings, grow their own gardens, heat their homes with wood, and essentially see no distinction between work and play. In fact, work is often conceived of as a kind of sacred trust. They achieve complete fulfillment from their relationship to the land rather than as participants in the consumer culture of the dominant society. The back-to-the-landers of this category take many of their ideas, especially in the realms of environmental stewardship and worship, from an imagined, idealized concept of Aboriginal life. The word "tribe" is commonly used to describe the social groupings of this orientation (Scott, 1997:206).

The microfarmers are defined by Jacob (1997:57) as individuals who are committed to operating intensive small-scale productions that often function year-round. These entrepreneurs are ready to relinquish family independence by entering the marketplace full-time. In reality, they are small-scale free enterprisers who like to be in control of their own companies. Making one's own living on one's own terms and in accordance with one's own schedule is for them the fulfillment of the ultimate dream.

Naturally, this option means keeping up with the latest in technological developments because the competitive, fast-paced world demands it.

Finally, the last category of back-to-the-landers are labeled apprentices, a group best portrayed as learners. These would-be rural dwellers often come in on the heels of established back-to-the-landers who are willing to teach them the ropes. At times they procure positions as hired hands, working for room and board or even for free. In more fortunate circumstances, they may be supported by a government grant or program that teaches farming skills.

Over the past decades the back-to-the-land movement has emerged as a less unique lifestyle and adopted more structural characteristics. Activist roles, which were once a real part of the movement, have been substituted by efforts to get on with life. It is evident that back-to-the-landers have the kinds of educational credentials and professional experience that could make them valuable activists working on behalf of their communities. Jacob (1997:16) suggests that by working their farms, there is little time or energy left to get involved in community organization.

Gradually, a form of institutionalism has developed in the back-to-the-land movement. As an example, the *Georgia Straight,* a Vancouver publication venture, serves as a bulletin board and clearinghouse for would-be communalists in British Columbia. More traditional methods of operation have given way to more modern (albeit ecologically safe) devices such as solar power, composting toilets, photovoltaic cells, and retrofitted superinsulation. Some formerly strong proponents of the movement have discovered that the back-to-the-land alternative is only one route by which to achieve a sustainable future. It may constitute the fulfillment of the utopian dream for some, but it will also be subject to constant examination and revision.

BRUDERHOF

The Bruderhof, also known as the Society of Brothers, is essentially a copycat version of the better-known Hutterite society discussed in the next chapter. Initially this group called themselves the Hutterian Society of Brothers, but they have since been forbidden by law to use the term Hutterite. The Bruderhof originated in Germany in 1920 as a protest group against organized religion and the orthodox manner of interpreting the Scriptures. The founder was Eberhard Arnold (1883–1935), whose father, Carl Franklin Arnold, was a theology professor. The younger Arnold studied theology at Breslau University and became convinced that the Christianity of his day fell far short of the biblical mandate. As Baum (1996:41–42) notes, "Eberhard believed that a life in discipleship of Jesus Christ affirms life in a comprehensive sense—more encompassing and complete. . . . For Eberhard, belief in Jesus meant affirmation of life, not at all yearning for death. . . . affirmation of the body, not self-chastisement or contempt of sexuality, and affirmation of nature and its gifts, not false asceticism." In Eberhard's estimation, Christians were not sufficiently committed to living the Gospel of Jesus Christ as they should be. Not content merely to criticize Christian practice, he decided to devise an alternative form of communal living. Although initially successful, his experiment was eventually dissolved by the Gestapo (Eggers, 1988). He was then forced to relocate to Liechtenstein, then Holland, and eventually England. Later a Bruderhof community was established in Paraguay, but later disintegrated. By 1998 the group numbered about 2,000 with six communities in the United States, and one in Sussex, England (Hofer, 1998:133).

Creed and Activities

Essentially Christian in character, the Bruderhof must be regarded as an alternative Christian organization. Bruderhof theology tends to be conservative in print, but liberal in practice. Eberhard Arnold combined a multiplicity of sources in framing his theological stance including Anabaptist writings, the Salvation Army, Hutterites, and the Student Christian movement (Baum, 1996). Contemporary writings published by the Plough Publishing Company still reflect orthodox Christian beliefs, although some Bruderhof practices seem not to coincide with these. Hofer (1998) reports that Bruderhof elder Christoph Arnold personally carries a gun, allegedly for protection. This habit would not be approved by the

Hutterian Brethren whom the Bruderhof tried to copy. In addition, Hofer (1998:139) notes that "[t]he Bruderhofs have purchased a corporate jet and have been reported providing flights for the likes of Eddie Van Halen (glamour rock star) and Sharon Stone (of *Basic Instinct* movie fame) to many destinations." According to conservative Christian apologists, these are not the kinds of connections that orthodox Christians would make (Hofer, 1998:131).

French and French (1975:175) report that the residences in the various Bruderhofs they visited apparently afforded a pleasant environment; all rooms were brightly painted and all activities were undertaken with togetherness and joy. The sounds of choral and chamber music filled the halls in the evening, and individuals accorded the same attitude of enjoyment to their work as to their forms of entertainment. This was not our experience, since we had not made an appointment when we visited the Bruderhof in Farmington, Pennsylvania. Despite a request to visit some of the group buildings, we were only permitted to enter the visitor's center, which contains a bookstore and coffee shop.

Two primary sources of income for the Bruderhof communities in the United States are a factory (Community Playthings) that makes children's toys and the Plough Publishing Company. The toy factory manufactures a wide range of sturdy wooden toys such as blocks, trucks, chairs, tables, trains, gas stations, and slides. All aspects of production are done on site, including initial cutting of the wood, planing, varnishing, assembly, inspection, and shipping. The work of the publishing company is distributed between the Rifton, New York, and Farmington, Pennsylvania communities, the former being assigned the editing, designing, and distribution, and the type being set and books printed in Farmington. Many if not most of the published works are by the three Arnolds—Eberhard, his son Heini, and his grandson Christoph.

Although work is deemed to be a sacred trust and a vital part of the Christian obligation, it does not dictate the essence of one's daily tasks. French and French (1975) reported that during a visit to the Rifkin Bruderhof on a very beautiful summer day, they were surprised to find that the factory was closed down and everyone was outside enjoying a game of baseball. Together the workers had decided that the day was too pleasant to be wasted at the assembly lines so they shut down production and went outside to play. Enjoying life, it seems, is as important to the colony as getting things done. This same Bruderhof also made the decision to maintain production even though their share of the market was rising. By maintaining production instead of increasing it, they could work at a more moderate pace and they would not have to hire outside help.

The various colonies of the Bruderhof are tightly organized in terms of administration. A formal hierarchy exists by which roles and tasks are defined. Women called "housemothers" allocate rooms and personal supplies such as toothpaste, candy, and clothing. Work distributors assign jobs, and one or more "Servants of the Word" (lay ministers) provide spiritual guidance and help resolve personal conflicts. A senior elder presides over the Servants of the Word. Not all activities are dictated, however, for many daily decisions are simply decided by a group of people at a particular location. More important decisions are brought to a general meeting of all members.

Charisma plays a huge role in the Bruderhof. A case in point is the colony at Warwick, Massachusetts, which was begun in the late 1960s by a talented young man named Michael Metalica. As a youth he was both an honor student and drug user who had visions, which he claimed came from God and directed him towards a prophetic role. By 1971 he was the lead singer in a traveling rock band called "Spirit in the Flesh," and much admired by his worshippers in the Bruderhof. Under his leadership the colony soon built an attractive Swiss chalet-style dormitory; it, along with other buildings on the site, were kept very clean and cheerful. The establishment of a rock band seems a somewhat unusual enterprise for a group that had strict rules, but naturally all income accrued to colony coffers. According to Terjesen (1979), who visited there, Michael's influence in the settlement was so powerful that virtually everyone either began or ended their sentences with "Michael says." It became evident that Michael handled the finances for the colony and had veto power over all decisions made by the membership. Terjesen suggests that Michael's claim that he was both Saint Peter and General Robert E. Lee in former lives did not seem to bother colony adherents.

They also did not question his assertion that the world was on the threshold of an Aquarian Age, which will see the Second Coming of Christ.

Unlike the Amanas, Doukhobors, and Zoarites, Bruderhof members are forbidden to provide unauthorized information about the society to outsiders, and visits to the Bruderhof must be approved in advance. Tours by visitors are carefully monitored. When we (the authors) visited the Farmington Bruderhof in 1999, we requested to see the factory or the publishing house or one of the homes, and were told we would have to make an appointment. While we were conversing at the coffee shop with a friendly young woman about life in the settlement, she was suddenly called away. Two men appeared and informed us that they would answer any questions we might have about the Bruderhof. Once outside, I (John) took a picture of the visitor's center, and one of the men requested that I forfeit my camera to him, which I chose not to do. As soon as we could, we drove off. As Zablocki (1971:226–227) has noted, "It is curious that the Bruderhof is able to extend its net of observation so thoroughly over the community without giving the impression at all of being a totalitarian society."

The Bruderhof illustrates the interdependence between deep religious faith and successful communal living. This recipe can only be successful when carefully designed safeguards are in place. Applicants for membership, for example, must serve a minimum term of six months to a year in the community before they are officially admitted. Most applicants are not admitted on their first try, partly because the criteria for membership are very rigid and partly because such a process serves to weed out the weak.

Eggers (1988:192) lists five questions that are asked of prospective members. Answers given by applicants are judged by spiritual leaders within the Bruderhof. The questions that candidates have to answer may be summarized as follows:

1. Are you certain that this way of brotherly community based on a firm faith in God and Christ, is the way to which God has called you?

2. Are you ready to put yourself completely at the disposal of the church community of Christ to the end of your life—all your faculties, the whole strength of your body and soul, and your entire property?

3. Are you ready to accept every admonition and admonish others if you should sense within our community life something that should be clearer or would more fittingly bespeak the will of God?

4. Are you firmly determined to remain loyal and true, bound with us in mutual service as brothers and sisters, so that our love may be burning and complete in the building of the church community?

5. Are you ready to surrender yourself completely and to bind yourself unreservedly to God, to Jesus Christ, and to the community?

Zablocki (1971:66, 114) outlines three steps for novices to undertake in formalizing commitment to the Bruderhof. The first stage consists of the "stripping" ritual, in which the novice tries to rid himself or herself of their past affiliations. Talk about the past is discouraged but admitting to guilt feelings about past deeds is encouraged. As the old self is being renounced it is recast as a pitiful state, but there is hope of a new self emerging.

In the second stage the convert tries to formulate a new identity with emotional support and assistance from the group. He or she is assured that all members of the group once felt the same way. Members then share their own struggles and victories. Now the novice is called upon to reassess the former self and realign it to the group norm.

In the third stage the newcomer experiences the death and resurrection of "self," during which time a final confession is made and conversion is completed. The individual is now committed to be open to new growth experiences. It is only after undergoing this final stage that the individual is permitted to be baptized. At this point converts are required to make a lifetime vow and turn all of their personal property over to the colony. According to Zablocki (1971:264–267), the final rebirth of the individual occurs during the third stage.

Rosabeth Kanter (1972:71) points out that reinforcement for conversion usually includes sacrifice, investment, renunciation, communion, mortification, and transcendence. To illustrate this, in the Bruderhof communitarianism is accomplished through communal work activities, dancing and singing joyously together at meals which Terjesen (1979:279) described as a "soul stirring experience."

Deviant members can be treated quite harshly. Ruth Baer Lambach (1993:255), whose parents and siblings lived with the Bruderhof for a number of years, describes the Bruderhof approach to community reinforcement: "In Pennsylvania, after less than a year at the Bruderhof, they felt it best for my spiritual development that I experience the outside world. They took me to Pittsburgh, gave me twenty dollars, and dropped me on the street. I found a job and lived on the outside for nine months." Lambach claims that as a result of her being raised in both Hutterite and Bruderhof societies, despite 30 years on the outside, she still finds it difficult to meet her conflicting needs of individuality and community.

Eberhard Arnold

World War I brought home the horrors of war to many European countries. After the war, in Eberhard Arnold's estimation, Germany was in disarray. Those who were promoting the Christian faith were not of much help. Eberhard and Emma Arnold gathered together with a group of like-minded believers in an effort to seek an alternative way of presenting the Gospel as a positive and uplifting philosophy. After an initial thrust in 1920 to establish a colony (Bruderhof), six years later as many as 40 people met regularly for such a purpose. They searched for quarters where they could live together and celebrate their faith, and eventually chose a location near the Rhön Mountains, convinced that their experiment was led by the Spirit of God.

As the Nazi regime began to permeate Germany, laws were passed that all children had to attend compulsory German schools, which would indoctrinate them to a new way of thinking. As a result the Bruderhof sent their children to Switzerland and Liechtenstein. When conscription became mandatory, the Bruderhof saw to it that their young men were safely out of the country. Still, these pressures proved too much, and in

1937 the group migrated to England. The idea of a group of Germans moving to a country like England, which was at odds with Germany, had social and cultural repercussions, and the Bruderhof relocated to Paraguay in 1940. Here poverty and disease were their constant companions. When the group finally emigrated to America and established themselves at Rifton, New York in 1954, they were able to see the future in more promising terms. This particular colony also became known as Woodcrest, and the people as Woodcresters.

Eberhard Arnold died in 1935 and was succeeded by his son Heini, who served the Bruderhof until his death on July 23, 1982 (Mow, 1991). He was succeeded by his son, Christoph, who (as was told to the authors by an informant at Farmington, Pennsylvania), is presumably in hiding for fear of his life. Apparently Arnold believes that some Bruderhof expatriates might wish to do him harm.

Merger Moves

The Society of Brothers was initiated without first-hand knowledge of the Hutterian Brethren, although they had read literature about them. Eberhard Arnold visited the Hutterites of South Dakota in 1930, then spent a year with them, and ultimately became an ordained Hutterite minister. He returned to Germany and began reorganizing his community along the lines of the Hutterite lifestyle—clothing, worship patterns, child rearing practices, and so on. When his group migrated to Paraguay they were given financial support by the Hutterian community in hopes that the Bruderhof would eventually become faithful Hutterites. But suddenly it was discovered that the Bruderhof had no restrictions against practices that the Hutterites disdained, such as smoking, folk dancing, divorce, watching movies, letting women vote on colony matters, and participating in other unapproved "worldly" practices. Financial contributions to the welfare of the Paraguay Bruderhof discontinued and the colonies were shut down. In addition, in 1953 merger talks with the Hutterites were cancelled (Hofer, 1998:131).

In 1955, under the leadership of Heini Arnold, Eberhard's son, the plan to unite with the Hutterian Brethren was revived. One Hutterite

198 | THE PALGRAVE COMPANION TO NORTH AMERICAN UTOPIAS

colony, the Forest River Colony in North Dakota, which already had its share of dissident members, appeared to be interested in merger talks with the Bruderhof. A deal was struck, and soon 36 Bruderhof members arrived in North Dakota. Hofer (1998:132) describes them as "a group of eccentrics, intellectuals, dissident seekers of truth, and creative practitioners of radical Christianity." Soon the group took control of the colony and forced the resident preacher, Andreas Hofer, to return to his parent colony in Manitoba. Schmiedeleut Hutterite elders then stepped in and excommunicated the Bruderhofers, most of whom departed for the Woodcrester community in Rifton, New York. (The Schmiedeleut—"blacksmith people"—are one of the three groups of Hutterites who left Russia and settled in the United States in the early 1870s.) A few original members of the Hutterite colony remained and sought help from the Schmiedeleut conference to regain both their financial standing and spiritual connection.

Almost ten years passed; then in 1964, Heini Arnold visited the Schmiedeleut in Manitoba with hopes of reconciliation. He offered his personal apologies for developments before a meeting of 71 Schmiedeleut ministers, who ultimately approved a tentative merger between the two bodies. One minister, Jacob Kleinsasser of the Crystal Springs Schmiedeleut Colony, who later became bishop, was particularly impressed with the idea of merger and enthusiastically promoted it. By 1973 it appeared that the union would work, and as one observer put it, some Schmiedeleut were most impressed "with the childlike submission and unreserved obedience by the common people to an hierarchy-type government" (Hofer, 1998:133). Younger Hutterites were excited about the move since Bruderhof colonies allowed a lot of practices that their elders had always believed to be worldly. There was more openness among the Bruderhof and they were actively engaged in missionary work, something that Hutterites only talked about.

One of the reasons Jacob Kleinsasser favored a union between the Society of Brothers and the Hutterites was because he saw the day coming when the latter could not survive solely on agriculture. He surmised that in a shrinking society with a global economy, they eventually would have to enter other professions. He also liked the idea that the Bruderhof endorsed higher education. Surely they could serve as a model in these respects. In order to convince his constituents that the move was a good idea, Kleinsasser informed them that the advantage was in Hutterite hands; *they* would teach Christianity to the Bruderhof. However, many Hutterites disagreed with Kleinsasser's interpretation, and became concerned about the liberal ways of the Society of Brothers and their dictatorial manner of administration. When the opportunity came, they voted not to proceed with the merger.

In December, 1992, 160 Schmiedeleut ministers presented a list of 12 grievances against Kleinsasser and he asked for a formal vote of confidence. He lost, and subsequently the Schmiedeleut informed the Bruderhof that there would be no union. Consequently, a split in the Schmiedeleut camp divided them into two factions, those who followed Kleinsasser and those who did not. Events pertaining to the schism were closely watched by the outside world and caused much pain in the Hutterian community. A number of Mennonites (cousins of the Hutterites) followed these developments with great concern. As a final episode, the Schmiedeleut, under the leadership of Samuel Kleinsasser, Jacob's brother, published a tract explaining the failed union (Kleinsasser, n.d.).

Meanwhile, the Bruderhof attempted to give support to Jacob Kleinsasser, but they were hindered by two developments in their own circle. One was the formation of KIT (Keep in Touch), an organization begun by Ramón Sender, a former member of the Bruderhof, intended to broadcast unhappy stories of people who had left the society. More than 300 ex-Bruderhofers are on the mailing list (Hofer, 1998:138). Charges of cruelty and unfair treatment to women as well as other such topics are discussed in this publication. In 1997, the Bruderhof launched an unsuccessful court case against the KIT organization. Then for some reason the Bruderhof changed tactics and thanked Sender and KIT for the free publicity.

The September 1, 1995 issue of the *Kit Newsletter* labels the Bruderhof a totalitarian sect with serious cultic aspects. Alderfer (1995:194) suggests that the Bruderhof is in some respects a twentieth-century version of Ephrata. Both communes have drawn their share of negative press. Since its origins the Bruderhof has been charged with using severe punishment and repressive attitudes towards young people who showed a normal, early childhood curiosity about body parts and sexuality. During the 1960s this necessitated sending many young people to local psychiatrists and mental institutions, until the Bruderhof hired their own psychiatrist. The condition of these young people is tentatively called "The Society Syndrome." Young boys were allegedly beaten in the commune by Bruderhof overseers, and at one time several of them were hit in the face as punishment. There are reports of youth who underwent deep depression, some of whom were taught, even as children, that they were harboring evil spirits within them. One boy was apparently struck so severely that he suffered severe flashbacks for the next 25 years *(Kit Newsletter,* September 1, 1995).

A second anti-Bruderhof development was the publication of a book by Elizabeth Bohlken-Zumpe, a granddaughter of Eberhard Arnold. In *Torches Extinguished,* Bohlken-Zumpe claims that the Bruderhof have disregarded her grandfather's teachings and have developed into a "cult." Following publication of the book, an exodus of Bruderhof members ensued, some willingly and others through excommunication. Ironically, Eberhard Arnold, founder of the Bruderhof, once suggested that the first generation of any utopian enterprise has the spirit; the second generation has a good example to follow; and the third generation has only a vivid memory. By the time the fourth generation takes control they are stuck with all the rules and regulations that are left and, according to Arnold, turns them into a sect or a cult.

The late John Hostetler, former anthropologist and Professor Emeritus at Temple University, was at one time a supporter of the Bruderhof, and published a forward in one of their books (Eggers, 1988). On investigating the group further, he had a change of mind and published a pamphlet entitled *The Society of Brothers who call themselves Hutterites: Some Personal Concerns.* Hostetler described some of the actions of the society against its members as totalitarian, especially the act of intensely interrogating children. Raised in an Amish community, Hostetler was well acquainted with the restrictions on individuality in closed communities. He could not, however, in any way reconcile the self-annihilating tactics of the Bruderhof even with what he had experienced as an Amish youth.

The reality of Bruderhof growth underscores the fact that even unorthodox formats for the fulfillment of utopian dreams still appear attractive to some members of society. Sadly, some of them develop cult-like characteristics which no longer classify them as utopian. There is reason to believe that unless more humane alternatives can be developed, this trend will continue.

THE FARM

Dozens of communes were founded in the United States during the 1960s, many of which are still in operation. One of the longest lasting is The Farm, a community of 250 people in Summertown, Tennessee. This utopia was envisioned by a group of "hippies," as they were called, in the late 1960s and established in 1971 (Scott, 1997:192). The Farm is a cooperative enterprise of families and friends living on three square miles in southern middle Tennessee. It started in the hope of establishing a strongly cohesive, outwardly directed community, a base from which the group could, by action and example, have a positive effect on the world (Bates, 2000).

The Farm was inspired by Stephen Gaskin (born in 1935), an instructor at San Francisco State College. Gaskin was in charge of a lecture class on cultural upheaval, which was attended by thousands in search of meaning and peace. Each class began with group meditation, and included lectures about the highlights of major world religions, and endless discussions about building alternative social structures. When Gaskin decided to expand his following, a caravan of converts followed him to Tennessee, where they purchased 2,000 acres and built The Farm. At its peak the community consisted of 1,500 people (Miller, 1999).

Today The Farm consists of 1,750 acres of rolling farmland on which there are 27 multifamily dwellings. All buildings utilize solar energy and are designed for energy efficiency. Many members sustain themselves by working in nearby towns or on site. They pay rents ranging from $75.00 to $125.00 per month, depending on what the group decides is needed at its regular townhouse meetings.

Beginnings

The established philosophy of The Farm is to live a simple lifestyle much in the tradition of the Amish. Initially Farm members even nicknamed themselves "Amish in Technicolor." One major departure from Amish ways when the group started was to grow marijuana, an offense for which Gaskin and three others spent a year in jail. Today the group continues to adhere to the idea of living in harmony with nature and places a great deal of emphasis on the protection of the environment. They are quite serious about wanting to save the planet from exploitation, and try to integrate their daily activities into the natural world in a way that is supportive of healthy human development and will successfully enable The Farm to continue into the indefinite future.

Members of The Farm community are strict vegetarians who avoid meat, eggs, milk products, honey, leather, and anything of animal origin. A major farm crop is soybeans from which they develop a series of marketable products. The group shuns abortion, and practices a form of natural birth control related to the rhythm method. Naturally, the colony has had a very high birth rate. They are so opposed to abortion that they once placed advertisements in local newspapers that read: "Hey Ladies! Don't have an abortion, come to The Farm and we'll deliver your baby and take care of it, and if you ever decide you want it back, you can have it" (Miller, 1999:121).

Farm Update

Today The Farm continues to operate in a relatively orderly fashion. Although members meet weekly for inspirational services of an interdenominational nature, they like to think of themselves as "Free Thinkers," because they discuss religion and philosophy in terms that do not exclude any possibilities (see www.thefarm.org). In addition to talks by Stephen Gaskin, group members participate in offering meditations of one kind or another. In keeping with their deep reverence for life, they are pacifists or conscientious objectors.

They operate a successful book publishing company, a solar electronics operation, a soyfood business, a medical clinic, an ambulance service, and a midwifery program. The latter program has been responsible for delivering more than 2,000 babies with outcome statistics significantly higher than hospitals. Cesarean rates, for example, are only 1.8 percent, compared with a hospital rate of 20 percent. However, they may also be catering to a very select clientele.

The underlying creed of the Farmites is simple: do what you can to save the earth and help your community members. To this end the standard of living at The Farm has always been quite modest. Miller (1999:121) suggests that living conditions at The Farm are not much better than that of Third-World countries. Gaskin has always served as a model for his people, never giving in to the temptation to demagoguery as most leaders of such experiments do. He has always lived at the same standard as his followers. When his loyal adherents built him a comfortable home, he refused to move into it, insisting that economic equality should be maintained in the colony. At one point a group of insurrectionists insisted that he step down as leader and he immediately did so. Still, he remained a staunch supporter of the community. It was because of this kind of leadership approach, as well as the commune's commitment to "make it work," that the colony has continued to this day.

In the early years of the experiment, like other hippie communes, members of The Farm experimented with the institution of marriage and practiced a very liberal sexual code. This practice has since been modified. At one point Stephen and Ina May Gaskin participated in what was called "four marriage," which consisted of two couples joining together as a marital union. Threesomes were also established, but the resultant complications proved to be too much. Eventually the colony decided to revert to a conventional form of marriage. Initially Farmites regarded conventional schooling with much the same attitude as they did marriage, so they built a private elementary school as well as a high school on the premises.

Changes

In 1974, The Farm founded an organization named Plenty, which was aimed at helping the poor in surrounding areas and aiding with disaster situations such as tornado damage. Workers representing Plenty also established an ambulance service at a much lower cost to patients than regular companies. They also experimented with developing ecologically sound technology such as passive solar construction, wind-powered systems, and electric automobiles. About a decade ago The Farm gained self-sufficiency in food production and established a construction company with 80 skilled craftsmen. They also built greenhouses, dry goods and grocery stores, and automotive welding, woodworking, and machine shops.

During the 1970s the era of the hippie movement came to an end, and The Farm did not escape unscathed. A crisis loomed when a worker was hurt and the commune faced a bill of $40,000 because they had no medical insurance. Many projects that had been operated at or below cost had to be curtailed and, left with no viable source of income, many members were forced to leave. Some of those who left were influenced by changing social values and gave in to the urge to live the good life offered by dominant society. Satellite communities established by The Farm had to be closed down. The organization found itself at a crossroads; should they go on as usual or try to reconstruct the basis of their operations? They chose to do the latter, and began by decollectivizing The Farm and charging monthly fees to their membership. This meant that members would need to go outside the community to look for jobs in order to pay their dues. This proved to be a very difficult task in a region of Tennessee where steady-paying jobs are a luxury. By 1983 the membership dropped to 225, and in 2003 stood at 250.

Despite these challenges Farm leaders labored on. During the 1990s they constructed a senior citizens' complex. They also built a visitors' center called the Ecovillage Training Center and some revenue is garnered from visiting tourists who come to learn about alternative building styles, solar power generators, hybrid vehicles, and passive solar heating and cooling. The Farm "helped launch the *Ecovillage Network of the Americas* (ENA), headquartered initially at The Farm Ecovillage Training Center. ENA links together the efforts of a wide variety of green communities, Eco-City projects, and incipient ecovillages to make the way easier for future ecovillagers and to lay the foundation for a major shift in Western consumer lifestyles across the broader culture" (Bates, 2000:4).

The Farm is one of a very few modern intentional communities with a sound economic base, inclusive philosophy, and positive future. They welcome visitors, who are asked to make reservations, and tours of the site are available. A "primitive" campground facility is available, as is modest lodging for a fair price. Swimming is available for a dollar per guest, and The Farm Store stocks an assortment of food and supplies. The Farm serves as a strong workable model for anyone wanting to design an alternative lifestyle in today's hurried world.

NEW AGE COMMUNES

A study by Popenoe and Popenoe (1984) reveals that the 1960s highlighted the origin of literally dozens of communes that sprang up within the counterculture, many of them based on New Age thinking. A few such organizations were begun earlier. This development has occurred in Australia, Great Britain, France, Israel, Japan, New Zealand, South Africa, and the United States. Examples of those in the United States include the Ananda Cooperative Village in the Sierra Nevada Hills of California, the Zen Center of Los Angeles, The Stelle Group in Illinois, The Renaissance Community of Gill, Massachusetts, The Abode of the Message in Mount Lebanon, New York, and the Rochester Folk Art Guild.

Ananda Cooperative Village

The Ananda Cooperative Village was founded in Nevada City, California in the 1940s by Paramahansa Yogananda, who considered himself the last of a line of great thinkers, including Krishna and Jesus Christ. Yogananda named the village "Ananda," which means "Divine joy" in Sanskrit. Yogananda envisaged that his village would become a gathering place for all religions and stressed such virtues as cleanliness, stewardship, and caring. Adherents were cautioned to avoid violence, greed, lying, stealing, and sensuality. When he died in 1952, one of his disciples, Donald Walters, established a second Ananda community.

Walters was soon ordained a monk and given the name Swami Kriyananda. He attracted a group of young people from the San Francisco area and managed to purchase 650 acres of land not far from the city. There he built a second Ananda Colony. The new community formulated a few rules, most of them spiritual in nature. Individuals were allowed to develop their own mores about sex, marriage and divorce. When they applied to the state to incorporate as a municipality, they experienced some opposition from locals who were not too enthused about having an unorthodox spiritual community in their midst. Eventually the Anandas gave up their goal and decided to leave things as they were. Still, they nursed the hope that soon the day would come when their movement would catch fire. The membership of Ananda grew to include 750 adult members with 70 children in its period of rapid growth during the 1970s, and has retained that number. Total membership today stands at 800 adults and children settled in seven locations in California, Washington, Oregon, Rhode Island, and Italy.

The aims and ideals of the World Brotherhood Colonies is to "spread a spirit of world brotherhood among all peoples and to aid in the establishment, in many countries, of self-sustaining world-brotherhood colonies for plain living and high thinking" (Ananda, 2002).

The Zen Center of Los Angeles

Zen is a form of Buddhism that has had strong appeal among intellectuals since the decade of the 1960s. The Zen Center of Los Angeles began in 1967, the prime mover being Bernard Glassman, who was an aeronautical engineer. Glassman began with a following of 15 people and together they raised enough money to purchase a $26,000 property. The resident priest was Taizan Maezum, and the lifestyle he advocated could best be described as voluntary simplicity. Still in operation, rules about moral behavior are generally quite relaxed at the Zen Center. A board of voting members run the affairs of the commune, guided by decisions made at town meetings. The commune runs several businesses such as a stitchery, a publishing center, a bookstore, and a medical clinic. A number of residents are Zen monks. The Zen Center conducts daily classes at their residential community, offering both short-term and long-term training. Current membership of the Zen Center ranges between 75 and 100 (WaterWheel Web Edition, 2003).

The Stelle Group

The Stelle Group consists of 44 privately owned houses with approximately 125 people. The theme of the organization is cooperation rather than communalism. The movement was founded in 1973 by Richard Kieninger and grew to 30 members by 1969. At one time the commune had over 200 members but personality conflicts reduced its size. The colony was fraught with factionizing from the beginning, but in 1970 managed to purchase 240 acres of land some 75 miles south of Chicago.

Several years ago the Stelle Group developed a water purification plant and started the Stelle Woodworking Corporation and Stelle Industries. Today no single organization oversees all aspects of community life. The Stelle Group considers itself as only one organization among many others with the principal mission to engage in educational and philosophical outreach through the promotion of books and tapes. Unique features of the Stelle Group include innovative ideas in social relations, education and science, and technology. Residents support themselves in a variety of ways, some through private businesses and others by working for the various associated industries. The fundamental goal of the organization is to assist individuals, within the sphere of the organization, in their ascent along the spiral of states of consciousness toward self-realization. Adherents can come and go as they please; they can seek guidance when they feel it appropriate to do so. Economic ventures are seen as a means to an end, but they must also be compatible with universe stewardship.

The Stelle Group is home to the Midwest sales office of SunWize Technologies, a solar power manufacturer. They also manage a plastics plant, an automatic screw machine company, and a printing operation (Popenoe and Popenoe, 1984:42). Related interests include holistic, preventive health practices, homeopathy, nutrition, kinesiology, herbology, mental and emotional balancing, and physical fitness.

The Stelle Group's unique cooperative educational center has attracted the interest of pedagogues from around the globe. Never a large group, the inhabitants number about 100. According to their website, most participants are actively expanding their love and awareness of inclusiveness. On Monday nights members partake of a shared dinner for fellowship and share information about community operations (The Stelle Group, 2002).

The Renaissance Community

The story of the Renaissance Community is an unusual one. In 1968, 17-year-old Michael Metelica and a group of other teenagers decided to live together in a tree house that they had built in the woods near Leyden, Massachusetts. They based their bond on love, excitement, friendship, and openness, and eventually took the name Brotherhood of the Spirit. Other young people joined them in such numbers that the group soon had to build a cabin to accommodate everyone. However, that was not enough. By the summer of 1973 they had 365 members. Two years later they changed their name to the Renaissance Community. Metelica changed his name to Michael Rapunzel after the fairy tale by that name. Rapunzel became a rock musician and claimed to have visions pertaining to being the reincarnation of St. Peter and Robert E. Lee. The Renaissance Community experienced success during the 1970s, but in the years that followed, like many other New Age communes the group lost many members, eventually shrinking to less than 100. Rapunzel died in 2003 at the age of 52.

The philosophy of the original community was that everyone would work at whatever jobs they could find in nearby communities and contribute their funds to the cause. Originally many of the members were musicians, so they formed a number of touring groups. They soon discovered that this nomadic kind of lifestyle was not the best way to build an organization. They built a recording studio and started a business to convert old buses into touring motels. Later a performance theatre was added, followed by a natural foods restaurant, a grocery store, and a youth center. All industries were developed with a keen eye for conservation, respect for the environment, and spirituality.

Today, the group remains philosophically reflective of the 1960s. All gatherings are begun with an "attunement" session emphasizing group meditation. Religious services for reflection, working out conflicts, and decision making are held three times a week. Governing is by consensus (Kraft, 2003).

The Abode of the Message

In 1910 an Indian musician, Murshid Inayat Khan, began a spiritual movement called the Sufi Order of the West. Emphasizing the close link between the physical and spiritual realms, Khan urged his followers to discover the true meaning of life in every sphere of activity. He was succeeded by his son, Pir Vilayat Inayat Khan, who, together with a group of followers, purchased a piece of ground in Mount Lebanon, New York in 1975. They named their new venture the Abode of the Message (meaning "place of truth"), and soon attracted 75 members.

Although the plan was to operate an egalitarian system, when some members complained of contributing more than others, the group moved to a more individualized format. A number of industries enabled the commune to operate a bakery, a Volkswagen repair shop, an alternative energy company, a food distributing company, and a health center. Later the commune switched to a more agrarian base and concentrated on growing vegetables, fruits, and grain crops.

In 1981, a large segment of members departed for Santa Fe, New Mexico, but the remaining members persisted. Three years later the membership of the Abode of the Message was 60 adults and 20 children, with an annual turnover of 10 to 15 percent. Their numbers have remained fairly stable through the years. Today their plant consists of a cluster of Shaker buildings dating from the 1800s located in the Taconic-Berkshire Mountains of upstate New York. On site are a series of buildings such as a gathering hall, and rooms for short-term rental. A secluded campground is available for rest nearby. Most residents work in the surrounding areas and pay a monthly board-and-room fee. Spiritual activities are held daily in the meditation hall and the Abode also offers weekly classes and frequent summer retreats. Since the commune does not demand a particularly high level of commitment due to its emphasis on individualism, there is no guarantee that it will expand in the future.

The Rochester Folk Art Guild

In the fall of 1957, a number of artists gathered in New York State to form a community to learn and practice the principles of inner development formulated by George S. Gurdjieff (1866–1949). Gurdjieff was a charismatic Greco-Armenian born in Russia, where he established The Institute for the Harmonious Development of Man in 1919. He promoted a litany of mystical notions about the universe that he claimed he was taught by wise men in Central Asia. He later relocated his organization to France and traveled and lectured in Central Europe.

Mrs. Louise March, the guild's founder, worked with Gurdjieff in Switzerland, then began the Rochester Folk Art Guild with 12 members. The group purchased a farm in the heart of New York's Finger Lakes Region near Middlesex, New York, and called it East Hill farm. They divided maintenance responsibilities, which are occasionally up for review. A new Japanese-style country home was built in 1975, with all of the work done by members. Many members have contributed large amounts of time and energy to maintain and develop East Hill Farm and to establish the guild as a renowned center for quality craftsmanship.

The objectives of the community are to link the material and spiritual elements of life in art forms, with little emphasis on financial gain. Activities include a variety of art, with performances, exhibitions, concerts, and demonstrations. The governance and financial makeup of the commune is a mixture of democracy and individualism: new members are never recruited, although individuals may apply. The guild is incorporated as a not-for-profit educational organization and is supported by its sale of crafts, contributions of members and friends, and educational programs it provides on an ongoing basis. The small membership of a few dozen has remained constant (The Rochester Folk Art Guild, 2002).

The Church Universal and Triumphant

The Church Universal Triumphant (CUT) was begun in the late 1950s by Mark Prophet, an Army Air Corps veteran from Chippewa Falls, Wisconsin, and his wife, Elizabeth. Although raised in a Pentecostal church, Prophet took up with a New Age group in Washington, D.C. known as Summit Lighthouse. Elizabeth joined Mark in his search for the truth by rejecting her family's affiliation with Christian Science. Together the pair formed the Keeper of the Flame, based on the assumption that America was in need of spiritual realignment. The group moved to Colorado Springs in 1966, then to Malibu, California, and ultimately to Montana in the mid-1980s. When Mark Prophet died in 1973 his wife took over his position as leader and reconfigured the movement to its later format as the CUT.

Essentially the CUT is an apocalyptic organization on the edge of mainline Christianity with New Age leanings. Elizabeth Prophet taught that America is in a mindset of moral and spiritual disaster, but she believed that regeneration was possible through her teachings. At its peak the movement attracted a mailing list of 25,000, only 5,000 of whom were considered communicants. Whitsel (2003) notes that CUT authorities do not currently release actual membership figures.

Elizabeth Prophet's philosophy included a vital concern about an impending disaster for America, and she predicted that a Russian nuclear missile would shatter the earth's surface in America on March 15, 1990. In view of this, the CUT purchased 12,000 acres of land in Montana near Yellowstone Park and built the Royal Teton Ranch. They dug and equipped dozens of underground bunkers and armed themselves. When the predicted disaster did not occur on the assigned date, hundreds of disillusioned members left the ranch. These individuals had invested all of their life savings in the underground "town" built by the CUT. Now they had nothing to go back to and they were extremely frustrated. Of course, Prophet later denied that she had predicted a catastrophic event, insisting that she had only said that there was "good potential" for such a disaster (Whitsel, 2003:118).

It is easy to glean a very negative view of Prophet's philosophy from Whitsel's rendition. Apparently Prophet believed that a "new dark ages" was upon America. She feared a growing world dictatorship, and suggested that a ruling elite was governing America. She believed that their policies were infiltrated by Satan. She described the world economy as declining, and seemed obsessed with socialism. She described the AIDS virus as a "genetic threat" to the continued spiritual evolution of the Lightbearers (her adherents) in a universe growing morally dim (Whitsel, 2003:114).

When the disaster prophesied by Prophet did not materialize and many members left, the CUT fell into desperate financial straits. Its leaders were forced to take drastic measures to pay their debts. This included reducing staff and selling off thousands of acres of land. The United States Forest Service bought half of the ranch holdings, about 6,000 acres, for $13 million. The move was prompted by the government's goal that no more development occur in the Yellowstone area. The CUT also had to struggle with the fact that Elizabeth Prophet divorced Edward Francis, whom she had married after Mark died. Already the mother of four children when she married Francis, at the age of 55, Elizabeth had a son, Seth, with Francis, two years before they divorced.

After being diagnosed with Alzheimer's Disease, on January 1, 1999, Elizabeth Prophet stepped down as leader of the CUT. Organizational leaders informed their membership that the "torch has been passed" and they should end their codependency with Elizabeth Prophet. In fall of that year, Prophet was legally declared to be an incapacitated person, and two guardians, one of whom was her daughter, Erin, were named as guardians.

After the catastrophe predicted by Elizabeth Prophet proved to be an empty prophecy, the CUT lost about one-third of its adherents. Membership decline continued through Prophet's divorce and failed health, and the new leaders decided to dilute aspects of CUT's theology. A corollary belief to the central doctrine of negativity about world conditions had motivated the CUT to stockpile weapons. In 1992, the U.S. Justice Department stripped the CUT of its tax-exempt status. After successful legal maneuvering, the CUT regained its nonprofit status in 1994, its lawyers arguing that the CUT had been the target of sustained religious bigotry.

The future of the CUT has at least temporarily been assured by successful international recruitment and restructuring. Biological succession has been ruled out since none of Prophet's four older children are affiliated with the organization. Two hundred worldwide teaching centers have been established to attract new converts.

WOMEN'S COMMONWEALTH

The history of the Women's Commonwealth of Texas (Sanctified Sisters) spans two centuries. Originating in the 1860s, the community kept up its spirit of hospitality until the last sister, Martha Scheble, died in 1983.

The Sanctified Sisters (or Sanctificationists) began as a religious group of zealous women who challenged male authority in the Protestant churches of Belton, Texas. Their leader, Martha White McWhirter (1827–1904), was born in Gainsboro, Tennessee. So strong were the Sanctificationists' convictions that they found it necessary to form their

8.1   McWhirter House, Belton, Texas

own communal organization in order to live out and preserve their anti-thetical belief system. The group challenged traditional female roles and experimented with new ideas about the relationship between men and women, childrearing, sexuality, and communal ownership of property. Their unique history leaves a rich and unique legacy in the areas of economics, religion, and politics (Chmielewski, 1993).

Beliefs

The fundamental underlying beliefs of the Women's Commonwealth are not explicitly spelled out in formal documents. Instead, the many writings (mostly letters) of Martha McWhirter and other members provide the basis for discerning their theological leanings. The belief system of the Women's Commonwealth was essentially orthodox Christianity, save for a few alterations and special emphases.

The doctrine of sanctification adhered to by the Woman's Commonwealth was not unique to them. Ecstatic religious experiences were quite common to the Texas frontier after the Civil War. Revival services, similar to those conducted by the Reverend Charles Finney of Oberlin College in the East, were all the rage in Texas. People who took up with these doctrines usually came from evangelical denominations whose creeds lent themselves to this kind of interpretation. The idea was that once individuals experienced rebirth through faith in Jesus Christ, their lives still required an additional cleansing. Often called "the Second Work of Grace," this event involved total commitment of the individual to the Holy Spirit. Once individuals yielded themselves completely to the will of God, they became sanctified, and they were somehow above sin.

All of the women who joined McWhirter's group claimed to have had such an experience. The Civil War was a contributing factor since it had severely upset peoples' lives. People were looking for something new, something to hang onto, and the times were changing. These were women who had carried the brunt of the breadwinning role while their husbands were away at war and were not sufficiently appreciated for their efforts when the men came back. The opportunity to join

McWhirter's group with its emphasis on sanctification gave them just the break they were looking for.

The principle of community was obviously strong in the Women's Commonwealth, partly because of their communal set up. McWhirter emphasized the virtues of honesty, frankness, sharing, and "feeling deep." The latter concept was interpreted to mean that members should never hide their feelings. If they were upset or displeased with a particular situation, they were encouraged to speak up. If relationships became strained, McWhirter blamed the devil, who always liked to interfere in human relationships. Members were warned that they would have to give themselves completely over to the will of God in her community. One rather suspects that McWhirter would have a ready interpretation for any situation in which God's will might not be immediately discernable.

Like most reformers of the day, it was McWhirter's opinion that church denominations were failing in their Christian practice. She set out to examine the error of their ways and illustrate what right living was all about. She once made the comment that "theologians are to blame for much of the evil and unhappiness from which people suffer in this world" (Kitch, 1993:246). It was McWhirter's perception that believers ought always to acknowledge the superior knowledge and power of God. A Christian community could be built on that principle alone and should not become convoluted through too much theological hair-splitting.

McWhirter drew a sharp distinction between the church and the world, the former being interpreted as the Women's Commonwealth community. In the world, men had all the advantages. It was a place where women were dominated, controlled, and exploited; it was a place where false, hollow values were practiced. Believers were cautioned to remain separate from the world and only interact with it on a selective basis.

Martha White McWhirter

In 1845, at the age of 18, Martha White married George McWhirter and took his surname. In 1855 the couple moved to Bell County, Texas, where they farmed for ten years and gave birth to 12 children. Later they moved to Belton, the county seat, and George served as a major in the Confederate Army. His army service assured Martha of a military pension when he died even though they divorced (Kitch, 1993:140). After his discharge George went into business and eventually owned a number of stores in Belton.

A religious woman, Martha McWhirter regularly attended the local Methodist church, and one evening as she was returning home from a prayer meeting, she became depressed. She was convinced that the meeting had been an empty ritual and her experience could just as well have been the work of God or the devil. The same negative thought kept bothering her for days, and she was unable to sleep at night. Desperately she prayed for sanctification, to be cleansed completely from all evil thoughts. She gathered a small group of women about her and together they prayed for the same result. Local church leaders were only mildly interested in McWhirter's concerns, and when the congregation moved into a new building, Martha's group remained in the old quarters. Eventually, the church saw McWhirter's efforts as a form of direct competition with their program and her group was subsequently locked out of the building.

In 1874, a number of Belton congregations banded together to build an interchurch edifice and McWhirter's group joined them. She became somewhat of a preacher in this new environment, though she was impatient with those who wanted to keep their denominational identity intact. The women began by sharing their materials resources, a practice that was strongly opposed by their husbands. In 1877, the McWhirter home became a haven for women, Martha having relegated her own husband George to the attic. She accused him of flirting with a hired girl and as a result of the dispute George never returned to the marriage bed. Eventually he moved to an apartment above a store he owned.

It was 1879, and the setting was arranged; the McWhirter home would be the location of the Women's Commonwealth. They began their treasury with the $20 savings of a sister who was a teacher in a local school (Chmielewski, 1993:59).

The Women's Commonwealth had a troublesome beginning. Several husbands were not exactly enthused with the movement, and a

8.2   Doorway where a warning bullet from a mob of angry husbands and outraged townsmen struck McWhirter House, February 13, 1880, Belton, Texas

group of them attacked the McWhirter house on the night of February 13, 1880. They were particularly upset that two men had joined the new commune, and gossip about their exact role in the house spread rapidly. A warning bullet was fired at the front of the house and the men, Matthew and David Dow, were taken out of the house and beaten. No one was ever punished for the incident. The record shows that the Dow men stayed in the commune for many years, always fulfilling a servile role. By 1883 there were 42 women in the community. When they joined, the women always brought their children, who were treated as full-fledged members.

During the first few years the Sanctificationists tried hard to be successful at their new arrangement. They hauled wood, took in laundry, sold dairy products, and did housework for their neighbors. Some women did not move into the commune but assisted from their homes. In 1885, the group purchased steam laundry equipment and took in washing from nearby Baylor College. They were not afraid to take jobs traditionally held by men. One sister, for example, directed the firewood business. They bought trees cut down for firewood for 25 cents a cord, then chopped, piled and loaded it, then sold it for $3 per cord. A steady income allowed them to add several houses on the McWhirter property and eventually build a hotel. Some of their wealth was accumulated through the purchase of property seized by the bank in foreclosure. This practice added to the consternation of male locals, who lost their property to the bank.

The first hotel venture of the Sanctified Sisters was the Central Hotel, which was built in 1886. Boarders were accommodated for $50 per month. Belton's economy boomed during the 1880s and the Sanctificationists benefited greatly. Always financially alert, they formed two holding companies, one for the hotel and the other for investments such as their two farms. All of these maneuvers were accomplished without legal sanction because women's property rights did not exist in the state of Texas until 1913. As Kitch (1993:44) points out, this accounts for the fact that the Women's Commonwealth property was registered in the name of *femes soles* before the law was passed. It also explains why prior to 1913, the sisters had made it a point not to purchase much property until their husbands were deceased.

By 1887, the year that Martha's husband George died, business at the Central Hotel was so successful that it took the energy of everyone in the group to maintain it. A second hotel was completed in 1892, and the locals were so impressed with the success of the Women's Commonwealth that they invited Martha McWhirter to sit on the Belton Board of Trade. She was the first woman in the state to serve. As business expanded, so did their reputation. The Women's Commonwealth was visited by representatives of the Shakers, and the Women's Commonwealth members returned the visit, as well as traveling to the Harmonists' colony in Pennsylvania. On one of her visits to a Shaker colony in New Hampshire, McWhirter lectured the women about equal rights. She had only been in the community for a day when it appeared evident to her that men were making all the decisions. Evidently McWhirter's preaching did not mar relations between the two communities, which kept in contact with one another for several years.

Leisure time in the Women's Commonwealth included instrumental and vocal music, painting, and reading. A reading circle was formed that was so successful that the commune donated 350 books to the local Belton library. A few sisters traveled, sometimes to represent the colony on business matters. One destination was the Chicago Exposition, for the purpose of learning more about improved farming techniques. Later travels were undertaken in order to find a new location for the colony.

As the Women's Commonwealth grew in prosperity, additional properties were purchased in Waco, Texas, and several businesses were established in New York state. Despite their steady growth, in 1895 a young woman, Susie Carter, became the first defector. She was the first in a long list of unhappy adherents who sought their fortunes elsewhere. Although reasons for her leaving are not clear, Susie's story suggests that the community focus could not meet younger members' needs. Indeed, daily life in a commune could appear to young women like Susie as dull as life in an ordinary family (Kitch, 1993:54). Although Susie returned to the commune a year later, McWhirter punished her by compelling her to get rid of all clothing she had accumulated during her absence. Susie remained with the Sanctified Sisters and became politically very active. In 1902 she and several colleagues participated in local suffrage associations and paid dues to the National Suffrage Association. For a time Susie served as secretary of the Federal Women's Equality Association.

Relocation

Even though the Sanctificationists eventually gained respect in the Belton community, in 1898 they decided to relocate, perhaps to retire or because Washington offered them a more stimulating environment. The exact reason for the move is not known to researchers, and in fact, some of the Sanctificationists' neighbors in Belton begged them to stay (Chmielewski, 1993:62). The women purchased a home in the Mount Pleasant suburb of Washington, D.C., and officially incorporated their commune as the Women's Commonwealth of Washington, D.C. They had never liked the name Sanctified Sisters, and so they made an official change of name. Their new residence contained both private rooms and communal quarters, and occasionally the sisters opened their home to boarders. Every woman did her share of domestic work and together they managed very well. In Washington the group became more visible to the media and a great number of articles were written about their activities.

Martha McWhirter died in 1904 and Fannie Holtzclaw took over leadership of the home. By 1910, only 18 adult women were left, but they continued to be financially successful through the sale of products from a farm they had purchased in Maryland. Most of the older members had died and the organization did not attract new members. The women sold garden produce, preserves, eggs, milk and butter, and a homemade wine called Koumiss. An added financial thrust consisted of cooking meals for customers from Washington. During the 1920s and 1930s, after the house in Washington was sold, the community members remained on their Maryland farm. The spirit of hospitality for which they became known in Belton was maintained until the last survivor, Martha Scheble, died in 1983. According to an attorney's estimate, Martha was worth about $170,000 in 1973, $70,000 of which was deposited in passbook savings accounts or stock investments. Ten years later her wealth had grown to a quarter of a million dollars (Kitch, 1993:112).

In many ways, the Women's Commonwealth broke new ground in establishing that nineteenth-century women could be financially successful on their own. The Women's Commonwealth was an organization designed for its time and place. According to observers, when the reforms it promoted were realized, its purpose had been fulfilled and it did not need to be maintained. The Women's Commonwealth experiment had immense influence on subsequent lawmaking and in recognizing women as full equals in society. As suffragettes, the Sanctified Sisters participated in a number of these activities and even formed their own organization, known as the Commonwealth Suffrage Association. As legislative changes occurred and public awareness of the need for sexual equality grew, the women were able to reduce their efforts for the cause. By 1904, most of the members were older, of course, and the record shows that they were minimally involved in the suffrage movement.

In large part the success of the commune and the quest for women's rights were due to the personal role of Martha McWhirter. Above all, she was committed to her community. This dedication, coupled with her upbeat personality and resolute philosophy, qualified her well for a leadership role. Though she probably did not know it, her name was added to the roster of major contributors to the women's cause in nineteenth and twentieth-century America.

A visit to the Belton Museum will provide an abundance of information and displays regarding the Women's Commonwealth. The McWhirter house is also available for inspection by appointment.

CHAPTER 9

HUTTERITE COMMUNALISM

*Ultimately, all utopias are doomed. The goal is unattain-
able, but also strangely relevant; only the journey towards the "good place" has true value.*
                        —*Andrew Scott (1997:17).*

It often happens that the diligent pursuit of a utopian vision can propel
individuals to such great motion that to observers it may appear that the
obvious has been bypassed. This is the case with the Hutterite Brethren,
whose atypical lifestyle appears to have satisfied generations with very
little adjustment in either belief or policy. Few of their members ever
question their way of life and they are quite happy to maintain it. In fact,
and not surprisingly, a closer examination of their unique way of life
shows the makings of a model by which to develop the primary elements
of utopian living. After all, the successful operation of a 471-year experiment ought to count for something.

The history of Jacob Hutter's followers is well-known to scholars of
utopian history since their organization is the longest-lasting form of
communalism known to modern times. Little is known about Hutter's
early life and the date of his birth is unknown (Peters, 1971:13). He was
martyred in 1536. Promoters of the Protestant Reformation like Martin
Luther, John Calvin, John Knox, and Ulrich Zwingli probably never
dreamed that the radical left wing of the movement could spawn an

enduring utopian segment like the Hutterites. Still, that is exactly what happened. In contrast with Scott's pronouncement above, Hutterites have endured for nearly five centuries and their colonies are currently experiencing rapid growth.

BELIEFS

In the early part of the sixteenth century in Central Europe, an Augustinian monk and Wittenburg professor named Martin Luther posted a series of reforms for the Roman Catholic Church, which resulted in the formation of the Lutheran movement (or Lutherans). Luther deplored the name, but his adherents adopted it. Luther's foundational doctrine that separated him from the state church was the notion that individual salvation occurs by faith alone, not by works nor by following church dogma and tradition. On January 3, 1521, a papal bull was issued against Luther, and although he was imprisoned for heresy, he did not change his mind about his beliefs.

Luther's proposals for reform were paralleled by many other priests, and many groups of separatists formed by following various leaders. The most radical wing of the Protestant Reformation, as it was called, were a group known as Anabaptists. Their leaders—Felix Manz, George Blaurock, Conrad Grebel, Dirk Philipps, and Menno Simons—renounced infant baptism, opposed war, refused to take an oath, and believed that the Sacraments should be regarded as mere symbols. They committed themselves to a life of strict discipleship, refused to participate in political events or hold office, and declared the Bible to be an open book to everyone (Friesen, 1993:126). Since Scriptural interpretation became a private affair, many splinter groups soon emerged. One such group, the Hutterian Brethren, or Hutterites, originated in 1530 over the issue of common property.

JACOB HUTTER

Following the Anabaptist penchant for individualism in biblical interpretation, in 1530, Jacob Hutter, a hatter by trade, gave literal meaning to the text, "All the believers were together and they had all things in common" (Acts 2:44). Quickly gaining a following, Hutter's people adopted his name and initiated a communal way of life, thereby causing a division in the Anabaptist camp. Hutter was a man of strong conviction with an aggressive personality, and was a strict disciplinarian. He followed Georg Blaurock as leader of the Tyrolean Anabaptist group and immediately advocated significant changes in congregational life. Hutter insisted that a complete break with the past was necessary; a communal way of life was the immediate solution to spiritual deterioration. Believers were urged to leave their homes and kindred and share with their fellow pilgrims what little possessions they had as a pledge of their resignation (*Gelassenheit*) to the cause (Hostetler, 1977). By 1530, Hutter's followers had split with the main body of Anabaptists and became known as Hutterites. Today there are about 40,000 Hutterites comprising 400 colonies living in the northwestern United States and western Canadian provinces (Hofer, 1998).

Migration

Within a century after the Anabaptist Reformation began in Europe, persecution of such sects as Amish, Hutterites, Mennonites, and other pietist groups became commonplace. While the Swiss Mennonites and Amish migrated to the United States, Catherine the Great lured the Hutterites and Mennonites to Russia in the 1770s on the condition that they would farm the land assigned to them, pay taxes, minimally respect the state government, make no converts, and essentially mind their own business. In exchange, these Anabaptists were promised a form of self-government, and the right to maintain their own language and operate their own schools and churches.

In due course, Catherine the Great died, things changed, and Russia began to militarize. Immediately things changed. Privileges previously extended to the Mennonites were quickly revoked, including freedom from military conscription. State officials were rigorous in enforcing the new laws. Many young men of Anabaptist background who refused to serve in the military were rounded up during the night and either sent to concentration camps or were never heard from again. The same situation prevailed among the pacifist Russian Doukhobors (Janzen, 1990). Hutterite leaders believed emigration was the only way out and both the United States and Canada beckoned. The exodus began in the 1870s with the Hutterites moving to South Dakota and the Mennonites opting for Kansas, Manitoba, and Minnesota. The Doukhobor exodus to Canada occurred two decades later for basically the same reasons (Friesen and Verigin, 1996).

In 1876 the three Hutterite groups—Dariusleut, Lehrerleut, and Schmiedeleut—relocated to South Dakota. The Dariusleut derived their names from their leader, Darius Walter; the Lehrer ("teacher") group was renowned for their emphasis on teaching/learning. The Schmiedeleut ("blacksmith") people specialized in that trade. The word "Leute" means "people" in German. As time has passed the three groups have developed slight differences in dress, appearance, and character. The Lehrerleut tend to be the most conservative, and the Schmiedeleut are usually more open to worldly influences. The Dariusleut are somewhere in the middle (Hofer, 1998:172).

9.1   Signpost for Tschetter Hutterite Colony, Freeman, South Dakota

As the Hutterites and fellow Mennonite colleagues prepared to leave Russia, government officials suddenly realized that they were about to lose 45,000 of their best farmers. They therefore tried to put pressure on both groups to stay. Instead of compulsory military service the government promised alternative ways to fulfill that requirement. Many Mennonites acquiesced and remained in Russia, but only two Hutterite families did so. In all, during the 1870s some 18,000 Hutterites and Mennonites migrated to North America (Hofer, 1998:93).

Hutterites are agricultural communalists, pacifists, biblical literalists, and to a certain extent, isolationists. Essentially their way of life has consistently endured, with the exception of a few years in Russia when several of their districts abandoned that way of life. The Hutterites suffered severe losses in membership when they migrated to South Dakota, and on arrival in America most families chose not to live communally. This contingent of Hutterites became known as Hutterite-Mennonites or "Prairieleut" (Hostetler, 1977:121f). In 1874 there were only 425 Hutterites who chose to live communally. Since then they have grown to include more than 40,000 people.

As the Hutterites tried to tame the prairies for agricultural pursuits, they faced the same hardships as other immigrants. There were problems with marginal rainfall, winter blizzards, prairie fires, mosquitoes, gophers, and grasshoppers. Still, the Hutterites prospered, but when World War I came, they found themselves faced with the same dilemma as they had in Russia—join the military or suffer the consequences. As the war went on a number of young men were incarcerated at Alcatraz prison, and some of them died there (Hostetler and Huntington, 1971). Consequently, in 1918, many Dakota Hutterites began their move to Alberta and Manitoba. The Dariusleut and Lehrerleut chose Alberta and the Schmiedeleut relocated to Manitoba.

COMMITMENT

Why the Hutterian Brethren have endured and grown when other communal groups have failed is a mystery to some scholars. When Hutterite beliefs and practices are systematically compared to other communes, the mystery is diminished to some extent. Most of the characteristics required to maintain a separate lifestyle identified by Kanter (1972:75f) are carried out by Hutterites. These include: (i) sacrifice (Hutterites essentially give up any element of individualism); (ii) renunciation (they take vows to the colony that they equate with salvation itself); (iii) investment (they give all of their time, thought, and energy to colony projects); (iv) communion (all colony activities are done in groups; seldom do Hutterites engage in any kind of individual activity); (v) mortification (individual identity is synonymous with group identity; the self is fulfilled only when it lives up to the model set by the community); and, (vi) transcendence (Hutterites believe that the whole purpose of life is to respond to a higher spiritual mandate).

The process of sacrifice demands that members give up the major components of individuality when they join a commune. Once individuals agree to give up something for the sake of the organization, their motivation to remain participants is intensified. In the case of Hutterites, however, it is important to note that for the last several centuries Hutterite membership has almost exclusively been gained through birth. Thus, when members join, they do so as an act of confirmation of the only lifestyle they have ever known. When they are young adults they are expected to make their vows and endorse community principles. In most cases this decision is made without any real consideration of any alternatives, since the members know little of anything other than colony living. Unlike most adults in society who choose alternative lifestyles after due consideration of the options, Hutterite young people at the time of baptism tend to confirm the only lifestyle they know as part of the natural process of remaining in the community.

Rosabeth Kanter (1972:80) defines investment in terms of how individuals tend to "profit" by membership affiliation in a distinct group. Hutterites tend to gain a great deal, including social and economic security, personal and group identity, and community support. Rarely do individuals find it necessary to make difficult decisions. These are left to members of the colony board. This arrangement greatly reduces personal stress but enhances the dependency factor for Hutterite adherents.

The extremely small number of converts to the Hutterite cause from the outside illustrates that though the brethren are admired for their cultural tenacity, few individuals care to submit to the level of renunciation required to become members. For Hutterites, renunciation means relinquishing relationships that might be potentially disruptive to group cohesion, economic independence, and individual freedom of choice. Colony commitment also requires the mortification of personal identity. Personal self-esteem is subjugated to group identity and true meaning comes through colony auspices rather than through personal attainment. The use of religious language, appeals to transcendent responsibilities, and the promise of greater heavenly rewards by denying self assist in strengthening these convictions.

When the profile of Hutterian communalism is compared to that of other such North American experiments, their superior functionality is almost immediately evident. This genius may be sketched along three lines—philosophical, administrative, and practical.

PHILOSOPHICAL REASONS

Perhaps the strongest underlying reason Hutterites have been successful is because they are foundationally orthodox Christians. They believe in the inerrancy of the Holy Scriptures, and hold to the doctrine of the Trinity, the incarnation of Jesus Christ, the need for individual salvation, and the Second Coming of Christ. The Hutterites emerged from the main branch of Anabaptists, who were regarded as the leftwingers of the Protestant Reformation; but, as with other groups who originated at that time, Hutterite beliefs may now be regarded as typical of mainline Christianity. Although once considered somewhat reactionary by state churches, most Anabaptist groups clung tenaciously to the beliefs incorporated in the Apostle's Creed:

> I believe in God, the Father Almighty,
> creator of heaven and earth.
> I believe in Jesus Christ, his only Son, our Lord,
> who was conceived by the Holy Spirit,

born of the Virgin Mary,
suffered under Pontius Pilate,
was crucified, died, and was buried;
he descended to the dead.
On the third day he rose again;
he ascended into heaven,
is seated at the right hand of the Father,
and will come again to judge the living and the dead.
I believe in the Holy Spirit,
the holy catholic (universal) church,
the communion of saints,
the forgiveness of sins,
the resurrection of the body,
and the life everlasting. Amen.
(The United Methodist Book of Worship, 1999:34).

It is only on the mandate of "living together" that there is a departure from orthodoxy on the part of the Hutterites. In fact, the Hutterites
are not entirely without Scriptural substantiation for their beliefs. Most
theologians would agree that the pivotal passage in Acts did or *does* decree communalism, at least for that time and place. The Scripture reads:

> They devoted themselves to the apostles' teaching and to the
> fellowship, to the breaking of bread and to prayer. Everyone
> was filled with awe, and many wonders and miraculous signs
> were done by the apostles. All the believers were together and
> *had everything in common.* Selling their possessions and goods,
> they gave to anyone as he had need (Acts 2:42–45, italics ours).

What is left to be argued are the specifics of that command. Biblical
hermeneutists are in agreement that communality *did* occur at the happening to which the passage in the Book of Acts refers, but these scholars
generally interpret this to be a temporary arrangement, brought about by
the urgency of the moment. Anabaptists followed the principle that any
believer could interpret Scripture at any time and apply it to daily living.

Jacob Hutter, therefore, was entirely within his Anabaptist theological rights when he offered a literal interpretation to the passage in question. No doubt exhilarated by the sense of freedom brought about by the Anabaptist notion that the believers are their own priests, Hutter one day saw something new and meaningful in the above passage from the Book of Acts. Not hindered by such scholarly roadblocks as translating from original Biblical languages, interpreting idiomatic meanings, taking cultural implications into account, or noting contextual inferences, Hutter literally described what he saw. Then he shared the news with his colleagues. Clearly, the Christian church was in error in not obeying an explicit command of Scripture, he argued, and many believed him. The rest is history, except that in the case of the Hutterites it is also living history.

When Hutter's bombshell landed, controversy immediately arose among the Anabaptists over this new-found truth. It soon heightened to the point that Hutter and his followers broke with mainline Anabaptists and proceeded on their own, thanks to the Anabaptist emphasis on individualism. They were only one of several groups who eventually chose to go it alone theologically. For Hutterites, however, the point stood firm; the practice of communalism was mandated in the Bible and they would obey it. For other Anabaptists, what remained to be determined was whether or not the mandate had only an immediate application.

Hofer (1998:170) suggests that a major plank in the platform of Hutterite tenacity stems from the unshakable foundation that they have built up from frequent attacks and moves. In Europe, persecution forced them to leave their lands, flee from their tormentors, and start over. This has made them a vigilant people. Historically, Hutterites have often found themselves in countries and neighborhoods where they had no friends or previous contacts, and this has helped them to become dependent upon each other and on no one else. Their persecution experiences influenced them to become mistrustful of other groups, particularly of state governments.

ADMINISTRATIVE REASONS

Kanter (1972:64) has detailed the primary issues with which a utopian group must cope in order to have solidarity in its human organization. In practical terms this means how work gets done without coercion, how decisions are made to everyone's satisfaction, how some measure of individuality is maintained, and how consensus is attained regarding community values. Committed members work hard, participate actively, derive love and support from the communal group, and strongly believe in community values. Hutterite colonies are able to manifest these characteristics for several reasons, primarily because they segregate themselves from mainstream society and limit or at least regulate outside influences. They stress a spiritual foundation to community obligations, and individual members are taught that fulfilling their work commitment offers some guarantee for a favorable life in the hereafter. The historical evidence of their longevity further bolsters the call for individual commitment and virtually assures retention of members, group cohesiveness, and social control. It was to Robert Owen's dismay that he saw his utopian dream melt before his very eyes, partially because he had not established any criteria of responsibility for the community. Fourier's partying phalanxes faced a similar dilemma when they prioritized good times above responsibility.

Unlike most utopian societies, Hutterites do not have heroes, and they do not practice hereditary succession or yield to dictatorial or autocratic leaders. They do not have to read or listen to readings of the works of an Arnold, Bimeler, Beissel, Lee, Metz, or Rapp, but basically trust the Spirit of God to make Himself known to them through Biblically based preaching. Although operating very much like the Amana colonies in structure and function, they have no allegiance to any particular leader, administrative or spiritual. Like other orthodox Christians, they revere no literature other than the Holy Bible. The fact that each colony democratically chooses its own leaders diminishes the possibility of insurrection. Hutterites have an effective educational system that begins in kindergarten and concludes when the state allows—usually after the eighth grade. Concerned about cultural maintenance, Hutterite elders supervise member interactions with dominant society, and outsiders (except for friends and neighbors) are permitted to visit only in controlled situations—that is, for business or school field trips. In many instances neighboring farmers have been known to make friends with Hutterites and visits back and forth are common.

In comparing Shaker orientations with those of Hutterites, one is somewhat amazed at the extent to which the former would protect their leader from criticism. As Foster (1991:20) notes, if at any point a rebel Shaker might question Mother Ann's personal behavior or teachings, he or she might be informed that Mother Ann herself was not as important as her teachings. Even if she were personally to deviate from her prescriptions, or fall from grace, the Shakers would continue to follow the truth of the basic principles that she taught while she remained in a perfect state. This ability to separate personality from "truth" obviously helped ward off possible criticisms of Ann Lee's behavior. By contrast, Hutterites have never raised Jacob Hutter to such a position. Hutter had a vision that was recognized as timely, but it was certainly not Divine. Unlike Ann Lee, Hutter was not seen as imparting additional truth to his people; he was merely reemphasizing or clarifying beliefs established much earlier by the apostles.

Daily Hutterite operations assume a form of modified, representative democracy in which only men can participate. Hutterites base their exclusion of women's rights on the apostle Paul's first letter to the Corinthian Church: "As in all the congregations of the saints, women should remain silent in the churches. They are not allowed to speak, but must be in submission, as the Law says. If they want to inquire about something, they should ask their own husbands at home; for it is disgraceful for a woman to speak in the church" (I Corinthians 14:33b–35).

On a Hutterite colony, the day-to-day operations are pretty well decided by a council of three or four individuals consisting of the colony boss (or steward), the preacher, and the field boss (Friesen, 1993:133). On occasion the assistant preacher or the German teacher may be consulted if the management group feels his input would be useful. Although all baptized males have a vote, they are seldom called on to vote except when new leaders are elected.

A similar arrangement prevailed among the Doukhobors. Their leader, Peter the Lordly, made many personal decisions concerning the CCUB's welfare, but he always had advisors with whom he consulted.

Unfortunately, his son, Peter the Purger, utilized this form of representative democratic input to a much lesser degree. Among the Hutterites, if an elected leader does not fulfill the obligations of his office, he is given three opportunities to rectify the situation. If he fails to do so, he is removed from office. Nevertheless, he continues to be part of colony life in every other way.

The Amana people operated in much the same way, separating somewhat the spiritual elements from the mundane. The former were handled by people deemed to be Divinely inspired, and the latter by supervisors appointed by the communal council. By contrast, theological and administrative matters in the Society of Brothers (Bruderhof) are dictated by the writings and presence of someone descended from or approved by Eberhard or Christoph Arnold (many books by the Arnolds are published by the Plough Publishing Company). At present the whereabouts of the current leader, Christoph Arnold, Eberhard Arnold's grandson, are held secret, thereby adding mystique to his transmitted admonitions. Ephrata is probably an extreme example of autocracy, with Beissel personally involving himself in all matters, whether spiritual, economic, or practical. The Harmonists similarly revered George Rapp, to the extent that Rapp could not successfully be succeeded even by his own son. The Shakers demonstrated a marked inability to get past the personal impact of Mother Ann Lee when she passed away. Financial success as well as winning additional members were merely academic exercises after her death. In comparison with these groups, Hutterite ways look remarkably conventional.

In studying communes, a marked similarity emerges between philosophical orientation and village format. Those societies that have operated according to a very strict set of beliefs reflect their rigidity in their village floor plan and austere architectural designs. This applies specifically to the Bruderhofs, Ephrata, Harmonists, and Shakers, but to a lesser extent to Hutterites, Amanas, Doukhobors, and Zoarites. The villages of the latter communities were clean and well-kept, but they looked lived in and had a bit more of an informal air about them. The community of Zoar, for example, never did elect to establish a uniform style of housing. Homes were constructed of materials that were available and built to the size and shape desired at a given time. Similarly, when the orthodox Doukhobors relocated several families from British Columbia to Alberta in 1915, the society bought existing farms and simply added homes on each farmyard as needed. By contrast, the Harmonists and Shakers left no stone unturned in making their dwellings look picture perfect. Perhaps this inflexibility was too much for the human spirit of the inhabitants and aided in the dissolution of these communities.

PRACTICAL REASONS

Aside from being bored from time to time, Hutterites, like former Amana, Doukhobor, and Zoar communal dwellers, report that life is meaningful and relaxing. Life can be happy and carefree even though technological devices are limited, and when duty calls for hard work it is rarely done alone. At the same time, colony life does allow for a measure of freedom from group fellowship and pressure, since individual families do live in private suites. This arrangement allows nuclear families to have some time to themselves, to bond as a family unit, and develop an identity apart from that of the community.

On Saturday afternoon on a Hutterite colony, everyone quits work a bit early and makes preparations for Sunday, the day of worship and fellowship. However, there is one point of departure from the practice of other parallel groups. The citizens of Amana, Zoar, and the Doukhobors primarily worked to maintain life, not to build or conquer empires. Theirs was a spirit of cooperation, not competition. They were not primarily work-oriented people, but laced their daily life and work with leisure activities and spiritual overtones. Members of all three of these societies worked to get through the day so that during the evening they could go to rest with a feeling of satisfaction that they had contributed something to the well-being of their brothers and sisters. Unlike Hutterites, these groups never worried about growth, assuming that the future would look after itself. Most Hutterite colonies differ in this regard, having caught the urge to expand their community because of their high birth rate. Their argument is that economic success is both expected and necessary. It is the Biblical mandate, they argue, quoting in support Scriptural passages such as these: "Whatever your hand finds to do, do it with all your might . . ." (Ecclesiastes 9:10). "You will eat the fruit of your labor; blessings and prosperity will be yours" (Psalm 128:2). The Anabaptist (Hutterite) mandate to revere work as a form of Christian discipleship was not a focus in Amana, Doukhobor, or Zoar philosophies. True, individuals should earn their bread, but at the same time members of these three communes heeded the Biblical warning, "Do not store up for yourselves treasures on earth, where moth and rust destroy, and where thieves break in and steal" (Matthew 6:19). In their final years, Amanas, Shakers, and Zoarites all found it necessary to hire outsiders to assist with menial maintenance tasks because of their declining work ethic.

The Hutterite response would be that idleness per se is sinful. Besides, colony leaders must always be ready to branch out to a new community when their numbers reach around 130, and this challenge requires ready cash in today's society. Hutterites plan to have plenty of cash on hand when such a day arrives. Not all colonies operate according to this prescription, depending on leadership style, and much of the economic success of the more well-to-do colonies is also due to the motivation of colony leadership. The fact of variation in Hutterian leadership style and philosophy supports the contention that a degree of group deviance, while limited, is permitted within the Hutterite movement.

CONCLUSION

The foundations of Hutterite society are primarily spiritual and economic. Today, technological changes, regulatory restrictions (primarily bureaucratic in nature), and the limiting of expansion due to changes in the surrounding farm population are exerting pressure on the old way of life (Peter, 1987:185). The emergence of modern machinery has reduced the need for manpower and brought the need to manage leisure to a new high. Traditional restrictions on travel are being lifted, particularly for unbaptized males, who frequently go to town to live a "wilder pace of life." Increasing numbers of them also leave the colony for good, no doubt lured by the "good life" outside. Technology has also brought new wealth, new conveniences, and such commodities as more modern homes.

In the bureaucratic sphere, a variety of government agencies have attempted to place restrictions on Hutterite production of farm products such as eggs, chickens, hogs, and so on. In some cases production of these commodities has been eliminated by the Hutterites because of lost profits. Neighboring farms that have been consolidated have successfully competed with Hutterites and forced them to abandon certain industries. These developments have brought to light emerging signs of internal weakening and enhanced assimilation among Hutterites. Outside agencies are no longer feared as they once were. Hutterites are engaging in an ever-widening circle of business, and making more extensive use of clinics and hospitals. Some Hutterite leaders are delivering university and school lectures about their way of life and inviting school tours (for a fee) onto colonies. As time goes on, more young people will likely leave colonies, lured by the attractions of the outside world. Instances of outside influence are also invading the colonies; cameras, radios, and even television sets are slowly being accepted. If colony leaders are serious about maintaining their traditional way of life, they may want to consider undertaking a formal analysis of current developments and trends among their people.

On a more somber note, it is important to note that Hutterites are not perfect, and their social system does have flaws. There are times when young people do leave colony life and seek to assimilate into mainstream life. From time to time there are also deviances among them that contradict the moral standards of dominant society, even though they are rare. In 1998, for example, four men from two colonies in southern Alberta were found guilty of sex offenses against children and youth in their colony. In May 1999, three families from the Berry Creek Colony in central Alberta left the community and launched a court case against the colony for monies owed them in the form of unsigned family allowance and GST (Goods and Services Tax) tax credit checks. Although the group won their battle in a local court, the colony appealed and the matter is now in a higher court. Years ago, colony leaders would never have resorted to the courts to settle matters among themselves.

Despite these realities, as well as outside jealousies, misunderstandings, and deliberate persecution, the Hutterite vision of utopia has succeeded where others have failed. Only a small fraction of their members have ever violated societal norms, social or moral. Perhaps it is this very success that leads constantly to new and premeditated campaigns on the part of society and government to attempt to dismantle this amazing human endeavor. Hutterites have been accused of breaking down small communities by not purchasing goods locally. This has proven to be false (Hofer 1998:176). Hutterites have been accused of inbreeding because of intermarriage, and so allegedly they hire non Hutterites to impregnate their women. There is no truth to this charge. In 1944, the Alberta Government passed a law prohibiting Hutterites from purchasing land in the province: there was public fear that the Hutterites were "taking over the province." A government investigation proved that there was no basis to the charge (Friesen, 1977:186). An alternative and more sensible route would have been to initiate a careful study of the utopian system that Hutterites have managed to preserve so well for the last few centuries. It is possible that from such study a utopian model could emerge that would more fully meet the urge for peace, happiness, and contentment that is within us all.

CHAPTER 10

TOWARD A MODEL OF UTOPIA

It is not difficult to find proposals for creating ideal lifestyles—most people have some idea of what their concept of an ideal lifestyle would be if they had opportunity to formulate it. The fulfillment of utopia, as perceived by its frequent promoters, offers potential opportunity for steady employment, fellowship, and a strong support group. Such dreams have many times been realized in the not too distant past, and there are many splendid models from which we can learn. The experiences of all the communities discussed in this book offer valuable insights into what might improve society as we know it.

Residents of the various communities discussed in this book were content to live as they did, partly because they *chose* to live in their respective communities. The exception would be individuals born to parents who were members of an alternative organization and raised within the bounds of that community. Usually they too learned to value their upbringing, although a fraction of them may have left their home communities when they found opportunity to do so. This, of course, is not unusual. Many young people in North America, particularly those in rural areas, leave home on reaching adulthood. In many cases this is necessitated by the lack of economic opportunity, but there are also instances where these individuals simply prefer to live somewhere else.

Many of the alternative organizations that we have described lasted for many years. These include Amana, Harmonists, Zoar, Shakers, and

Hutterian Brethren. The latter group, in fact, despite a history of ups and downs, has persisted for 474 years. This includes migrations to several countries. At one time during their Russian sojourn, due to persecution their numbers were reduced to less than 100, but their vision was strong enough to drive them forward (Hostetler, 1977). A handful of Shaker women still proudly carry the Shaker banner as "The United Society of Believers."

Most of the groups described in this book have been hindered or persecuted by both governments and the body politick. Most were not viewed as contributors to the maintenance of a stable society. Surprisingly, many of these communities rigorously adhered to traditional values and fostered conventional family relations. Many intentional communities showed that they were resourceful, creative, and economically independent; the agricultural and technological fruits of their labors were in high demand.

ABILITY TO CHANGE

One of the surprising features of successful intentional communities is their ability to adapt to change. Groups like the Hutterites have a long record in this regard, but they are not alone. The Harmonists, for example, relocated across state lines several times for economic as well as philosophical reasons. All of their moves were successful. When the Amana people sold their industrial plant and relied solely on agricultural income, they did so in order to keep up with the times. The people of the Oneida community stopped the production of animal traps when the market dried up and switched to manufacturing silverware. The Farm nearly went bankrupt in 1976, regrouped, and came back.

CRITICISMS

Public perceptions of alternative communities as atypical, unusual, or even suspect are too often inaccurate, insulting, and wrong. People who live in them are usually quite well-adjusted and content, much like their peers in dominant society. Through the five centuries of North American life since the arrival of Christopher Columbus, many groups have struggled to establish successful lifestyles and often succeeded. Dreams like theirs can (and still are) being realized by individuals and groups who plan *and* actualize them. According to Stephen Gaskin, founder of The Farm: "We were hippies who wanted to live together. . . . [Now] we've got our families and kids. It's not a crash pad for the summer. The farm is a family person now. It used to be a wild teen-ager, but it has matured and settled down. . . . we're all veterans of the spiritual movement. We're atheists, freethinkers, Christians, and Catholics. Like Buckminister Fuller said—man you gotta be a generalist!" (Trausch, 1987).

Campaigns to belittle or discourage the formation of alternative organizations are an ongoing phenomenon, many of them wrought out of ignorance. Every group described in this book has at one time or another been severely criticized for some aspect of their philosophy or lifestyle. Hutterites, for example, have been charged with being cruel to their women because women are not given the opportunity to vote on colony matters. In response, Hutterites are quick to refer to St. Paul's first letter to Timothy (2:11), "A woman should learn in quietness and full submission." Critics charge that the Hutterite birth rate is too high; they intermarry with close relatives; and they do not pay taxes. An Alberta government report proved all of these criticisms without merit (Report on Communal Property, 1972).

The fact that Hutterites believe in pacifism, like some of the other communities described here, bothers those who support military service. The complaint is that pacifists are quite willing to benefit from the freedom that exists in Canada and the United States, but will not defend it when called on to do so. Pacifist groups like Hutterites and Mennonites claim they can make civil contributions in other ways.

A frequent criticism of Hutterites is that their children are sheltered from life in dominant society because colonies operate their own state-approved schools. Some contemporary educators claim that Hutterite-operated schools are a waste of taxpayers' money but these critics are unaware that the cost for educating Hutterite children on-site is entirely borne by the colony. If there are costs not covered by colony taxes, the local county bills the colonies.

In 1817, the Zoarites faced similar criticism while they were still in Germany. Their refusal to send their children to public schools, which at that time were controlled by the clergy, and their opposition to war brought persecution upon them. They were stigmatized as fanatics, and flogged, fined, and imprisoned by ecclesiastical authorities (Nordhoff, 1966:100). Oddly enough, through the years that they operated in America the Zoarites were seldom criticized, probably because they worked hard, demanded little by way of community resources, and gave back at least as much as they took. Their lifestyle was sufficiently orthodox that, at most, they were viewed as objects of curiosity.

It is commonplace to blame Hutterites for the demise of nearby small rural towns because colony leaders allegedly purchase most of their supplies from larger urban centers. Critics claim that Hutterites can buy most needed items from wholesale outlets because they purchase products in large amounts. This practice bypasses local merchants who rely on business from neighborhood residents in order to survive. At times, Hutterites *do* purchase large amounts of goods from wholesalers, often buying products that society at large considers outdated and obsolete. It has been proven that Hutterites generally purchase about one-third of needed items from local businesses, nearby small towns, and larger urban centers (Friesen, 1993:185f). Despite these and other unfounded charges, Hutterite life goes on. Most criticisms are simply ignored by colony leaders whose noncombative beliefs apply equally to unfair daily verbal assaults as they do to possible military conscription.

Negative onslaughts against a host of other intentional communities in North America parallels the Hutterian experience. For example, in 1906 a local resident in Iowa took the Amanas to court on a charge of unfair advantage. It was charged that the Amanas, as a legally constituted religious organization, were exceeding their corporate powers by holding too much real property and establishing "purely secular industries." The implication was that the Amanas had forfeited their corporate franchise, but the courts determined otherwise (Shambaugh, 1988:87).

The story of the Christian Community of Universal Brotherhood (CCUB) is an account of unfair treatment at the hands of a multiplicity of parties—governments, neighbors, and financial institutions (Friesen,

1995b). In 1899, the Doukhobors were forced to leave their native Russia because of persecution. In 1903, their Saskatchewan settlement lands were confiscated because as pacifists they refused to take an oath to the government, a condition of their immigration that they had not been informed of beforehand. They were investigated by four government commissions. After their migration to British Columbia from 1908 to 1912, some Doukhobors had their children taken away from them and incarcerated in fenced, government-run schools. In 1938 the CCUB was forced into bankruptcy through secret government collaboration with two financial institutions, which suddenly called in a demand note of $319,276 based on $6 million of assets. In a short time some 10,000 Doukhobors living in the three western provinces of Canada were homeless.

At the point of their greatest economic success, the Oneida people were objects of scorn and accusations of being out of touch with the times. Their practice of "free love, complex marriage, and scientific breeding" was more than nineteenth-century America could accept (Kephart and Zellner, 1994:87). Martha McWhirter's Women's Commonwealth suffered similar accusations because it was unusual for women both to enter the business world and to experience success in it. The presupposition of Ann Lee's Shakers that economic success was unrelated to the institution of marriage caused them considerable criticism, inconvenience, and upset.

POSITIVE FEATURES

Daily routines in most of the intentional communities we surveyed followed expected lines. There were chores to do, expectations to meet, and responsibilities to assign. Arrangements had to be made regarding sexual relations, marriage, death, and child-raising. Many tasks were assigned on the basis of gender or age. Routine has a way of ensuring stability and relieving stress.

In communal societies such as Amana, Harmonists, Hutterites, Shakers, and Zoar, the scene would be quite predictable. Young people over a certain age were assigned daily chores. No one worked particularly hard, and even mundane tasks like preparing chickens for market or cleaning a barn took on an element of joy in that they were undertaken in tandem with other members of the commune. While they worked people shared stories and memories and laughed and sang. They found that time passed quickly. As standard procedure, communal peoples rarely engage in tasks by themselves because most obligations are designed for group effort. Among Hutterites there are times when the minister prepares sermons alone and the steward (financial secretary) scrutinizes colony accounts by himself, but these are rare though necessary undertakings.

A workable utopia for the twenty-first century must reassess the obsessions of the last century for continued growth, increased use of resources, and the relentless commitment to building a proverbially better mousetrap. Recent catastrophes have given North Americans the opportunity to undertake this assessment to formulate more meaningful values. There is some indication that this message has not fallen on deaf ears.

Many intentional communities of the past were designed on a patriarchal or benevolent dictator model, although elements of democracy were woven into them. Jane Addams (Hull House), Ann Lee (Shakers), and Martha McWhirter (Women's Commonwealth) showed that women could successfully direct utopias with some form of input from participants. Robert Owen (New Harmony), for all his good intentions, overworked the concept of democracy, and people wearied of so much decision making. Doukhobor leader Peter Verigin always relied on the input of a group of advisors in making decisions. As the operations of several intentional communities have shown, administrative patterns may vary from one experiment to another and be quite successful. A design for the twenty-first century would have to take local variables into account in formulating a workable system, but with some effort a workable plan could surely be formulated.

A patriarchal approach appears to have worked for the Hutterites, but as Peter (1987) points out, Hutterite women tend to influence colony decision-making by lobbying their men privately. There are indications that in matters that affect the women, they have a great deal of informal control. Like other societies, Hutterites are in a change mode regarding their philosophy and operation, even though the pace of change is exceedingly slow. Pressures from rapid technological innovations greatly affect the operation of intentional communities and must be anticipated so that appropriate adjustments can be made (Rothstein, 2003:15). As the examples of the Harmonists and Zoar illustrate, "keeping up with the times" is very important if cultural maintenance is to be assured.

CRITERIA FOR EFFECTIVE UTOPIA

Analysts of any persuasion would be quick to agree that many elements of our current social system could be improved. Poverty, crime, inequality, and dishonest politicians are only a few items on the shopping list of social reform, and the adoption of the stronger features of past experiments would certainly alleviate some of these devastating conditions. The building of a new social order does not imply the adoption of a communal model. In fact, many of the attributes that have enabled alternative communities to survive and indeed prosper are the ones required for the development of improved social institutions, communal or otherwise. Terjesen (1979:272) contends that there are four specific criteria that assure the longevity of utopian experiments. The first three criteria mandate the potential framework or structural possibility for an improved social system, and the fourth criterion requires a relevant focus. Terjesen's criteria include: (i) a dynamic form of leadership, charismatic or otherwise; (ii) successful boundary maintenance mechanisms; (iii) a fervent religious bent or at least a forceful, consistent philosophical orientation; and (iv) firm commitment apparatuses.

Leadership

Most observers of the utopian scene seem to agree that the success of any utopian experiment is directly related to the kind of leadership it attracts. History bears this out to some extent, for indeed most intentional communities in the past have been originated by men or women with driving visions. These unique inspirational leaders seem to spring up from time to time, irresistibly inclined toward improving the lot of humankind. These individuals are not simply reformers; they are people whose particular message is in tune with the times. They are not merely tinkers or tailors, but have strong convictions about creating new designs. They may properly be called social architects, who would not be satisfied with anything less than a most thorough, vital, and permanent reconstruction of the very fundamentals of human society. Their dreams cannot fade as long as society has the foresight and tools to develop this kind of dreamer/thinker. It is the responsibility of educational institutions to see that they do not mold imitators or strait-jacketed thinkers, or people who fear the unknown. As Godwin (1972:7) states: "In the history of human society, there is one peculiar and significant fact. . . . It is this: that a set of [people] have appeared from time to time who have been led by the oppressions and disorders of society, into a position apart from others as the projectors of an entirely new and radical reorganization."

The origins of those intentional communities that grew out of a specific need tend to resemble one another. A number of German Separatist groups such as Amana, Harmonists, and Zoar came into being through unfortunate circumstances that impelled the originators to envisage a better world. These people were persecuted and punished for their beliefs and sought a way out—a way to freedom. Jane Addams, Martha McWhirter, Stephen Gaskin, and John Noyes sought to improve aspects of society through demonstrating their ideas. All were successful to some extent even though in many ways they were ahead of their time.

Analysts point out that the charismatic impact of individuals who influence the formation of social factions seldom lasts more than three generations. When these chapters come to an end there is often conflict among adherents about leadership or, if they cannot carry on, arguments about the nature of dissolution or division of assets. Exceptions to this tendency include the experiences of Amana, Brook Farm, the Iowa Icarians, and Zoar, all of whom settled their final accounts with a minimum of discord. For the most part, Hutterite leadership has been successful because elected leaders cannot usurp command over their people. If their leadership style is not acceptable, they are replaced by a democratic vote of baptized males. Founder Jacob Hutter himself was once removed from office by his peers, just as Stephen Gaskin of The Farm was.

Both remained with their constituents, faithfully serving in their reduced capacities.

Although Canada and the United States are democratic societies, and leadership is supposedly determined through reasonable means after due consideration, North Americans still yield too often to the temptation to ascribe extraordinary attributes to certain individuals who can make music, dance, play sports, model clothing, or star in movies. This debilitating phenomenon is the ultimate contradiction in a democratic society that does its best work through reason, discussion, and analysis.

The attainment of a just and reasonable lifestyle, as we all know, is tedious, painstaking, and sometimes boring work. It requires commitment to fundamental principles, and not a mere yielding to the whims of charismatic individuals. The adulation of celebrity personalities draws energy away from the serious business of building an equitable, reasonable social order. Superheroism may make a lot of money for a few investors, but in the long run it belittles any serious effort to improve society. As the Hutterite example shows, supplemented by such long-term experiments as Amana, Shakers, and Zoar, individualism and the desire for personal property can be replaced with genuine concern for community welfare. Utopian societies do not need to have superstar leadership, but can function quite successfully in a democratic framework.

In the final analysis, everything we have learned about successful effective utopian leadership formats shows that they must include several important criteria. Leaders must be capable, charismatic individuals who are democratically representative of their constituency, elected by the membership subject to periodic review, and replaceable when the greater interest of the community is violated. If these criteria are applied, it is highly unlikely that despots, autocrats, or tyrants would be drawn to these offices or be long sustained in them.

Boundary Maintenance

Effective utopian communities tend to have strong boundaries, including physical, social, and behavioral. What goes on in the community is sharply differentiated from what goes on outside. It is important that any long-lasting community have creeds, beliefs, and rituals that may at times be kept hidden from outsiders in order to provide members with the feeling that they alone have access to special knowledge. Physical boundaries often help adherents define with whom it is acceptable to have a relationship (Kanter, 1972:170). When these characteristics take on an unusual or peculiar bent, however, the stage is set for possible deviance. Both Amana and Zoar contributed to their own demise by developing institutions, such as hotels, factories, and retail outlets, which necessitated and even encouraged extensive outside contact. On occasion the Shakers suffered a similar fate. After a time, changes occurred within these utopias and differences in belief and practice between them and the outside became minimized. When this happened the very foundation and future of the communities was threatened.

The strengthening of community boundaries may sometimes be attributed to outside agencies rather than the community itself. Prejudice, discrimination, jealousy, severe criticism, and outright persecution often foster a tightening of boundaries, with the group increasingly isolating itself from outside contact. On the positive side, however, lasting utopias usually concentrate on providing a satisfactory and meaningful lifestyle for their people, void of too much unpleasantness, strife, or stress. When unbaptized members leave a Hutterite community, for example, they are always welcomed back to visit in hopes that they will eventually change their ways and permanently return to the colony. When *baptized* individuals leave, however, they are shunned, and no one is supposed to have anything to do with them. There are exceptions to this rule, of course, especially in cases where loved ones become seriously ill or pass away.

American patriotic loyalties were expanded to their limits when the World Trade Center was destroyed. Americans quickly rallied to the cause, helping out in every way conceivable, never tiring in their support for those who were suffering. The tragedy brought Americans strength and renewed patriotism. As the months following the tragic event have demonstrated, this was not a temporary emotional outburst of sympathy; it was a genuine effort that showed what Americans are made of. Even Canada pitched in, including Prime Minister Jean Chrétien, who made a special visit to New York to show that Canadians shared in the nation's suffering. The ultimate test will be to see if this mature spirit of nation-building can persist. An improved society will necessarily prioritize human relationships and human caring above temporary lustful fulfillment.

Credal Loyalty

Although a strong belief system is essential to maintaining a utopian vision, a balance between fervency and laxity must be assured. Most of the groups surveyed in this book demonstrated that there was little that could be classified as particularly unusual or eccentric about their philosophies. Like other creed-oriented communities or subcultures, with minor interruptions or deviations, their lifestyle exhibited a remarkably stable pattern of daily living. Their institutional life was structured, but not stifling. The fortunate experience of all North American groups was that they had adequate resources favorable to expansion. Their children engaged in various forms of play; the women tended gardens, sewed, and crocheted; and the men worked in the fields, tended to their crafts, and gathered to discuss community and world events. Outsiders who visited traditionally oriented communities to purchase produce often lingered to share a meal or visit. These exchanges allowed community residents to gain information about the outside world, which they could later discuss in more detail among themselves. New information was utilized to justify the status quo of living one day at a time. It was rarely exploited as a means of social reform.

Visionary groups that thrive on an extensive amount of religious fervency frequently dissolve after a short duration. On the contrary, many short-term experiments demonstrated that the human spirit is not geared to endure excesses of any kind for very long periods of time. As St. Paul warned the Philippian Church, "Rejoice in the Lord always: and again I say, Rejoice. Let your *moderation* [gentleness] be known unto all men. The Lord is at hand" (Philippians 4:4–5 KJV, italics ours). But as our survey has shown, there are exceptions. The Harmonists, Amanas, Zoarites, and Ephratans lasted several generations before waning. In the meantime, though mostly misunderstood through recent centuries, a number of alternative organizations have managed to preserve the integrity of their faith in belief and practice.

The adoption of workable principles unique to many intentional communities is possible and could greatly improve aspects of the North American way of life. In fact, a few generations ago, most North Americans lived in accordance with those principles. Technology and new forms of entertainment in the last few decades have influenced concomitant changes in human desire. Most North Americans have responded to this challenge in this way; "If we can make those machines, replace those traditional values, and follow our natural urges without too much restraint, why not do so?" Utopianist goals may require a break from our hedonistic value system and the draining of our natural resources may require a hard look at what we are doing to the environment. It might be advisable to consider seriously if we need to make changes to our way of life now, rather than wait until they are forced upon us by circumstances. The utopian examples discussed here may provide valuable input to these considerations.

Commitment Apparatus

Significant technological or social change in mainstream society can greatly affect the lifestyle of alternative communities. The Shakers, Harmonists, and Zoarites discovered this a bit too late. They were not quite prepared to deal with the challenge of shifting economics. The Hutterian Brethren faced one of the greatest challenges to their way of life when the Bruderhof temporarily merged with them in 1930. Always operating most efficiently on their own, the Hutterites broke with their own tradition when they yielded to the pleas of Eberhard Arnold to unite the two societies. Although the Hutterites were financially aided in their settlement period by the Harmonists and the Amanas, thereafter they had little interaction with these groups. This is regrettable to some extent, for they might have learned a great deal from one another. Certainly their philosophy was more in keeping with Amana and Harmonist beliefs than those of the Bruderhof. Alternatively, the isolationist tendencies of the Hutterites may have served to safeguard their way of life.

The marriage with the Society of Brothers was short-lived when the Hutterites discovered that the Bruderhof tolerated practices that the Hutterites regarded as worldly. The union came to an abrupt end. A few years later another courtship developed, this time with Julius Kubassek, founder of the Community Farm of the Brethren in Ontario. Several Hutterite families took up with the movement, until it was discovered that Kubassek had dictatorial tendencies, was too individualistic, and had leanings towards celibacy (Hostetler and Huntington, 1971). Once again the appeal to merge vanished and the Hutterites continued their journey in isolation following the patterns set by the Scriptures and tradition.

Utopian Promise

Despite the success of many utopian experiments, particularly those that survived for at least three generations, in the end most of them dissolve. Reasons for dissolution are legion, many of them perhaps indicative of the restless nature of the human spirit. There are exceptions. The Doukhobors, for example, did not fall apart because of any internal weakness. They were forced into bankruptcy by the government and insurance companies. Although the event occurred in 1937, many older adherents still nurse the dream that some day their form of communal living will be revived (Friesen and Verigin, 1996:126f). To that end, in 1980 the Doukhobor Youth Commission recommended that an experimental commune consisting of several villages be set up to exemplify traditional ways. To date no one has accepted the invitation to join the experiment, once again underscoring the fact that the Doukhobor utopian dream belonged to a specific time and place. The challenge now remains for individuals to emerge with timely visions for the twenty-first century.

During the 1960s many American youth migrated to Canada to avoid the draft, and later decided to return home. As time passed, some of them got lonely, and the idea of spending the rest of their lives on the seashore amid piles of washed up driftwood was no longer appealing. They were now ready to face what they perceived to be undesirable philosophical conditions head-on. Similarly, the Women's Commonwealth made their point about universal suffrage, but the women, successful but weary and elderly, simply wanted to live out the rest of their lives in peace. Robert Owen was not so successful, and the somewhat unusual adherents whom he attracted to New Harmony did not necessarily share his vision and so abandoned the place.

Those intentional communities that successfully alter aspects of their systems to time and place (such as The Farm, Amana, and Hutterites) continue to influence society. A cost is involved, of course, if mainstream society is to be enriched by new visions of how things *could* be. Individuals have to be willing to trade temporal, visceral satisfactions for the enduring values of sacrifice, commitment, renunciation, mortification, transcendence, and communion. The reward for such an undertaking is the possibility of developing a more meaningful lifestyle, the fulfillment of the passion for utopia. We need utopian thinkers, planners, and builders. Without them, society's creative juices will stagnate. As Karl Manheim put it, "With the relinquishment of utopias, man would lose his will to shape history, and therewith his ability to change it" (Rothstein, 2003:14).

REFERENCES

Abrahamson, Mark. (1996). *Urban Enclaves: Identity and Place in America.* New York: St. Martin's Press.

Abrams, Philip, Andrew McCulloch, Sheila Abrams and Pat Gere. (1976). *Communes, Sociology and Society.* Cambridge, U.K.: Cambridge University Press.

Addams, Jane. (1990). *Twenty Years at Hull-House: With Autobiographical Notes.* Chicago, IL: University of Chicago Press.

Albertson, Ralph. (1973). *A Survey of Mutualistic Communities in America.* New York: AMS Press.

Alderfer, E. G. (1995). *The Ephrata Commune: An Early American Counterculture.* Pittsburgh, PA: University of Pittsburgh Press.

Ananda. (2002). http://www.ananda.org/ananda/colonies/index.html.

Andrews, Edward Deming. (1963). *The People Called Shakers: A Search for the Perfect Society.* New York: Dover Publications.

Bates, Albert. (2000). http://www.thefarmcommunity.com/faq.htm.

Baum, Markus. (1996). *Against the Wind: Eberhard Arnold and the Bruderhof.* Farmington, PA: The Plough Publishing Company.

Beard, Charles A., and Mary R. Beard. (1960). *The Beard's New Basic History of the United States.* Garden City, NY: Doubleday & Company, Inc.

Bellamy, Edward. (1951). *Looking Backward: 2000–1887.* New York: Random House.

Bender, Harold S. (1964). *Mennonites and Their Heritage: A Handbook of Mennonite History and Beliefs.* Scottdale, PA: Herald Press.

Berton, Pierre. (1990). *The Promised Land: Settling the West, 1896–1914.* Toronto, ON: McClelland and Stewart.

Bestor, Arthur Eugene. (1959). *Backwoods Utopias: The Sectarian and Owenite Phases of Communitarian Socialism in America: 1663–1829.* Philadelphia, PA: University of Pennsylvania Press.

Bowen, Lynne. (1994). *Muddling Through: The Remarkable Story of the Barr Colonists.* Vancouver, BC: Greystone Books.

Brewer, Priscilla. (1986). *Shaker Communities, Shaker Lives.* Hanover, NH: University Press of New England.

Brown, Dee. (1995). *The American West.* New York: Simon and Schuster.

Browning, Robert. (1942). "Andrea del Sarto," in *The Selected Poems of Robert Browning.* New York: Walter J. Black.

Buber, Martin. (1949). *Paths In Utopia.* Translated by R. F. C. Hull. London: Routledge & Kegan Paul.

Burnet, Jean R., and Howard Palmer. (1988). *Coming Canadians: An Introduction to a History of Canada's Peoples.* Toronto, ON: McClelland and Stewart.

Calverton, Victor Francis. (1969). *Where Angels Dared to Tread: Socialist & Communist Utopian Colonies in the United States.* Freeport, NY: Books for Libraries Press.

Carden, Maren Lockwood. (1998). *Oneida: Utopian Community to Modern Corporation.* Syracuse, NY: Syracuse University Press.

Carmony, Donald F., and Josephine M. Elliott. (September, 1980). "New Harmony, Indiana: Robert Owen's Seedbed for Utopia." *Indiana Magazine of History,* XXXVI, 161–261. Reprinted in 1999.

Carpenter, Delburn. (1975). *The Radical Pietists: Celibate Communal Societies Established in the United States Before 1820.* New York: AMS Press.

Carter, Novia. (1974). *Something of Promise: The Canadian Communes.* Ottawa, ON: Canadian Council on Social Development.

Carter, Velma, and Levero (Lee) Carter. (1989). *The Black Canadians: Their History and Contributions.* Edmonton, AB: Reidmore Books.

Cavan, Ruth Shonle. (1979). "The Future of a Historic Commune," in *Communes: Historical and Contemporary.* Ruth Shonle Cavan and Man Singh Das, eds. New Delhi, India: Vikas Publishing House, 257–71.

Chmielewski, Wendy E. (1993). "Heaven on Earth: The Women's Commonwealth, 1867–1983," in *Women in Spiritual and Communitarian Societies in the United States.* Wendy E. Chmielewski, Louis J. Kern, and Marilyn Klee-Hartzell, eds. New York: Syracuse University Press, 52–73.

Cohen, J. M., and M. J. Cohen. (1985). *Dictionary of Quotations.* New York: Penguin.

Coontz, Stephanie. (1992). *The Way We Never Were: American Families and the Nostalgic Trap.* New York: Basic Books.

Crum, Dorothy. (1998). *Life in Amana.* Iowa City, IA: Penfield Press.

Davis, J. C. (1984). "The History of Utopia: The Chronology of Nowhere," in *Utopias.* Peter Alexander and Roger Gill, eds. London, UK: Duckworth, 1–18.

Dieter, Melvin E. (1991). "Mormons," in *New 20th Century Encyclopedia of Religious Knowledge.* Second edition. J. D. Douglas, ed. Grand Rapids, MI: Baker Book House.

Donskov, Andrew, John Woodsworth and Chad Gaffield, eds. (1995). *The Doukhobor Centenary in Canada.* Ottawa, ON: Institute of Canadian Studies, University of Ottawa.

Douglas, J. D. (1991). *New 20th Century Encyclopedia of Religious Knowledge.* Second edition. Grand Rapids, MI: Baker Book House.

Dyck, Cornelius J., ed. (1967). *An Introduction to Mennonite History: A Popular History of the Anabaptists and the Mennonites.* Scottdale, PA: Herald Press.

Eggers, Ulrich. (1988). *Community for Life.* Scottdale, PA: Herald Press.

Emerson, Ralph Waldo. (1904). *The Complete Works of Ralph Waldo Emerson,* vol. 10. Boston, MA: Houghton-Mifflin, 359–69.

Florinsky, Michael T. (1955). *Russia: A History and Interpretation.* Volume 1. New York: Macmillan.

Fogerty, Robert S. (1972). *American Utopianism.* Itasca, IL: F. E. Peacock Publishers.

———. (1990). *All Things New: American Communes and Utopian Movements 1860–1914.* Chicago, IL: The University of Chicago Press.

Foster, Lawrence. (1991). *Women, Family and Utopia: Communal Experiments of the Shakers, the Oneida Community, and the Mormons.* Syracuse, NY: Syracuse University Press.

Francis, E. K. (1955). *In Search of Utopia: The Mennonites in Manitoba.* Altona, MB: D. W. Friesen & Sons.

Francis, R. Douglas. (1989). *Images of the West: Changing Perceptions of the Prairies, 1690–1960.* Saskatoon, SK: Western Producer Prairie Books.

French, David, and Elena French (1975). *Working Communally: Patterns and Possibilities.* New York: Russell Sage Foundation.

Friebert, Lucy M. (1993). "Creative Women of Brook Farm," in *Women in Spiritual and Communitarianism: Societies in the United States.* Wendy E. Chmielewski, Louis J. Kern, and Marilyn Klee-Hartzwell, eds. Syracuse, NY: Syracuse University Press, 41: 75–88.

Friesen, Bruce K., and John W. Friesen. (1996). *Perceptions of the Amish Way.* Dubuque, IA: Kendall/Hunt.

Friesen, Gerald. (1984). *The Canadian Prairies: A History.* Toronto, ON: University of Toronto Press.

Friesen, John W. (1977). *People, Culture & Learning.* Calgary, AB: Detselig Enterprises.

———. (1983). *Schools With A Purpose.* Calgary, AB: Detselig Enterprises.

———. (1993). *When Cultures Clash: Case Studies in Multiculturalism.* Second edition. Calgary, AB: Detselig Enterprises.

———. (1995a). *Pick One: A User-Friendly Guide to Religion.* Calgary, AB: Detselig Enterprises.

———. (1995b). "'Welcome to Our World': The Sad Saga of Doukhobor Immigration and Settlement in Canada," in *Freedom Within the Margins: The Politics of Exclusion.* Caterina Pizanias and James S. Frideres, eds. Calgary, AB: Detselig Enterprises, 215–30.

Friesen, John W., and Virginia Lyons Friesen. (2001). *In Defense of Public Schools in North America.* Calgary, AB: Detselig Enterprises.

Friesen, John W., and Michael M. Verigin (1996). *The Community Doukhobors: A People in Transition.* Second edition. Ottawa, ON: Borealis Publishing Company.

Geortz, Rueben. (1995). *Princes, Potentates, and Plains People: The Saga of the Germans from Russia.* Sioux Falls, SD: The Center for Western Studies, Augustana College.

Godwin, Parke. (1972). *A Popular View of the Doctrines of Charles Fourier.* Philadelphia, PA: Porcupine Press.

Goodwin, Barbara. (1984). "Economic and Social Innovation in Utopia," in *Utopias.* Peter Alexander and Roger Gill, eds. London, UK: Duckworth, 69–84.

Hacker, Andrew. (1956). "In Defence of Utopianism," in *Utopias: Social Ideals and Communal Experiments.* Peyton E. Rickter, ed. Boston, MA: Holbrook Press, 1971, 307–12.

Harder, M. S. (1949). "The Origin, Philosophy, and Development of Education Among the Mennonites." Unpublished Doctoral Dissertation. Los Angeles, CA: The University of Southern California.

Harris, Michael. (1999). "The Kibbutz: Uncovering the Utopian Dimension." *Utopian Studies,* 10(1), 115–27.

Heidebrecht, Herbert V. (1973). Values of Mennonite Youth. Unpublished Master's Thesis. Calgary, AB: The University of Calgary.

Hill, Daniel G. (1981). *The Freedom Seekers: Blacks in Early Canada.* Agincourt, ON: The Book Society of Canada.

Hillary, Jr., George A. (1968). *Communal Organizations: A Study of Local Societies.* Chicago, IL: University of Chicago Press.

Hine, Robert V. (1983). *California's Utopian Colonies.* Berkley, CA: University of California Press.

Hofer, Samuel. (1998). *The Hutterites: Lives and Images of a Communal People.* Saskatoon, SK: Hofer Publishers.

Holbrook, Stewart H. (1957). *Dreamers of The American Dream.* Garden City, NY: Doubleday & Company Inc.

Holloway, Mark. (1966). *Heavens on Earth: Utopian Societies in America, 1680–1880.* Second edition. New York: Dover Publications.

Hostetler, John A. (1977). *Hutterite Society.* Baltimore, MD: The Johns Hopkins University Press.

Hostetler, John. (1993). *Amish Society.* Fourth edition. Baltimore, MD: The Johns Hopkins University Press.

Hostetler, John A., and Gertrude Enders Huntington. (1971). *The Hutterites in North America.* New York: Holt, Rinehart and Winston.

Hwang, Yong G. (Summer, 1995). "Student Apathy: Lack of Self Responsibility and False Self-Esteem are Failing American Schools." *Education,* 15(4), 484–90.

Jacob, Jeffrey. (1997). *New Pioneers: The Back-to-the-Land Movement and the Search for a Sustainable Future.* University Park, PA: The Pennsylvania State University Press.

Janzen, William. (1990). *Limits on Liberty: The Experience of Mennonite, Hutterite, and Doukhobor Communities in Canada.* Toronto, ON: University of Toronto Press.

Kach, Nick. (November, 1984). "The Acculturation of Old Believers." *Multicultural Education Journal,* 2(2), 19–26.

Kanter, Rosabeth Moss. (1972). *Commitment and Community: Communes and Utopias in Sociological Perspective*. Cambridge, MA: Harvard University Press.

Kephart, William M., and William W. Zellner. (1994). *Extraordinary Groups: An Examination of Unconventional Life-Styles*. Fifth edition. New York: St. Martin's Press.

Kitch, Sally L. (1993). *The Strange Society of Women: Reading the Letters and Lives of the Women's Commonwealth*. Columbus, OH: Ohio State University Press.

Kleinsasser, Samuel. (n.d.). *Our Broken Relationship With the Society of Brothers*. San Francisco, CA: KIT Information Service.

Kline, David. (1990). *Great Possessions: An Amish Farmer's Journal*. San Francisco, CA: North Point Press.

Kraft, Stephanie. (2003). www.valleyadvocate.com/gbase/News/content.html?pid=:5413.

Kraushaar, Otto F. (1980). "America: Symbol of a Fresh Start," in *Utopias: The American Experience*. Gardner B. Moment and Otto F. Kraushaar, eds. Metuchen, NJ: The Scarecrow Press, 11–29.

Kraybill, Donald B. (1990). *The Riddle of Amish Culture*. Baltimore, MD: The Johns Hopkins University Press.

Kraybill, Donald B., and Carl F. Bowman. (2001). *On the Backroad to Heaven: Old Order Hutterites, Mennonites, Amish, and Brethren*. Baltimore, MD: The Johns Hopkins University Press.

Kraybill, Donald B., and Steven M. Nolt. (1995). *Amish Enterprise: From Plows to Profits*. Baltimore, MD: The Johns Hopkins University Press.

Kring, Hilda Adam. (1973). *The Harmonists: A Folk-Cultural Approach*. Metuchen, NJ: Scarecrow Press.

Kumar, Krishan. (1993). "The End of Socialism? The End of Utopia? The End of History?," in *Utopias and the Millennium*. Krishan Kumar and Stephen Baum, eds. London, UK: Reaktion Books, 63–80.

Laird, Gordon. (November/December, 2000). "Closing Kemano: Pulling the Plug on a British Columbia Small-Town Utopia." *Canadian Geographic*, 120(7), 82–96.

Lambach, Ruth Baer. (1993). "Colony Girl," in *Women in Spiritual and Communitarian Societies in the United States*. Wendy E. Chmielewski, Louis J. Kern, and Marlyn Klee-Hartzell, eds. Syracuse, NY: Syracuse University Press, 241–55.

Liffring-Zug, Joan. (1975). *The Amanas of Yesterday: A Religious Communal Society*. Iowa City, IA: Penfield Press.

Mariampolski, Hyman. (1979). "Religion and the Survival of Utopian Communities: The Case of New Harmony, Indiana (1924–1827)," in *Communes: Historical and Contemporary*. Ruth Shonle Cavan and Man Singh Das, eds. New Delhi, India: Vikas Publishing House, 215–34.

Marty, Martin E. (2003). "'But Even So, Look at That': An Ironic Perspective on Utopias," in *Visions of Utopia*. Furaha D. Norton, ed. New York: Boston University Press, 49–88.

McLean, Elizabeth. (1997). *The Promise of Paradise: Utopian Communities in B.C.* Vancouver, BC: Whitecap Books.

Mehl, Bernard. (1963). "Education in American History," in *Foundation of Education*. George F. Kneller, ed. New York: John Wiley and Sons, 1–42.

Melnyk, George. (1985). *The Search for Community: From Utopia to a Cooperative Society*. Montreal, PQ: Black Rose Books.

Miller, Timothy. (1999). *The 60s Communes: Hippies and Beyond*. Syracuse, NY: Syracuse University Press.

Milne, Mike. (April, 1994). Cults or Faith on the Fringe?" *The United Church Observer*, 57(10), 15–30.

Morhart, Hilda Dischinger. (1981). *The Zoar Story*. Strasburg, OH: Gordon Printing.

Mow, Merrill. (1991). *Torches Rekindled: The Bruderhof's Struggle for Renewal*. Ulster Park, NY: Plough Publishing Company.

Mumford, Lewis. (1962). *The Story of Utopia*. New York: Viking Press.

Neubauer, Peter B. (1965). *Children in Collectives: Child-Rearing Aims and Practices in the Kibbutz*. Springfield, IL: Charles C. Thomas.

Newman, Cathy. (1989). "The Shakers' Brief Eternity." *National Geographic*, 176(3), 302–25.

Nolt, Stephen M. (1992). *A History of the Amish*. Intercourse, PA: Good Books.

Nordhoff, Charles. (1966). *The Communistic Societies of the United States: From Personal Visits and Observation*. New York: Dover Publications.

Noyes, George Wallingford. (1923). *Religious Experience of John Humphrey Noyes: Founder of the Oneida Community*. New York: The Macmillan Company.

Palmer, Howard. (1972). *Land of the Second Chance: A History of Ethnic Groups in Southern Alberta*. Lethbridge, AB: The Lethbridge Herald.

Peake, Frank. (1983). "Anglicanism on the Prairies: Continuity and Flexibility," in *Visions of the New Jerusalem: Religious Settlement on the Prairies*. Benjamin G. Smillie, ed. Edmonton, AB: NeWest Press, 55–68.

Pease, William H., and Jane H. Pease. (1963). *Black Utopias: Negro Communal Experiments in America*. Madison, WI: The State Historical Society of Wisconsin.

Peter, Karl A. (1987). *The Dynamics of Hutterite Society*. Edmonton, AB: The University of Alberta Press.

Peters, Victor. (1971). *All Things Common: The Hutterian Way of Life*. New York: Harper & Row.

Pitzer, Donald E., and Josephine M. Elliott. (September, 1979). *Indiana Magazine of History*, LXXV(3), 225–300.

Polikoff, Barbara Garland. (1999). *With One Bold Act: The Story of Jane Addams*. Chicago, IL: Boswell Books.

Pope, Alexander. (1963). "Essay on Man," in *The Poems of Alexander Pope*. John Butt, ed. London: Methuen.

Popenoe, Oliver and Cris Popenoe. (1984). *Seeds of Tomorrow: Communities that Work*. San Francisco, CA: Harper & Row.

Popoff, Eli A. (1982). *An Historical Exposition on the Origin and Evolution of the Basic Tenets of the Doukhobor Life Conception*. Grand Forks, BC: POP Offset.

Pyle, Howard. (1889). *A Peculiar People: A Tale of the Ephrata Cloister*. Ephrata, PA: The Aurand Press. Reprinted from *Harper's Magazine*.

Randall, E. O. (1904). *History of the Zoar Society From Its Commencement to Its Conclusion*. Third edition. Columbus, OH: Fred J. Heer.

Rasporich, A. W. (Fall, 1987). Utopia, Sect and Millennium in Western Canada, 1870–1940. *Prairie Forum*, 12(2), 217–44.

Rawls, Thomas H. (1995). "Iowa's Amana Colonies," *National Geographic Traveler*, XII(4), 70–77.

Reibel, Daniel B. (1993). *A Guide to Old Economy*. Harrisburg, PA: The Pennsylvania Historical and Museum Commission and the Harmonie Associates.

Reimer, Gustav E., and G. R. Gaeddert. (1956). *Exiled by the Czar: Cornelius Jansen and the Great Mennonite Migration, 1874*. Newton, KS: Mennonite Publication House.

Religious Movements Homepage. (2003). religiousmovements.lib. virginia.edu/nrms/Shakers.html.

Report on Communal Property. (1972). Select Committee of the Assembly (Communal Property). Government of Alberta, Edmonton, AB: Queen's Printer.

Rexroth, Kenneth. (1974). *Communalism: From its Origins to the Twentieth Century*. New York: The Seabury Press.

Riasanovsky, Nicholas V. (1969). *The Teachings of Charles Fourier*. Berkeley, CA: University of California Press.

Richter, Peyton E. (1971a). "Introduction," in *Utopias: Social Ideals and Communal Experiments*. Richter, Peyton E., ed. Boston, MA: Holbrook Press, 1–26.

———. (1971b). "Community of Celibates: The Shakers," in *Utopias: Social Ideals and Communal Experiments*. Richter, Peyton E., ed. Boston, MA: Holbrook Press, 87–89.

Robertson, Constance Noyes. (1972). *Oneida Community: The Breakup, 1876–1881*. Syracuse, NY: Syracuse University Press.

Rochester Folk Art Guild. (2002). www.rfag.org

Rothstein, Edward. (2003). "Utopia and Its Discontents," in *Visions of Utopia*. Furaha D. Norton, ed. New York: Oxford University Press, 1–28.

Schilling, Rita. (1989). *Sudeten in Saskatchewan: A Way to Be Free*. St. Walburg, SK: St. Walburg Sudeten German Club, Saskatchewan German Council, Inc. Edited by Anne Szumigalski.

Schroeder, Adolf E. (1990) *Bethel German Colony, 1844–1883: Religious Beliefs and Practices.* Bethel, MO: Historic Bethel German Colony, Inc.

Scott, Andrew. (1997). *The Promise of Paradise: Utopian Communities in B.C.* Vancouver, BC: Whitecap Books.

Shambaugh, Barbara. (1988). *Amana: The Community of True Inspiration.* Ames, IA: State Historical Society of Iowa.

Shenker, Barry. (1986). *Intentional Communities: Ideology and Alienation in Communal Societies.* London, UK: Routledge & Kegan Paul.

Smith, C. Henry. (1957). *The Story of the Mennonites.* Newton, KS: Mennonite Publication Office.

Snyder, Eugene Edmund. (1993). *Aurora, Their Last Utopia: Oregon's Christian Commune, 1856–1883.* Portland, OR: Binford and Mort Publishing.

Spencer, Metta. (1990). *Foundations of Modern Sociology.* Scarborough, ON: Prentice-Hall Canada, Inc.

Spinrad, Leonard and Thelma Spinrad. (1979). *Speaker's Lifetime Library.* West Nyack, NY: Parker Publishing Company.

Stelle Group. (2002). www.thesetellegroup.org/120_120today.hym

Stoner, Carroll and Jo Anne Parke. (1977). *All God's Children: The Cult Experience—Salvation or Slavery?* Radnor, PA: Chilton Book Company.

Tagg, Melvin S. (1968). *A History of the Mormon Church in Canada.* Lethbridge, AB: Lethbridge Herald Printing Company.

Tarasoff, Koozma. (1982). *Plakun Trava: The Doukhobors.* Grand Forks, BC: Mir Publication Society.

———. (2002). *Spirit Wrestlers: Doukhobor Pioneers' Strategies for Living.* Brooklyn, NY: Legas Publishing.

Tarasoff, Koozma, and Robert B. Klymasz, eds. (1995). *Spirit Wrestlers: Centennial Papers in Honour of Canada's Doukhobor Heritage.* Ottawa, ON: Canadian Museum of Civilization.

Terjesen, Nancy Conn. (1979). "Longevity Factors in Past and Present Communal Societies," in *Communes: Historical and Contemporary.* Ruth Shonle Cavan and Man Singh Das, eds. New Delhi, India: Vikas Publishing House, 288–305.

Toews, John A. (1975). *A History of the Mennonite Brethren Church: Pilgrims and Pioneers.* Fresno, CA: General Conference of Mennonite Brethren Churches.

Trausch, Susan. (1987). www.uvm.edu/~jmoore/ sixtiesonline/ vtrausch.html

The United Methodist Book of Worship. (1999). Nashville, TN: The United Methodist Publishing House.

Utley, Robert M. (1984). *The Indian Frontier of the American West, 1846–1860.* Albuquerque, NM: University of New Mexico Press.

Walbert, David. (2002). *Garden Spot: Lancaster County, the Old Order Amish, and the Selling of Rural America.* New York: Oxford University Press.

Walters, Kerry S. (1989). *The Sane Society Ideal in Modern Utopianism.* Lewiston, NY: The Edward Mellon Press.

Warner, James A. and Donald M. Denlinger. (1969). *The Gentle People.* n.p.: Galahad Books.

Water Wheel Web Edition. (2003). www.zencenter.org/ SanghaLetters/ mayjun03_2.html

Weaver-Zercher, David. (2001). *The Amish in the American Imagination.* Baltimore, MD: The Johns Hopkins University Press.

Webber, Everett. (1959). *Escape to Utopia: The Communal Movement in America.* New York: Hastings House Publishers.

Wells, H.G. (1905, 1967). *A Modern Utopia.* Lincoln, NE: University of Nebraska Press.

Wetton, C. (1979). *The Promised Land: The Story of the Barr Colonists.* The Lloydminster, SK: *The Lloydminster Times.*

Whitsel, Bradley C. (2003). *The Church Universal and Triumphant: Elizabeth Clare Prophet's Apocalyptic Movement.* Syracuse, NY: Syracuse University Press.

Wilson, William E. (1984). *The Angel and the Serpent.* Bloomington, IN: Indiana University Press.

Wood, Daniel. (August 4, 2001). "Bountiful, B.C.," in *Saturday Night,* 116 (28), 24–31.

Wooster, Ernest S. (1924). *Communities of the Past And Present.* New York: AMS Press.

Yambura, Barbara S, and Eunice Willis Bodine. (1986). *A Change and A Parting: My Story of Amana.* Ames, IA: Iowa State University Press.

Yount, Lisa. (1997). *Frontier of Freedom: African Americans in the West.* New York: Facts on File, Inc.

Zablocki, Benjamin David. (1971). *The Joyful Community: An Account of the Bruderhof, A Communal Movement Now in its Third Generation.* Baltimore, MD: Penguin Books.

Zielinski, John M. (1975). *The Amish: A Pioneer Heritage.* Des Moines, IA: Wallace Homestead Book Company.

GLOSSARY

ACTIVIST COMMUNES: Activist communes are formed for the purpose of objecting to some aspect of the existing social structure. They are sometimes regarded as a species of petty-bourgeois protest.

ALTERNATIVE ORGANIZATIONS: A recently-coined sociological concept intended to describe the resultant structure when groups of people band together to build communities that improve aspects of the dominant society.

ANARCHIST INTENTIONAL COMMUNITIES: A utopian form primarily designed for the indulgence of individual or group appetites.

ANABAPTISTS: A European group of religious protesters in the early part of the sixteenth century.

ARCADIANISM: A form of utopia with an aesthetic or moral purpose.

BIG CHANGE: The name for an event when the Amana people of Iowa decided to dissolve their commune and form a secular company that completely separated church and state.

BOUNDARY MAINTENANCE: Boundary maintenance implies specific actions undertaken by an intentional community to eliminate the possibility that members may deviate through too much interaction with the outside world.

BRANCH DAVIDIANS: A unique religious commune at Waco, Texas, founded by self-proclaimed prophet David Koresh. The commune burned to the ground in 1993 after an armed government siege.

BURNING OF ARMS: The burning of guns, swords, and other military arms sponsored by Russian Doukhobors on June 29, 1895.

CCUB (Christian Community of Universal Brotherhood): A communal Doukhobor organization that operated in Canada from 1908 to 1939.

CHARISMA: Charisma is often viewed as a spiritual characteristic individuals manifest that allows them to attract and influence followers.

CHILIASM: The Biblical belief that Jesus Christ will someday return to the earth and establish a one-thousand-year reign of peace (Revelation 20:1–5).

COMMUNAL UTOPIA: The best-known utopian form. This kind of intentional community is highlighted by living together and sharing resources. All resources of the group are held in common.

COMMUNITARIANISM: The belief that society would best be organized if its participants had all things in common. The term is sometimes used synonymously with the term communism.

COMPLEX MARRIAGE: A form of marriage invented by Oneida founder John Humphrey Noyes, in which every member in the community was considered wedded to all other members of the opposite sex.

CONFIRMATION: A public act during which individuals who have been baptized as infants make their vows before a Christian congregation.

EHEBUCHLEIN: A book belittling marriage, written by Conrad Beissel of the Ephrata Cloister. Many women who read the book left their husbands to join Beissel's solitary commune.

EPHRATA CLOISTER: A Pennsylvania commune founded in 1733 by Conrad Beissel.

EUCHARIST: A Sacrament consisting of eating bread and drinking wine to denote the death of Jesus Christ, celebrated by most Christian religious denominations. It is also called the Lord's Supper or Holy Communion. In the Catholic faith the Actual Presence of Jesus Christ is believed to be in the elements of the Sacrament; this is known as transubstantiation.

GARDEN OF EDEN: A utopian location described in the early chapters of the Holy Bible (Genesis 2:15–17).

GELASSENHEIT: Applies to Amish culture and refers to submissiveness on the part of baptized members to the rules of order established by the church elders.

GREAT DIVISION: A seventeenth-century movement within the Russian Orthodox Church that caused dozens of church sects to emerge, including Doukhobors and Molokans.

HOLY COMMUNION: See Eucharist.

HULL HOUSE: An early twentieth-century Chicago headquarters for a humane society initiated by reformer Jane Addams.

INTENTIONAL COMMUNITIES: A concept employed by sociologists to describe utopian communities involving both communal and noncommunal communities and other social movements aimed at preserving a unique collective purpose.

ISKRA (DIVINE SPARK): A Russian term used by Doukhobors to denote that a touch of Divinity exists within each individual. The spark motivates individuals to undertake tasks or missions unique to themselves.

JESUS PEOPLE: A term used to define the beliefs and actions of groups of youth who displayed fundamentalist religious behaviors during the 1960s.

KEDAR: A son of Ishmael and ancestor of the Arabic tribe of Kedar. The Kedarites were known for their wealth in flocks (Jeremiah 49:28–29), and their men were famed as architects (Isaiah 21:16–17).

KIBBUTZ: A unique communal form launched by Zionist pioneers in Palestine prior to World War I.

KIT: An organization of former Bruderhof (Society of Brothers) members called "Keep it Touch."

LEUTE: The German word for people. Hutterites prefer the term "Leut."

LORD'S SUPPER: See Eucharist.

MARTYRS' MIRROR: A recordbook of sixteenth-century Anabaptist heroes who suffered cruel deaths at the hands of the state in Central Europe.

MEIDUNG: The German term for shunning or avoiding. It signifies that excommunicated members of Amish, Hutterite, or Mennonite groups are to be ignored by members in good standing.

METLAKATLA: An Aboriginal settlement established on the west coast of British Columbia by an Anglican named William Duncan. The community lasted from 1862 to 1887.

MIGRANT UTOPIA: An intentional community that is willing or has found it necessary to relocate to another geographic location in order to practice its unique way of life.

MILLENNIALISM: The belief that nature and humankind will be transformed by a force arising and acting independently of the wills of men and women. Most such forms have a solid Christian basis.

MORAL REFORM INTENTIONAL COMMUNITIES: These are generally designed to correct economic or social inequality and alleviate the poverty and suffering that inequality engenders.

MUTUAL CRITICISM: An innovation of John Humphrey Noyes, founder of the Oneida Community. The event consisted of members criticizing and encouraging one another for their personal growth and improvement.

MYSTICISM: The belief that it is possible to achieve communion with Deity through contemplation and love without the medium of human research.

NEW JERUSALEM: A future city of peace envisaged by Christians and described in the New Testament Book of Revelation (21:10–27).

NONCOMMUNAL UTOPIAS: Intentional communities that acknowledge the importance of influencing social change, with the stipulation that private property is not viewed as a deterrent to this accomplishment.

ORDNUNG: A set of rather strict rules established by leading elders in the Amish community. Adherents who do not follow the rules of the *Ordnung* are often excommunicated and shunned.

ORTHODOXY: A position of conformity to usual or established beliefs or doctrines.

PACIFISM: The belief that any kind of military effort or involvement is morally wrong.

PHALANX: An ancient military formation of infantry in close and deep ranks with shields drawn together and spears overlapping. Later, it was a term used by François Fourier in the early nineteenth century to describe a group of individuals united for a common purpose.

PIETISM: A theological position that originated in seventeenth century Germany and stressed the devotional ideal in religion.

POLITICAL-ECONOMIC INTENTIONAL COMMUNITIES: These are organized for the purpose of drawing attention to the need for reform in such areas as labor exploitation, urbanization, health care, and poverty.

POLYTHEISM: The theological position that there are many gods in the universe.

PRAIRIELEUT: A group of Hutterites who chose to own property independently when they migrated to America from Russia in the 1870s.

PROTEST MOVEMENTS: These are formed for the purpose of objecting vigorously to some aspect of the existing social structure. Protest groups often utilize public gatherings as a device for attracting attention to their cause.

PSYCHOSOCIAL INTENTIONAL COMMUNITIES: These usually arise in response to individual visions to transform society from its unnatural, competitive, and depersonalized state to a more healthy form.

RELIGIOUS-SPIRITUAL INTENTIONAL COMMUNITIES: These generally rely on a Christian base in formulating social reform.

REVIVALISM: Describes the fervent evangelistic methods characteristic of religious movements to attract adherents. It is the tendency to bring back former ways, customs, or institutions.

SACRED: Refers to any phenomenon within the realm of the church or religion.

SANCTIFIED SISTERS (SANCTIFICATIONISTS): The name of a women's organization started by Martha McWhirter in the 1860s in Belton, Texas. The group believed that over time, Christians could overcome sin and live in a sanctified or sinless state.

SECULAR: Refers to the worldly realm as distinguished from the church and religious affairs.

SEPARATISTS: A term to describe religious groups in Europe who broke away from the established state church.

SHUNNING: An Amish, Hutterite, and Mennonite practice, which requires that excommunicated members be ignored by those in good standing. Shunning means that regular members cannot eat with, speak with, or do business with those excommunicated by the church.

SOCIETY OF BROTHERS: Another term for a twentieth century group that originated in Germany who patterned their lifestyle after that of the Hutterian Brethren of North America.

SPIRIT WRESTLERS: A nickname given the Doukhobors by Russian Orthodox Church Archbishop Ambrosius in 1785 because they allegedly wrestled against the Spirit of God. The Doukhobors accepted the label, arguing that they indeed wrestled "in the Spirit of God."

SUDETENLAND: A mountainous region in northern Czechoslovakia annexed by Nazi Germany in October 1938, after the Munich Pact, and returned to Czechoslovakia in 1945.

THE REFORMATION: A sixteenth-century historical movement of priests and other religious leaders away from the Roman Catholic Church to start what became splinter Protestant groups.

THE REPUBLIC: An ideal form of society envisaged by the Greek philosopher Plato (427–347 B.C.).

THEOCRATIC DEVELOPMENT: The mystic union of the individual soul with God.

TRANSCENDENCE: The belief that a form or forms of beings and knowledge exist beyond the realm of human comprehension.

UNDERGROUND RAILROAD: A network of locations designed temporarily to house African Americans who were fleeing from slavery in the United States during the nineteenth century.

USCC (Union of Spiritual Communities in Christ): A noncommunal Doukhobor organization operated in Canada from 1939 to the present.

UTOPIA: An envisaged ideal form of society.

WELTANSCHAUUNG: German term for worldview. A personal perspective, a way of looking at the world; it comprises a philosophy of life.

WOMAN IN THE WILDERNESS: A millenarian, celibate, communistic community founded in Pennsylvania by pietist Johannas Kelpius in the late seventeenth century. Committed to self-denial, the group awaited the advent of Christ in the virgin wilderness of the frontier.

INDEX

ABOUT THE AUTHORS

John W. Friesen, Ph.D., D.Min., D.R.S., is a professor in the Faculty of Education and the Faculty of Communication and Culture at the University of Calgary, where he teaches courses in Aboriginal history and religious education. Of Mennonite background, he has written 40 books on cross-cultural education and ethnicity.

Virginia Lyons Friesen, Ph.D., is a sessional instructor in the Faculty of Communication and Culture at the University of Calgary. An early childhood education specialist, she holds a Certificate in Counseling from the Institute of Pastoral Counseling in Akron, Ohio. She has co-presented a number of papers at academic conferences and is co-author of several books.